SEAGAN EATING

SEAGAN EATING

The Lure of a Healthy, Sustainable Seafood + Vegan Diet

Amy Cramer and Lisa McComsey

Illustrated by Ed McComsey

Foreword by Chris Foltz and Todd Pesek, M.D.

A TARCHERPERIGEE BOOK

An imprint of Penguin Random House LLC
375 Hudson Street
New York, New York 10014

Author photos by Susan Woog Wagner / Ed McComsey photo by Angie Lombardi / Fish illustrations by Ed McComsey / Label art by Jo Anne Mastropasqua /

Library of Congress Cataloging-in-Publication Data

Names: Cramer, Amy, author. | McComsey, Lisa, author.
Title: Seagan eating : the lure of a healthy, sustainable seafood + vegan diet / Amy Cramer and Lisa McComsey ; illustrated by Ed McComsey ; foreword by Chris Foltz and Todd Pesek, M.D.
Description: New York, New York : TarcherPerigee, [2016] | Includes bibliographical references and index.
Identifiers: LCCN 2016019432 (print) | LCCN 2016020104 (ebook) | ISBN 9780399176944 (paperback) | ISBN 9780698411272 (ebook)
Subjects: LCSH: Cooking (Seafood) | Cooking (Vegetables) | BISAC: COOKING / Methods / Quick & Easy. | COOKING / Vegetarian & Vegan. | COOKING / Specific Ingredients / Seafood. | LCGFT: Cookbooks.
Classification: LCC TX747 .C79 2016 (print) | LCC TX747 (ebook) | DDC 641.6/92—dc23

Printed in the United States of America
1 3 5 7 9 10 8 6 4 2

Book design by Elke Sigal

To my wonderful husband, Ken, and my awesome children, Cai, Liv, and Cam, for loving, supporting, encouraging, and tasting.

—AMY CRAMER

To grandmother Alice, my very first grammar teacher and world's best meatloaf maker (sorry about the vegan thing). And to you, Mom and Dad, for feeding me all the love, support, and cocktails I need.

—LISA McCOMSEY

CONTENTS

Foreword by Chris Foltz and Todd Pesek, M.D. *ix*

1. Seduced by Seafood *1*
2. Why We Cheated on Plants *4*
3. What the Fluke Do Seagans Eat? *7*
4. Seagan Staples Shopping List *11*
5. The Health Benefits of Seafood *19*
6. Seafood Buyers' Guide *22*
7. Fish in a Flash—Five Easy Preparations *29*
8. Best (and Worst) Fish for Health and Sustainability *32*
9. Recipe Hacks—Prep Now, Use Later *48*
10. Cook's Toolkit—Kitchen Essentials *51*
11. Twenty-One Days of Swoon-Worthy Seagan Menus *54*
12. Decadent Seagan and Vegan Recipes *64*
    - Rich Seafood Dishes *65*
    - Simply Perfect Fish in Foil—Eight Variations *85*
    - Creamy Soups of the Sea *94*
    - Homestyle Classics and Comfort Food *98*
    - Sumptuous Sides and Snacks *113*

To-Die-For Dips and Dressings *125*

Wake-Up Call—Best Breakfasts *128*

Indulgent Desserts *132*

13. Restaurant Survival Guide and Sushi Primer *147*

14. Dissecting Food Labels—The Tips, Tricks, and Dirty Little Secrets *154*

15. Twenty-Three Vegan Foods You Should Ditch (and Their Healthy Replacements) *170*

16. Nuts and Seeds—Tiny Nutritional Powerhouses *194*

17. Herbs and Spices—The Spicy Seventeen *208*

18. Organic Foods—Worth the Price? *218*

19. GMOs—Safe to Eat? *223*

20. Superfoods—Super Hype? Or Superheroes? *227*

Resources *233*

Acknowledgments *239*

About the Authors *243*

Index *247*

FOREWORD

A MESSAGE FROM THE DOCTOR AND THE GROCER

You'd be hard-pressed to find a doctor who wouldn't tell you to eat more healthfully—but try finding one who can enable you to do so. That leaves patients to grapple with a dizzying array of tough choices and decisions on their own. Then there's the grocer who faces an ever-growing need to provide healthier options for customers. So when grocer and doctor team up, the result is superior sourcing and alternatives that are good for both people *and* the planet.

Our strategy is simple: Eat superfoods (nutrient-dense, calorie-sparse, plant-based, health-empowering whole foods), manage fats, get your dose of essential omega-3 fats, limit sugars, and know where your foods come from and how they were harvested (many practices are harmful to humans and the earth).

The Doctor

"Should I eat meat?" I usually get this question after a patient has had an epiphany following an illness. Their thought process is, "I've taken my health for granted and must now make healthier choices." Accordingly, diets laden with meat, dairy, and processed foods are suddenly replaced with low-fat, plant-based whole foods and other lifestyle changes. That drastic shift is usually never maintained, but equilibrium is eventually found.

I've learned over the years that meeting people where they're willing to be met is a good strategy. I start with the fact that those who eat less and do more live longer and more healthfully than those who overindulge and lead sedentary lives.

Data, such as that from the World Health Organization, now support the notion that processed meats—and likely even red meat—contribute to cancer, heart disease, and other ills.

After advising and helping people to eat less (strive for plant-based foods) and do more, I love watching their miraculous self-healing machines—their bodies—regain vitality and health.

I wholeheartedly endorse any effort that connects individuals to their food supply—and this book will help readers on their respective journeys.

The Grocer

As my team and I work to ensure that the rapidly evolving needs of our customers are met, it becomes clear that *everyone* wants to eat better and *nearly everyone* is confused about how to go about it. This presents an unprecedented opportunity for the grocery store to provide relevant food and service solutions.

Some 2,400 years ago, Hippocrates, the father of modern medicine, said, "Let food be thy medicine and medicine be thy food." That message is resonating stronger than ever today, but it's easier said than done. There's a mind-boggling amount of information—and misinformation—that leaves consumers bewildered and frustrated. What should I eat? What should I *not* eat? How do I prepare it? Where should I buy it? What's safe—and what's *not* safe?

Enter Amy Cramer and Lisa McComsey with their newest book, *Seagan Eating*. They present a comprehensive approach to a healthier lifestyle through a seagan (seafood + vegan) diet and share tons of great tips for delicious, nutritious eating. It answers all the questions we get as grocers in a way that makes it easy to menu plan, shop, and prepare. Rest assured, a copy of *Seagan Eating* will be on our shelves to purchase and in the library of each of our stores.

—Chris Foltz, chief operating officer, Heinen's Grocery Store (heinens.com)

—Todd Pesek, M.D., holistic physician and CEO of VitalHealth Partners (vitalhealthohio.com); chief medical officer of Heinen's Grocery Store; and author of the bestselling book *Eat Yourself Super . . . One Bite at a Time: A Superfoods Journey for the Happy, Healthy, and Hungry*

SEAGAN EATING

CHAPTER 1

SEDUCED BY SEAFOOD

Some Will Say We're Sleeping with the Enemy

Others will call it bait-and-switch. As authors of a how-to-go-vegan guide and cookbook, *The Vegan Cheat Sheet,* we know we're taking a bit of a risk by admitting to this doozy of a no-no: cheating with seafood.

Both of us went vegan for health reasons, and we followed that regimen for many years. Now we've converted to a seagan (seafood + vegan) diet, also for health reasons. Plant-based foods still comprise the bulk of our daily diets and deliver nearly every nutrient our bodies crave. But, after doing tons of research, we decided that the high-quality, essential omega-3 fatty acids you can get only from fish were a missing link—and it was time to take the plunge.

This wasn't an easy choice. Not all seafood is good for you (mercury!). Not all seafood is sustainable (overfishing!). And, of course, ethical vegans will find our infidelity unforgivable. But we believe there's a right way to go seagan, and we do our darndest to make thoughtful, well-informed decisions about which fish to eat (or not).

You Can Easily Get Hooked

For the gazillions of omnivores out there, becoming seagan is a healthy compromise that feels a lot more doable than going "whole-hog" vegan. While we found the vegan diet surprisingly easy and satisfying, we know most people will go vegan only—to quote a friend—"when hell freezes over."

Seaganism is both approachable and—we believe—the new gold standard for healthful eating. It not only allows for more meal variety and supplies our bodies with precious omega-3s, but it makes life easier when eating out.

This Book Isn't for One-Track-Mind Diet Purists

It's for those who:

- Flounder in the "messy middle" as they strive to look and feel their best but simply can't accommodate a militant, all-or-nothing approach
- Prefer to make small, incremental changes to their diets rather than drastic overhauls
- May ultimately long to go vegan but prefer to do it in baby steps—they can ditch the unhealthiest stuff first and use seafood as a bridge to full-fledged veganhood

Our Goal Is Overall Health

It's easy to be a fat, nutrient-deprived vegan or seagan (think potato chips and fried shrimp). That's why we share tons of tips on how to shop, cook, and eat better and more mindfully.

We don't believe in deprivation diets, or, for that matter, even counting calories. Our stance is simply this:

- Follow a well-balanced, mostly vegan diet
- Eat fish two to three times a week, as recommended by the American Heart Association (Note: while not all seafood is technically "fish"—crustaceans and mollusks, for

example—we use the term broadly to encompass all these sea creatures)

- Cut way back on junk
- Indulge now and then

We Take You to Market

Whether in a local fish market or a supersize grocery store, food shopping has gotten complicated and confusing: Should I buy the farm-raised or wild-caught salmon? What's all that gibberish on the ingredient label—and should I be wary? Do I really have to spring for the organic apples? Why all the fuss about GMOs (genetically modified organisms)? Which "superfood" is in vogue? Last week is was goji berries, this week it's bulletproof (buttered) coffee.

Argh!

We unravel all that and share some teeny-tiny ways you can punch up your nutritional intake (they're called nuts, seeds, herbs, and spices). We give you shopping lists, fish-buying recommendations, restaurant advice, weekly meal menus, and lots more scoop inside this handy, take-everywhere guide.

Best of all, you get tons of Amy's decadent recipes—proving you can eat luxuriously and healthfully every single day. Most are super easy to make, all are oil-free, and every single one is a crowd pleaser.

Anyone who knows us can vouch that we love food—rich, flavorful food, right down to our crab mac and cheese and frosted fudge brownies. You'll find those recipes (and many more) in the pages that follow.

Hooked yet? Read on—we think you'll love being seagan as much as we do.

CHAPTER 2

WHY WE CHEATED ON PLANTS

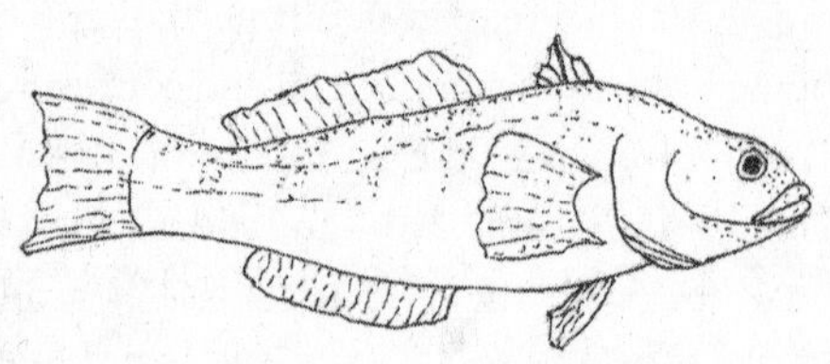

How did two random women—one living in Colorado, the other in New Jersey—come to follow a similar eating path and decide to write about it?

Quick rewind: Years ago, we met in New York City while working at *People* magazine and became fast friends, running sidekicks, and eating buddies. (If you'd ever tried Amy's homemade meatballs, you'd finagle a way to be her friend, too.)

Eventually separated by geography (Lisa moved to Costa Rica, Mexico, and New Jersey; Amy went to California, Ohio, and Colorado), we remained close and continued to share our passion for food, health, and exercise.

In 2013 we co-wrote our first book, *The Vegan Cheat Sheet*. Our friendship survived that collaboration and now we're back for round two.

Here's the rest of our vegan-to-seagan journey.

Amy's Story

My husband, Ken, and I swore off animal products in an effort to naturally lower his genetically high cholesterol (he'd been on meds for years and hated their side effects). For more than ten years, I was a fairly strict vegan.

The change in diet worked fabulously. We followed the stringent vegan, no-oil guidelines set forth by Dr. Caldwell Esselstyn Jr. in his book *Prevent and Reverse Heart Disease.* It didn't hurt that I was a chef and could turn out some pretty mean dishes. I loved experimenting with new recipes and eventually approached my writer friend (and now coauthor), Lisa, about collaborating on a simple guide to going vegan. That idea resulted in our first book, *The Vegan Cheat Sheet.*

Not long ago, while on vacation, I found myself in a famous New Hampshire lobster restaurant surrounded by veganish and carnivorous friends. For several years I'd hidden my "dirty little secret": I occasionally ate fish. Oh my! So I chose that moment to "come out" to my friends and boldly ordered a two-pound lobster. Go big or go home.

My so-called friends pulled out their phones and tried to snap pictures of my scandalous cheat. I quickly attempted to confiscate all electronic devices and declared that I was just being a tad naughty, since I was on the road and away from my home kitchen. I guess I wasn't ready to embrace my belief in the health benefits of eating seafood.

Over the next months, I did a lot more research on the reasons why eating fish can be a very good thing. I am now a proud seagan!

Lisa's Story

With the encouragement of Amy—and in the hopes of winning a family get-fit weight-loss challenge—I decided to go vegan "for a month," thinking it would be a boring starvation diet with little more than carrot sticks and tofu on the "approved" list.

Boy, was I wrong. Not only did I eat a ton, I discovered a whole new world of flavors and foods. It was an exciting change, I felt amazing, and going vegan was so much easier and more fun than I had ever imagined. I stuck with it for years.

But being the health fanatic and research-obsessed person I am, I started learning more and more about the importance of omega-3 fatty acids. Vegans will say you can get these essential fatty acids from certain plants—and that's true, to a degree. Fish, however, are the sole source of the healthiest forms of omega-3s—EPA and DHA (we explain all that in Chapter 5, The Health Benefits of Seafood, page 19)—and so I had to rethink my plan.

Seafood simply offered too many benefits for me to overlook its importance. So I started eating fish now and then. It wasn't an easy decision. I had a lot at stake in the vegan world—our book and my reputation, for starters. Like Amy, I "cheated" surreptitiously at first. The vegan police were out in hordes, pointing out my every transgression: "*That's* not vegan!" "Fish isn't vegan!" Arrest me then!

I've since made peace with all that, gone public with my vegan infraction, and have come to embrace the seagan way.

CHAPTER 3

WHAT THE FLUKE DO SEAGANS EAT?

Here's what we're not: doctors or nutritionists or scientists.

Here's what we are: a pair of health-enthusiast foodies and research fanatics. What follows is the result of our exhaustive nutritional "fishing expedition"—and the reason for our vegan-to-seagan transformation.

During our fact-finding mission, we became frustrated with all the misconceptions, misrepresentations, and industry "secrets" that make it hard to choose food wisely. We give you a road map for easier, healthier decision-making.

So What Exactly Do Seagans Eat?

We follow a vegan (plant-based) diet—that includes fruits, vegetables, legumes, nuts, seeds, and grains—with one allowance: seafood. No red meat, no pork, no poultry, no eggs, no dairy. And because we strive to be *healthy* seagans, we try to avoid a lot of sugar, oils, fried foods, artificial chemicals, and junk like that. (The operative word is *strive*. We're not perfect.)

There are arguments for and against just about any diet you can think of, and it's easy enough to hear what you want to hear (we're praying that the hot-fudge sundae will one day be declared a superfood).

It all boils down to this: Choose what works for you. We believe seaganism is an incredibly healthful, easy, and satisfying way to eat.

So let's start with why we ditched dairy and meat and limit our oil intake. For the detailed lowdown on seafood, check out The Health Benefits of Seafood on page 19.

Bye-Bye, Meat, Dairy, and Eggs

So long, Amy's veal Milanese. Good riddance, cheesy omelets. It was nice knowing you, ice cream. I'll never meet a smoother snack than you, Greek yogurt. Ah, breaking up is hard to do. But like many breakups, it can open the door to healthier relationships.

Our decision to go splitsville with these admittedly delicious foods was not a capricious one. No one in her right mind parts ways with Ben & Jerry's Peanut Butter Half Baked without a damn good reason. Or several. Here are ours:

Americans' waistlines are expanding, with more than a third of adults now classified as "obese" and two-thirds as "overweight or obese." Childhood obesity is on the rise, too.

We're a sick nation. Despite our access to one of the most advanced health-care systems in the world, we suffer from ever-increasing rates of chronic ailments and life-threatening illnesses, like heart disease, diabetes, cancer, and Alzheimer's.

We are what we eat—and if what we eat is high in fat, sugar, and other disease-promoting muck, we'll likely pay the price. (Hello, doctors, hospitals, and meds.) Cleaning up our plates is one of the simplest and most profound ways we can take better care of ourselves on a day-to-day basis. By decreasing our consumption of the nasty stuff—and boosting our intake of whole, nutritionally dense, plant-based foods and the occasional slab of omega-3-rich seafood—we'll enjoy a spike in health, energy, and maybe even longevity.

Doing away with foods rich in saturated fats (meats and dairy) and introducing those brimming in omega-3s (seafood) is part of our plan.

As it turns out, the government agrees. A 2015 report issued by the Dietary Guidelines Advisory Committee found that the American diet is "suboptimal and has major adverse health consequences"; it is "low in vegetables, fruit, and whole grains and high in sodium, calories, saturated fat, refined grains, and added sugars."

Their recommendation? A largely plant-based diet "higher in vegetables, fruits, whole grains, seafood, legumes, and nuts . . . and low in sugar-sweetened foods and drinks and refined grains."

A later 2015 report by the World Health Organization determined that consuming processed meats like hot dogs, ham, and bacon increases the risk of colon cancer and that eating red meats—including beef, veal, pork, and lamb—may heighten the risk as well.

Meat Packs a Nasty Environmental Punch

Raising livestock for meat exerts a huge toll on the environment. The industry has an unquenchable thirst for land, water, and other precious resources, and pollutes like crazy: More than half the global greenhouse-gas emissions come from, yes, flatulent cows and pigs; plus, untreated animal waste makes its ways into rivers and streams.

Speaking of water, it takes 850 gallons of H_2O to produce an 8-ounce portion of beef and 330 gallons for 6 ounces of pork. By comparison, an 8-ounce serving of kale "drinks" just 18 gallons.

Meat production also goes against the grain: About 13 pounds of the stuff is needed for just one pound of beef. That means more than half the world's crops are grown to feed livestock—not humans.

Oil, We Love You, But . . .

You've heard the news: Certain vegetable oils are good for your heart. Right? Well, like many claims in the food world, there's some controversy surrounding the oils-are-healthy assertion.

Detractors believe that oil—while plant based—is not a whole food, since its nutrients and fiber have been squeezed out. What's left is just a fat- and calorie-dense liquid that merely serves to pack on the pounds and clog arteries. (Better options: Eat the olives, not the olive oil; the sesame seeds, not the sesame-seed oil; the coconut, not the coconut oil. You get the idea.)

While all that's debatable and we haven't sworn off oil completely, we've learned to use it sparingly. For example, you don't need oil for sautéing—a dry pan with a touch of water or other liquid works beautifully. Oils in baked-good recipes have suitable replacements, like applesauce. Salad dressings can be made without oils and still taste rich and delicious.

Our collection of oil-free recipes (beginning on page 64) gives you plenty of proof. You'll save hundreds of calories and likely won't taste the difference.

So next time you reach for that bottle of oil, ask yourself: Do I really need it? Do I really want it? Will I even taste the difference? Instead of dousing your food in that caloric, high-fat olive or coconut oil, you may just want to slather it on your skin and hair—they make wonderful natural moisturizers!

CHAPTER 4

SEAGAN STAPLES SHOPPING LIST

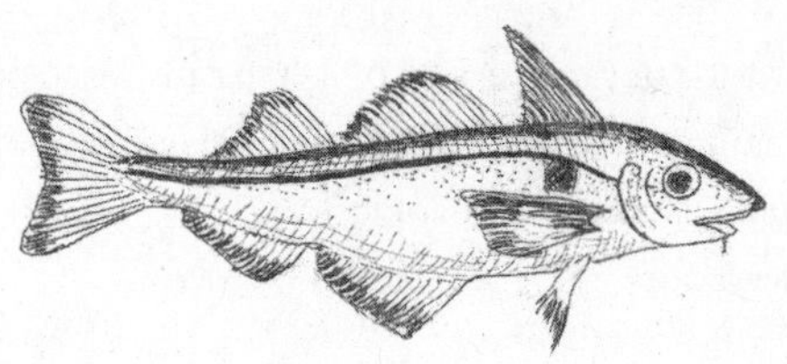

Wondering how a seagan stocks her kitchen? Here's what you'll find in our pantries, cupboards, and fridge—lots of healthful staples for easy, creative cooking at the drop of a hat.

BAKING INGREDIENTS

- Arrowroot powder (root starch that acts as a thickener)
- Baking powder (aluminum free)
- Baking soda
- Cacao nibs
- Chocolate chips—dark or semi-sweet; check label for no dairy (cocoa butter is *not* dairy—it's the cocoa's natural fat)
- Cocoa or cacao powder—unsweetened (avoid Dutch-processed or alkalized varieties, which strip the cocoa powder of up to 90 percent of its antioxidants)
- Cornmeal
- Flour (white whole-wheat and whole-wheat pastry are the best choices for baking)
- Maple syrup

- Molasses
- Sugar—brown, confectioners', and white cane (vegan or organic)
- Vanilla extract

BEANS AND LEGUMES

- Beans (dried or canned; buy BPA-free cans when possible)—black, cannellini, garbanzo, great northern, kidney, lima, navy, pink, white, and so forth
- Lentils (dried)

BEVERAGES

- Coconut water
- Coffee (preferably organic)
- Kombucha (only in Lisa's pantry; it makes Amy sleepy)
- Sparkling water—plain and/or flavored (no sugar or sweeteners)
- Teas—black, green, and herbal (dry, loose or in sachets, to make your own hot or iced tea)

BREADS

- Tortillas—corn (oil-free) and whole-wheat (100 percent whole grains)
- Whole-grain bread (100 percent whole grains)
- Whole-wheat breadcrumbs

CANNED/PACKAGED GOODS

Choose BPA-free cans when possible.

- Anchovies (preferably in water)
- Apple butter—unsweetened (good for baking)
- Applesauce—unsweetened (good for baking)

- Artichokes
- Clams—chopped or minced
- Coconut milk—light
- Fruit jams or preserves—no sugar added
- Marinara sauce—oil-free or low-fat (check labels for vegan)
- Nut butters and seed butters—almond, cashew, peanut, sunflower seed, and walnut
- Salmon
- Sardines—we like smoked (packed in water)
- Tomatoes (plum)—chopped, crushed, and whole
- Tomato paste
- Tuna fish—light (packed in water), sustainably caught (look for "hook and line," "troll and pole" or "troll caught" on label)
- Vegetable stock—oil-free

CEREALS

- Oats—we prefer standard rolled oats to eat raw and to make oatmeal
- Various cereals—100 percent whole-grain with no added oils (we love Nature's Path Smart Bran and Ezekiel Cinnamon Raisin)

CONDIMENTS

- Capers
- Chutneys (great to spice up wraps and rice and beans)
- Hot sauce (we love Cholula and Sriracha sauces)
- Mustard—Dijon style or whole-grain (check ingredients for dairy)
- Olives (in water)
- Salsa—peach, mango, and tomato
- Tamari and/or soy sauce (low sodium)
- Thai green curry paste

- Vinegars—apple cider (raw), balsamic, raspberry, red wine, rice, and white wine

"DAIRY" AND REFRIGERATOR ESSENTIALS

- Milk—almond, coconut, hemp, rice, or soy (our preference is unsweetened plain almond milk for savory cooking and vanilla flavored for desserts)
- Tempeh
- Tofu—firm or silken (light, if possible)
- Vegan cheese—we prefer Daiya (not all brands are casein-/dairy-free; check label)
- Yogurt—almond, coconut, or soy (plain/low-sugar)

FISH

- Ask your fishmonger what's fresh and local (consult our Seafood Buyers' Guide on page 22 for your healthiest, most sustainable choices); don't be afraid to substitute—you can usually swap out one fish for another in recipes

FREEZER SECTION

- Edamame—great for snacking
- Frozen-fruit bars (made with pure fruit—*no* high-fructose corn syrup)
- Fruit—blueberries, cherries, mangos, peaches, pineapple, and strawberries (perfect for pancakes, homemade sorbets, and other treats)
- Salmon (great for a backup dinner when you have no time to shop)
- Shrimp (great for quick dinners)
- Sorbet (avoid sherbets, which contain dairy products)
- Vegetables—artichoke hearts, broccoli, corn, green beans, pearl onions, peas, and spinach

- Veggie burgers (make sure they're vegan—many contain eggs and/or cheese)

GRAINS

- Amaranth
- Barley
- Buckwheat groats
- Bulgur
- Farro
- Freekah
- Grits
- Kamut
- Millet
- Popcorn kernels
- Quinoa
- Rice—basmati, black, brown (precooked for quick cooking), jasmine, short-grain brown, and wild
- Teff

HERBS AND SPICES—DRIED

- Allspice
- Basil
- Bay leaves
- Black pepper
- Cardamom—ground
- Cayenne
- Chili powder
- Cinnamon
- Coriander seeds
- Cloves
- Cumin
- Curry powder
- Dill weed

- Garlic powder
- Ginger
- Marjoram
- Mustard powder
- Nutmeg
- Oregano
- Paprika—smoked and sweet
- Red pepper flakes
- Rosemary
- Saffron
- Sage
- Salt—sea, kosher, and/or Himalayan
- Tarragon
- Thyme
- Turmeric

INDULGENCES

- Dark chocolate—70 percent cacao or more (not all is vegan; be sure to check)
- Marshmallows (vegan)

NUTS

Raw and organic are preferable; avoid salty, sweetened, fried-in-oil, and flavored varieties.

- Almonds
- Brazil nuts
- Cashews (a must for cashew cream)
- Coconut—unsweetened shredded or flakes
- Hazelnuts
- Macadamia nuts
- Peanuts
- Pecans
- Pine nuts

- Pistachios
- Walnuts

PASTA

- Lasagna noodles—whole-wheat
- Pasta of all shapes and sizes—made from whole wheat, brown rice, mung bean, quinoa, and other grains and legumes
- Soba noodles

PRODUCE

Shop the rainbow!

- Dried fruit (no sugar added):
  Apricots, cherries, cranberries, dates, figs, prunes, and raisins
- Fresh fruit—*tons*; we love:
  Apples, bananas, berries, cherries, grapefruit, grapes, kiwis, lemons, limes, mangos, melons, oranges, peaches, pineapple, plums, and pomegranate
- Fresh herbs and spices:
  Basil, cilantro, dill, garlic, ginger, marjoram, mint, oregano, parsley, rosemary, sage, and thyme
- Fresh vegetables—*tons*; our picks:
  Asparagus, bean sprouts, beets, bok choy, broccoli, Brussels sprouts, cabbage, cauliflower, celery, cucumbers, eggplant, green beans, green onions, mushrooms, olives, peppers, potatoes, radishes, shallots, sweet potatoes or yams, tomatoes, and zucchini (green and yellow)
  Load up on carrots, garlic, ginger, and onions for freezing and cooking (see our Recipe Hacks chapter, page 48)
- Salad and dark leafy greens:
  Arugula, beet greens, chard, collard greens, endive, escarole, green-leaf lettuce, kale, mixed-salad greens,

mustard greens, radicchio, red-leaf lettuce, romaine lettuce, spinach, and watercress

SEEDS

- Chia
- Flax and flaxseed meal (ground flaxseed)
- Hemp
- Pumpkin
- Sesame
- Sunflower (the kids adore these)
- Wheat germ

MISCELLANEOUS

- Aluminum foil (perfect for a quick fish dish without the messy cleanup)
- Nutritional yeast
- Parchment paper

COOKING WINE/ALCOHOL

My counter is always full of open bottles; for cooking, they last longer than you think.

- Marsala
- Mirin (rice wine)
- Port
- Red wine
- Rum
- Sherry (dry or sweet)
- Vermouth (dry or sweet)
- Vodka
- White wine

CHAPTER 5

THE HEALTH BENEFITS OF SEAFOOD

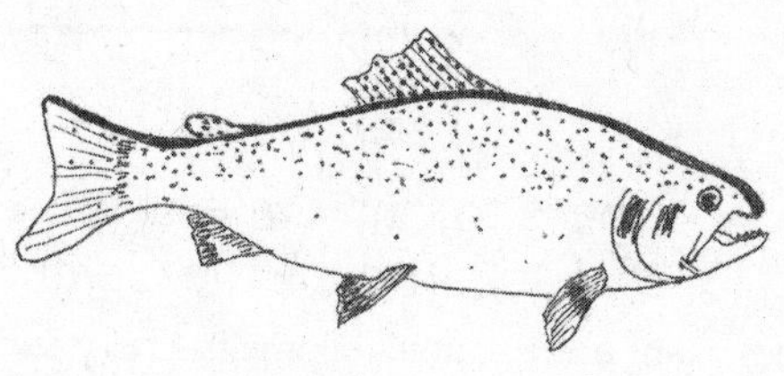

What's with all the fish hubbub? And why should I get hooked?

Fish is the perfect package: low in fat; high in protein; and overflowing with vitamins, minerals, and that thing we really love (and loves us back)—omega-3 fatty acids.

Here's the scoop. Omega-3s are essential fatty acids. Our bodies don't produce them, so we have to get them from the foods we eat.

And by the way, they're not called "essential" for nothing. These mighty little acids are workhorses—you might even call them miracle workers—crucial to healthy cell growth, proper fetal development, and robust immune functions. They're also critical for strong organs—including eyes, heart, and brain—and tissues.

Deprive yourself and pay the price: Omega-3 deficiencies have been linked to all sorts of health issues, including heart attacks, mood swings, circulatory problems, arthritis, macular degeneration, autoimmune diseases, attention-deficit disorder, allergies, asthma, and skin conditions.

NEED MORE CONVINCING?

Consuming omega-3s may help prevent and treat certain cancers, depression, dementia, Parkinson's disease, high blood pressure, high LDL ("bad") cholesterol, diabetes, allergies—and the list goes on.

Where to Find Omega-3s? That's Pretty Easy. And a Little Complicated.

The richest plant-based sources of omega-3 fatty acids are flaxseed (grind them for optimal benefit). They're also found in chia seeds, hemp seeds, sesame seeds, pumpkin seeds, walnuts, soybeans, navy beans, kidney beans, cauliflower, Brussels sprouts, kale, spinach, dark leafy greens, and seaweed.

ALA versus EPA and DHA (huh?)

Now for the tricky part (bear with us—science wasn't our strong suit): These vegetarian sources contain a type of precursor omega-3 called alpha-linolenic acid—ALA for short. Once ingested, ALA has to be converted into two other kinds of omega-3 fatty acids—the critical ones (called long-chained fatty acids)—eicosapentaenoic acid (EPA) and docosahexaenoic acid (DHA).

All of this converting business requires quite a bit of metabolic elbow grease, isn't terribly efficient, and can slow down absorption—leaving your body in want of the really good stuff, EPA and DHA.

That's Why We're Crushing on the Mother of All Omega-3 Sources—Fish

Eating fish is, hands down, the best way to get hefty doses of these essential EPA and DHA fatty acids. Eat two to three servings of seafood a week, says the American Heart Association, and you'll reduce your risk of death by heart attack, not to mention enjoy a host of other benefits we mentioned earlier.

Most fish contain at least some omega-3 fatty acids, but oily varieties like wild Alaska salmon (especially sockeye), Arctic char, Atlantic mackerel, rainbow trout, black cod, anchovies, herring, sardines, and mussels are among the richest sources.

A Love Affair with Limits

High omega-3 content isn't the Holy Grail if it comes from tainted sources. Some fish—especially the large ones, like swordfish, king mackerel, and albacore tuna—contain high levels of mercury and should be avoided.

Others are suffering from low populations, habitat destruction, and bycatch issues (fish and other marine creatures that are unintentionally captured while fishing for target species) and need to be left alone. Make wise, thoughtful choices—our Good Catch, Bad Catch guide (pages 36 to 47) will help light the way.

CHAPTER 6

SEAFOOD BUYERS' GUIDE

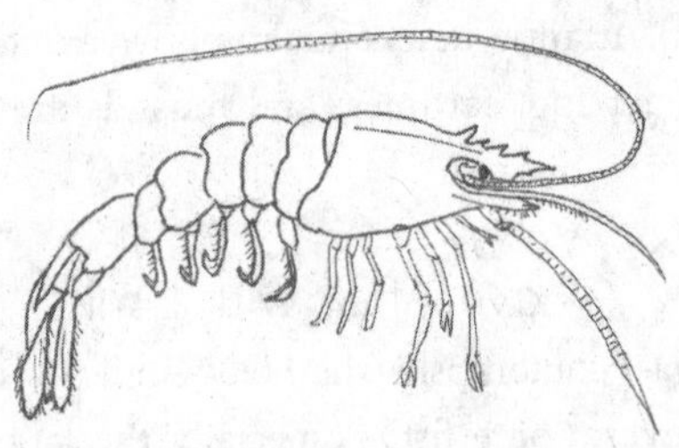

Angling for some fish tonight? While not quite as simple as squeezing melons, buying seafood can be relatively painless if you work with a trusted seafood professional and follow these guidelines. (Bring along our Good Catch, Bad Catch guide on pages 36 to 47.)

Shop at a Reputable Fish Market

Whether at your local grocery store or a neighborhood fishmonger, the person behind the counter should be able to answer questions such as:

- What is locally caught/super fresh today?
- When did this fish come in? (Don't buy anything more than two days old.)
- Is it endangered? Is it sustainably caught?
- Is the fish domestic or imported? If imported, where from?
- Has the fish been soaked in STPP (sodium tripolyphosphate—a preservative most commonly applied to scallops, shrimp, and very flaky fish)?
- Is it wild-caught or farm-raised?
    - If farmed, how was it raised (small, polluting pens; sustainable ponds; aquaculture, etc.)?

  - If wild, how was it captured? Using poles (preferable)? Or caught with longlines or trawlers (which produce bycatch)?
- What are the best ways to prepare this fish?
- Can you clean, bone, and fillet my fish?

Does Something Smell Fishy?

Fish stores should never smell, well, overly fishy. Nor should the seafood itself. Sniff around—you're aiming for a clean, briny ocean smell. Anything strong, acidic, or pungent could indicate decay.

Eye Your Surroundings

Fish should be displayed neatly and attractively on a bed of clean, shaved, flaked, or crushed ice.

Check the Label (with a Grain of Salt)

While the USDA requires that all seafood be labeled to reveal the fish's country of origin and catch method (farm-raised or wild-caught), there are exceptions to these labeling rules—so they're not totally reliable or even strictly enforced. That means we're back to double-checking with your fishmonger.

As for fish labeled "organic," be suspicious for now, as there are no standards in place for government-approved organic seafood. (Any "organic" label you stumble across may have come from an independent certification company that sets its own guidelines.)

Moreover, wild seafood is unqualified to be called organic because—unlike farmed fish—it's impossible to monitor the feral variety, and we can't control what they eat or how they live. Because of pollutants, environmental threats, and other issues, ocean-based fish farms are also ineligible. It's possible (and in discussion) that inland aquaculture farms could eventually meet organic criteria, but those certification programs have yet to be developed. Keep an ear out.

Look for a Certified Sustainable Seafood label from the

Marine Stewardship Council (MSC). This means the fish follows the United Nations' guidelines for eco-labeling and signals it was captured in a sustainable way (one that doesn't jeopardize the environment or deplete fish populations).

How to Buy Whole Fish

Press the Flesh

Most fishmongers will let you handle the fish; its flesh should be taut and spring back when pressed. The skin should be shiny and glistening, the tail moist and flat.

Peer into Its Eyes

Peepers should be bright, clear, and convex—not cloudy or sunken, which indicate the fish is old.

Take a Whiff

Seafood should smell briny—like seaweed—and not have an intense fishy odor. White fish smell a bit like melon or cucumber, and freshwater fish should smell like a clean pond.

Check the Gills

They should be wet and have a bright red or pink appearance. Dry, slimy, faded, or graying gills mean the fish is past its prime.

Scope out the Scales

Fish scales should be intact, cling tightly to skin, and appear moist and shiny—never dry.

Eat on Arrival—or Soon Thereafter

You can keep whole fish for two days in the fridge before it starts to go south. To retain freshness, keep it ultra cold by storing it in a plastic bag, and top with another ice-filled bag. If your dining plans change, stash your fish in the freezer within a couple days of purchase.

How to Buy Fillets and Steaks

Know Your Cuts

The two most common are:

- **Fillet:** Involves cutting the flesh away from—and parallel to—the backbone. Slices are bone-free except in species like salmon that may have "pins" or "intermuscular" bones—soft, small, annoying needlelike bones that are embedded in the flesh. You can ask your fishmonger to remove them, or try it yourself at home with needle-nose pliers, tweezers, or dedicated fish-bone tweezers.
- **Steak:** Usually reserved for larger fish (ten pounds or more), steaks are cut crosswise, through the backbone, giving you a thick cross-section, along with the bone.

Avoid the Gap

If you spot gaps in the flesh, walk away. The meat should be intact, tight, and moist. Any liquid on the fish should be thin and clear—not opaque or slimy.

Plastic Not Fantastic

Fish wrapped tightly in plastic packaging can breed bacteria and emit foul odors, so make sure there's no icky liquid floating around inside.

Spoil Alert

Dark spots. Discoloration. Dullness. Loss of texture. Sound like the makings of an anti-aging-cream ad? Well, in this case we're talking about fish flesh, which presents similar symptoms. Once cut, fish loses moisture and freshness by the minute. So steer clear of cuts with discolored blotches, dry patches, brown or yellow edges, or a spongy consistency.

Pack It In

A fish out of water (and in your shopping bag) is extremely perishable. To keep it cool, fresh, and moist, ask that it be packed in crushed ice.

Consume Quickly

Steaks and fillets can be stored up to two days in the coldest part of your fridge. For best results, wrap fish in a plastic bag and top it with an ice-filled bag to keep your catch super-cold. If you're not planning to eat it right away, toss it in the freezer.

How to Buy Frozen Fish

Stocking up on frozen fish can make your life so much easier. Keep it on hand for spontaneous meals without sacrificing quality or freshness. After capture, fish are generally processed and deep frozen right on board the vessel at the peak of their condition and healthfulness.

Dive Deep

Head to the depths of your store's freezer—below the freeze line—to find shiny, rock-hard frozen fish in well-sealed packages. Shun anything with white freezer-burn spots, frost, or ice crystals that may have formed after thawing and refreezing. There should be no sign of blood. Bypass any package that's ripped, torn, or crushed.

Check the Date

Don't buy frozen fish that's more than three months old.

Thaw Slowly

Keep your fish frozen at 0 degrees Fahrenheit until you're ready to use it, then thaw it in the fridge—never at room temperature. It takes six to eight hours per pound. For quicker results, place it under cold running water. You can also defrost frozen fish in the microwave, but be sure not to cook it, which will degrade the texture and flavor.

How to Buy Shellfish and Crustaceans

Clams, Oysters, and Mussels

These should be alive when sold (their shells will be firmly closed). If the shells are open, tap lightly and see if they shut. If they don't, they're dead meat—move on. Discard any with cracked or broken shells. Store them for no more than twenty-four hours in the fridge in a breathable bag (such as brown paper) that allows air to circulate. Scrub them clean before consuming.

Scallops

These usually come shucked. Look for meat with a firm texture and a clean, sweet, ocean smell.

BUY "DRY"

Scallops come "dry" and "wet." The wet variety is treated with a chemical solution called sodium tripolyphosphate (STPP), which gives seafood a firmer, smoother, glossier appearance, keeps it moist, and increases its shelf life. STPP bequeaths an opaque-white appearance, gummy texture, and bitter chemical flavor that soaks into the flesh and doesn't cook out. Buy dry or chemical-free scallops instead. If they're not labeled, ask your fishmonger.

Lobsters and Crabs

These should be purchased alive, as they spoil quickly after death. Look for leg movement. Lobsters will curl their tails under when picked up. If you're a total weenie like Amy and afraid to carry your creepy crawler home in a bag, you can ask your fishmonger to, um, "put it to sleep"—then dash home to prepare. (No dawdling, as quality will degrade swiftly.)

Shrimp

Raw shrimp flesh should be shiny and translucent with minimal odor. It's extremely perishable—eat it within twenty-four hours of purchase. Frozen shrimp is often a better (and much easier) choice and can be stored in the freezer for several weeks. Shells help protect the meat and preserve the flavor, so it's preferable to buy shrimp that has *not* been peeled and deveined before freezing.

Most "fresh" shrimp behind the fish counter have been shipped frozen, then thawed and displayed as fresh—so buying straight from the freezer case is just as good or better.

CHAPTER 7

FISH IN A FLASH—FIVE EASY PREPARATIONS

Amy here. I'm going to rat on Lisa: Prior to writing this book, she had *never* made a fish dish. Like many fish "chickens," she believed preparing seafood was time-consuming and complicated—and she only ordered it when dining out. Now she knows the truth (and feels a tad foolish): nothing could be faster or simpler. Here's proof:

1. BARBECUE BASH

- Top your grill with a triple layer of aluminum foil or a grill topper (with small holes) and heat to medium-high.
- Place whole fish or fillets on top of foil and coat with a marinade or barbeque sauce.
- Heat on an open or closed grill until fish is cooked through, 8 to 10 minutes.

2. FAKE FRY

- To oven-fry your favorite fish, make a crispy coating by combining whole-wheat breadcrumbs, a handful of ground nuts or coconut, and some seasoning.

- Dunk the fish fillets in an "egg" concoction (mix 1 tablespoon of ground flaxseed with 3 tablespoons of warm water and let sit for 5 minutes).
- Dip the coated fillets into the crumb-coating mixture, using your hands to firmly press the crumbs into the fish.
- Transfer to a baking sheet; bake for 8 to 10 minutes at 450°, flipping the fillets halfway through for crispness on both sides.

3. FISH IN FOIL

- Place a 4-ounce fillet in the center of a 9-by-12-inch piece of foil.
- Scrunch the foil around the fish, making it into a package with high sides.
- Top with fresh veggies, seasonings of choice, and 1 tablespoon of liquid (we love wine).
- Close the top to make a loose package; place the package on a baking sheet.
- Cook for 15 minutes at 425°—or heat on a preheated grill for 10 to 15 minutes.
- Serve in foil for a fun presentation or pour the contents of the packet over brown rice or another grain.

4. LOVELY LOX

Home-cured salmon is easy to make and so tasty—plus, it will impress your brunch guests. There are many variations (go online for more options), but I like to keep it simple:

- Combine ½ cup of sea salt with ½ cup of organic cane sugar.
- Take one whole, uncut piece of salmon (around 2 pounds), and cut it in half widthwise.
- Spread the mixture evenly on the flesh side of each piece.
- Place the pieces of salmon together, flesh sides touching.

- Wrap as tightly as possible in multiple layers of plastic wrap to prevent leaking.
- Place the wrapped fillets in the fridge and top them with a baking sheet weighted with cans, books, or other heavy objects.
- Turn the fish after 24 hours and re-weight.
- After two days (or more), remove the fish from the wrap and wipe or rinse off the salt/sugar mixture.
- Pat dry and slice thin.

5. TOSS IN SAUCE

- Prepare your favorite sauce, such as marinara, in a frying pan.
- Add the fish to the sauce.
- Cover and simmer for about 10 minutes, or until the fish is cooked through.
- Serve over whole-wheat pasta, brown rice, or another grain.

CHAPTER 8

BEST (AND WORST) FISH FOR HEALTH AND SUSTAINABILITY

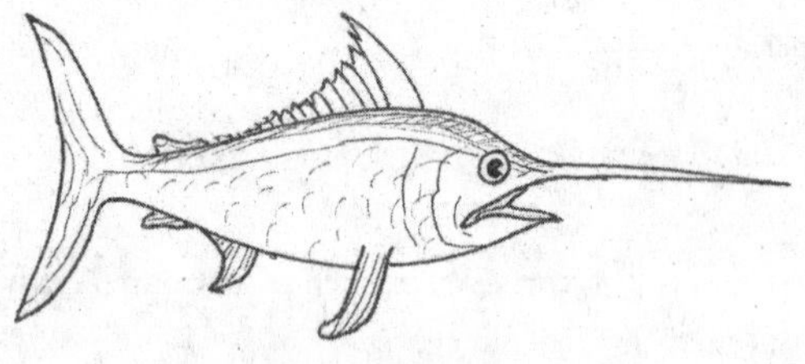

Fish Is Fraught

For the ethical vegan, eating seafood is murder. For the environmentalist, it's disastrous. For the clean eater, it's a nightmare—PCBs, DDT, dioxin, mercury, pesticides, antibiotics, and other gunk. And for stringent, health-focused vegans, one animal fat is as bad as another.

So what on earth is the lure?

Fish—the right fish—is a nutrition powerhouse, packed with protein, omega-3 fatty acids, and other vitamins and minerals. (For more on these benefits, see The Health Benefits of Seafood on page 19.) But finding the "right fish"—meaning it's plentiful, was caught in an ecofriendly manner (no bycatch or ravaging of coral reefs or ocean floors), and is relatively free of contaminants—requires some vigilance.

Unlike in years past, there's no more skipping into the supermarket and buying whatever shrimp or slab of salmon looks pretty and pink (hello, dye-infused pellets). These days, if we want to preserve our oceans and waterways and maintain our health, we have to choose our fish mindfully.

"Oh, fish sticks, like I have time for that!" we hear you say. And who does? Selecting the right seafood means committing to recon and research. But we've done a bunch of that legwork for you and compiled this guide to the good, the bad, and the ugly.

This List Is Fluid

The state of the oceans and their inhabitants is constantly in flux as conservation efforts are implemented (or ignored) and conditions change. Stay current on what to buy and what to avoid by checking in with organizations that keep tabs on these things, such as:

- EDF (Environmental Defense Fund) Seafood Selector—edf.seafood.org
- Food & Water Watch Smart Seafood Guide—foodandwaterwatch.org
- Monterey Bay Aquarium Seafood Watch—seafoodwatch.org
- Safina Center (formerly Blue Ocean Institute) Healthy Oceans Seafood Guide—blueocean.org/seafoods

You'll find up-to-date "best" and "worst" lists, wallet-size PDFs to download, apps for your smartphone, and more helpful tools.

And for tips on selecting your fishmonger and sniffing out the best, freshest catch, check out our Seafood Buyers' Guide on page 22.

A Few Fin Facts

Size Definitely Matters

Small fish at the bottom of the food chain (we're looking at you, anchovies, sardines, and herring) are generally more plentiful than their larger brethren, grow more quickly, and contain fewer contaminants—making them sustainable and healthy choices.

The large, top-of-the-food-chain predators that feast on other fish—think albacore tuna, swordfish, and king mackerel—absorb toxins and pollutants from their meals, which leads compounds like cancer-causing methyl mercury and PCBs (polychlorinated biphenyls) to accumulate in their flesh. Consumed in high doses, these can be harmful to humans, so watch your intake.

Domestic Rules

American fish are generally a more environmentally sustainable choice than imported varieties, since the United States imposes fairly stringent regulations that aren't necessarily instituted—or followed by—other countries. If you live near water, eat local catches whenever possible.

Pantry Raid

Don't shy away from canned, jarred, and pouched fish, which is inexpensive, shelf-stable, convenient, and perfect for spontaneous meals when unexpected guests arrive or the fridge is bare.

Salmon, sardines, anchovies, herring, crab, mackerel, and sustainably caught tuna (check the can for words like *hook and line*, *troll and pole*, or *troll caught*) make tasty pantry staples you can turn to for quick, healthful meals. Use them to fill sandwiches, enhance pasta sauces, or make marinades.

Keep It Clean

Sorry to state the obvious, but here goes: Fish that has been drowned in butter, drenched in white breading, fried in oil, coated with cream, slathered in tartar sauce, or smothered in cheese is no longer healthy. Check our recipe section (beginning on page 64) for just-as-decadent fish dishes that come minus all that sin.

The Mercury Mess

Mercury levels in certain fish—including large tuna, swordfish, and mackerel—have launched quite the publicity firestorm, especially with regard to pregnant women and their fetuses. But what's the scoop? And is the real danger real?

Mercury Rising

Spewed into the air by all manner of industrial, chemical, and power facilities, mercury can eventually make its way into our oceans and waterways. There it converts to methyl mercury, a form that's easily absorbed by humans. Small fish dine on contaminated aquatic organisms, larger fish prey on smaller fish, and the mercury builds in the flesh of those fish-eating fish. Once embedded in the animal's muscle, this colorless, odorless element cannot be removed by cooking, cleaning, or trimming off skin.

Is It All That Bad?

Mercury *is* known to harm the developing nervous system of fetuses and young children and can result in abnormal brain development and learning disabilities. And while no one knows what levels are safe for adult consumption (willing guinea pigs are hard to come by), mercury poisoning is real.

Sure, you may have to eat a lot of tainted fish before you experience symptoms such as impairment of peripheral vision, tingling, numbness, loss of balance, and muscle weakness—and your reaction (or not) depends on many factors, including your weight, mercury sensitivity, and gender.

That said, keeping a keen eye on your intake of mercury-prone fish is smart.

⚠ We've flagged these otherwise acceptable fish that have relatively high mercury content and/or other contaminants. The EPA recommends restricting intake of these species to one 6-ounce serving per week. And if you're pregnant, nursing, or looking to become pregnant, avoid them altogether.

Good Catch

Anchovy

Abundant in omega-3s, protein, iron, and minerals and low in mercury and toxins, these small, silvery, savory fish pack one heck of a flavor punch. They can be an acquired taste, but they'll add pizzazz to your dishes: Sauté or grill them and add them to pasta, pizza, and salads or use them to make marinades, tapenades, and, of course, the famous Caesar salad dressing (our recipe is on page 126).

If you buy fresh anchovies, they'll need to be filleted (not terribly difficult but see if your fishmonger will do the deed). Canned and jarred varieties are generally high in sodium, but you can soak them in water to reduce their saltiness.

Arctic Char

A distant relative of trout and salmon, this delicious, pinkish fish has a mild salmon-like flavor and is an ecofriendly choice that's brimming with omega-3s and protein. And because Arctic char farming practices don't lead to pollution or contamination, the farmed variety is acceptable (and wild may be hard to find). You can prepare it any number of ways, including poaching, pan searing, slow roasting, baking, and grilling.

Black Cod (Sablefish)

Thanks to its silky, buttery texture, chefs often refer to this North Pacific catch as "butterfish." It's low in calories, high in omega-3 fatty acids, rich in selenium, and sustainably fished. A highly versatile ingredient, black cod does well grilled, smoked, broiled, poached, or slow-cooked and makes excellent sushi.

Catfish (Domestic, farm-raised)

Low in fat and calories and containing omega-3s and high levels of vitamin B_{12} and magnesium, this predominantly freshwater catch is generally responsibly farmed, plentiful, and low in mercury. Its mild, firm flesh can be steamed, poached, baked, blackened, grilled, and smoked. Steer clear of imported catfish (see our Bad Catch section, page 42)—90 percent of it comes from Vietnam, which uses antibiotics that are banned in the United States.

Crab

Cleaning, cooking, cracking, and shelling these crustaceans are no easy feats. But once you've accessed their sweet meat, you'll find a delicacy that's loaded with vitamins, protein, minerals, and omega-3 fatty acids. Among the hundreds of species out there, blue crab is the most commonly eaten. Also popular are stone, Dungeness, snow, and Jonah crabs. They're delicious steamed; boiled; barbecued; and tossed into soups, stews, salads, dips, crab cakes, pasta dishes, and more.

Alaskan king crab is spiked with zinc (an antioxidant that helps support healthy bone mass and immune function); just don't mistake it for the overharvested imported king crab highlighted in our Bad Catch section.

Haddock

This firm white fish is a decent source of lean protein, selenium, and B vitamins but is low in omega-3s. Stick with bottom-longline- and hook-and-line-caught varieties from the United States and Canada. Its mild flavor makes it a versatile addition to recipes calling for white fish, including fish stews and chowders, and it's the perfect canvas for blackened or other highly seasoned dishes.

Halibut (Pacific)

Packed with almost an entire day's worth of omega-3 fatty acids and awash in potassium and vitamin D, this ecofriendly fish is low in overall fat and has a mild flavor that's palatable to even the finickiest fish eaters. Try it broiled, grilled, or marinated as ceviche. Avoid Atlantic halibut, one of our Bad Catch nominees, as it's vulnerable to overfishing.

Mackerel (Atlantic)

This small relative of the tuna is chock-full of omega-3s, comes packed with vitamin B_{12} (a serving has six times the RDA), and is low in contaminants. And because the species is so abundant, it's an environmentally friendly choice. With its strong, savory flavor, Atlantic mackerel is especially delicious grilled, smoked, and broiled. Beware its larger cousin, king mackerel (cited in our Bad Catch section), which contains high levels of mercury.

Rainbow Trout (Farmed)

While lake trout are generally high in contaminants, the protein- and omega-3s–packed farmed rainbow trout are shielded from toxins and score a "best choice" rating from the Monterey Bay Aquarium Seafood Watch, a consumer watch group. This freshwater white fish has a delicate, flaky texture and is tasty baked, broiled, roasted, pan fried, and grilled.

Salmon (Wild-caught Pacific/Alaskan species, including Chinook or king, chum, coho, pink, and sockeye; freshwater, farm-raised coho salmon)

Brimming with omega-3s, vitamins D and B_{12}, selenium, and protein, this heart-healthy fish is low in fat and contains minimal levels of mercury and other toxins. Chinook (or king) salmon has a rich, buttery texture, while sockeye salmon, an oilier variety, boasts deep-red flesh and bolder flavor and is perfect for grilling. Prefer a milder fish? Go for the lighter-hued coho. The budget-friendliest (and smallest) of the group are pink and chum, which are often used in canning and smoking.

Sardines

One of the most concentrated sources of omega-3s, sardines are bursting with vitamins B_{12} and D, as well as calcium, protein, and minerals. Sustainably fished and abundant, Pacific sardines even landed a spot on the Monterey Bay Aquarium's Super Green List.

Fresh sardines are delicious but extremely perishable, so they are often purchased canned. These tangy treats can be eaten straight from the can, topped with lemon juice or hot sauce, added to marinara sauces and served over pasta or spaghetti squash, or grilled fresh and topped with herbs. They also make a scrumptious dip (see recipe on page 125).

Shellfish (Bivalve mollusks)

You typically can't go wrong with nutrient-packed clams, mussels, oysters, and scallops. These little suckers serve as tiny water-filtration systems, sipping in the surrounding waters for food and cleansing it in the process—a huge boon to the environment, whether farmed or wild.

Safe to go raw? If you're healthy (and not pregnant), it's generally safe to eat raw clams and oysters that have been harvested from approved waters, packed under hygienic conditions, and properly refrigerated..

They may, however, pose a serious risk to those with illnesses like cancer, diabetes, and liver disease. When in doubt, enjoy them cooked.

Clams

One of best options for low-cholesterol shellfish, clams have more iron than beef and are a good source of protein, vitamin B_{12}, omega-3s, phosphorous, potassium, zinc, copper, manganese, and selenium. They're one of our nation's most sustainable seafood resources.

Mussels

Talk about flexing some nutritional muscle: These bivalves are among the most nutrient dense of all shellfish. They boast ample amounts of protein; vitamins A, B_{12}, and C; minerals such as manganese and zinc; and enough folic acid to give red meat a run for its money. Low in mercury and sustainably farmed, these mild, salty-flavored fish are delicious steamed; boiled; and when added to casseroles, pasta dishes, and salads.

Oysters

⚠ Known as an aphrodisiac due its high zinc content (more than any other food), the oyster is also a healthy catch for its vitamins A, B_{12}, and C, plus minerals like iron, calcium, and selenium. Serve them steamed, roasted, grilled, stuffed, and in soups and stews.

Scallops

An excellent source of protein, vitamin B_{12}, magnesium, and potassium. these succulent, mild-flavored mollusks are also low in calories and are generally a good, sustainable choice. Atlantic scallops (aka "giant scallops") are plentiful, but they're dredged, which can damage the seafloor. Opt for diver or day-boat scallops, which are retrieved with minimal impact on the environment. And be sure to buy "dry" over "wet" versions—the latter have been treated with chemicals that affect the scallop's texture and taste (not in a good way). These plump delicacies can be pan seared; grilled; broiled; and added to soups, stews, and pasta dishes.

Shrimp (Domestic and aquaculture raised)

Trapped Alaskan shrimp, pond-raised American and Canadian shrimp and prawns, and shrimp raised in recirculating aquaculture systems throughout the world are considered both safe and sustainable. Trawling, a popular method for capturing shrimp, is widely practiced in the United States but at a huge price: Many other sea animals are swept up and suffocate in these giant, dragging nets. Look for labels from independent agencies, including Wild American Shrimp, the Marine Stewardship Council, and the Aquaculture Certification Council, which certify best practices and sustainability.

Squid (Calamari)

Low in fat and calories (although higher in cholesterol than most fish), squid is an excellent source of omega-3s, protein, calcium, and vitamin B_{12}—and contains little in the way of mercury and contaminants. Try grilling this subtly flavored, slightly chewy, sustainable fish (actually a cephalopod), turn it into calamari salad, or toss it into soups and stews.

Tuna (Canned or pouched light)

⚠ Not all tunas are created equal: Light tuna (generally skipjack tuna) has the least amount of mercury. Albacore tuna is next but contains more than twice the mercury of light. And the highest mercury content is found in tuna steak and tuna sushi. Steer clear of Atlantic bluefin tuna, one of our Bad Catch headliners.

Toss canned light tuna (packed in water, not oil) into salads, pasta dishes, casseroles (see our Tuna Noodle Casserole recipe on page 78), and sandwiches—and look for brands that stipulate these catch methods on the packaging: "hook and line," "troll and pole," or "troll caught." Younger, smaller tuna (less than twenty pounds, versus hundreds of pounds for Atlantic bluefin) captured this way have much lower mercury and contaminant levels.

Bad Catch

Atlantic Flatfish (Flounder, sole, and halibut caught off the Atlantic Coast)

Overfished since the late 1800s, their numbers have been decimated, and they're loaded with contaminants.

Better catch: domestically farmed catfish, Pacific halibut, and tilapia

Chilean Sea Bass

Also known by their less eloquent name, Patagonian toothfish, these prehistoric-looking, cold water–loving beasts are prized for their rich, moist flavor. They're high in mercury, however, and their depleted stocks need a breather—badly. Take a pass for now.

Better catch: U.S. hook-and-line-caught haddock has a similar texture and feel

Catfish (Imported)

Itching for catfish? Nearly 90 percent of catfish imported to the United States comes from Vietnam, directly competing with American Delta–region catfish farmers. Vietnamese catfish has been linked with contaminated water, outdated facilities, and the use of antibiotics that are banned in the United States. Two varieties, Swai and Basa, aren't technically considered catfish by the federal government and are therefore not subject to the same inspection standards as other imported catfish.

Better catch: domestic farmed catfish

Cod (Atlantic)

Stocks of these once-plentiful fish collapsed in the mid-1990s and remain severely low. While vital to the economic health of New England fisherman, these fisheries need time to recover.

Better catch: Pacific cod

Grouper

High in mercury and perilously low in numbers due to their short reproduction cycles, grouper should be avoided.

Better catch: Pacific cod has a similar texture

King Crab (Imported)

Most of these long-legged creatures come from Russia, where harvesting limits are lax. Since 70 percent of the king crab sold in the United States is imported, it's important to ask its provenance.

Better catch: Alaskan king crab, which is more closely monitored

Mackerel (King)

This large, voracious predator's rich flavor makes it a highly desirable fish that once suffered from population decline. While stocks are healthier now, king mackerel contains extremely high levels of mercury and should be consumed rarely or not at all.

Better catch: Atlantic mackerel

Orange Roughy

These slow-growing fish take up to 40 years to reach full maturity, reproduce late in life, and can live to be 100, making it difficult for populations to recover from overfishing. They're also high in mercury. Don't be misled by "sustainably harvested" labels, as no orange roughy fisheries are considered well managed at this time.

Better catch: domestic catfish and tilapia have a similar texture

Red Snapper (Wild-caught, U.S. South Atlantic)

This tasty reef fish has been persistently overfished, putting tremendous stress on its numbers.

Better catch: black cod

Salmon (Wild-caught and farmed, Atlantic)

There's a sea of problems associated with this endangered fish that's now illegal to capture in the wild. Their already low numbers are suffering in part because of salmon farms, where fish are packed into pens often ridden with parasites and disease—and tainted with the antibiotics and pesticides used to combat these problems. Frequent escapes occur, which spreads disease and forces indigenous fish to compete with farmed fish for food and causes declines in native populations.

And the bright, rosy color of these farmed salmon? Thanks to "pinkifying" pellets, their naturally gray flesh turns a "natural-looking" (and buyer-friendlier) shade of pink. Wild salmon get their ruddy pigment from eating krill and shrimp, while farmed species feast on chicken litter and corn-and-soy fish pellets—which also means they have less of the omega-3s found in Alaskan wild-caught salmon.

Better catch: wild-caught Alaskan salmon

Shrimp (Farmed imported, Louisiana)

It may be time to stop the love affair with America's favorite seafood, most of which doesn't come from America. About 90 percent of our shrimp supply is farm-raised in faraway places like Vietnam, China, and Indonesia. With a few exceptions, most are grown in dirty, cramped conditions. The most contaminated of all seafood, this little crustacean frequently comes with a wealth of unwanted "sides," including pesticides; banned chemicals; carcinogenic antibiotics; cockroaches; and animal parts such as mouse hair, rat hair, and pieces of insects.

While up to 35 percent of imported seafood gets rejected due to all this nastiness, plenty ends up in our shrimp cocktail. And the scary part about that is, only 2 percent of imported shrimp is even inspected by U.S. regulatory agencies. Wild shrimp from Mexico and Louisiana are also on the hook for lax management, illegal fishing, and/or hefty bycatch—including endangered sea turtles—from trawling methods.

Better catch: certain domestic and aquaculture-raised shrimp (see shrimp in Good Catch)

Swordfish

Like other large fish at the top of the food chain, swordfish carry a heavy load of toxins, which they absorb from eating smaller fish and sea animals. Their high mercury level makes them undesirable. In addition, the preferred capture method is longlining, which can also kill other marine animals, like turtles, sharks, and seabirds.

Better catch: Pacific halibut, another meaty whitefish

Tuna (Atlantic bluefin)

These sleek giants are prized for their toothsome flesh, especially among sashimi eaters—creating a worldwide demand that has driven their numbers to near-extinction levels. With a voracious appetite for other sea life, including smaller fish, squid, crustacean, and eels, they're also extremely high in mercury and PCBs.

Better catch: wild-caught Alaskan salmon

Questionable Catch (You Decide)

Cod (Pacific)

While an excellent alternative to the overfished Atlantic cod, this western cousin is not without problems: Trawl-caught Pacific cod yields a good deal of bycatch, while those caught with bottom longlines can accidentally ensnare seabirds. The species also contains moderate amounts of mercury. Your best choice is Pacific cod captured in Alaska.

Monkfish

The "poor man's lobster" went from trash to treasure in the 1980s, and its popularity led to drastic overfishing. In addition, trawling for this warty, big-mouthed creature has led to collateral damage in the way of habitat and sea-creature destruction. Still, some watch groups argue that populations are recovering and that the environmental impact is "acceptable."

Lobster

Sweet-fleshed Atlantic lobster from the Gulf of Maine and Georges Bank is generally a good choice, but those hailing from fisheries in southern New England are suffering from population decline. Shun spiny or rock lobster from

Central America—much of which ends up in chain restaurants ("all you can eat lobster!")—as these species are overfished, illegally fished, or fished in unsafe conditions that harm divers.

Tilapia

The most popular farmed fish in the United States has been dubbed "the aquatic chicken" for its ubiquity, fairly low cost, and bland—but culinarily versatile—flesh. Most of our stateside supply comes from Latin America and Asia. Deprived of the high omega-3 content of most other fish (compare tilapia's 135 milligrams per serving to salmon's 2,000+ milligrams), this white, firm-fleshed fish is nonetheless high in protein and low in fat.

A hearty species native to lakes in Africa, tilapia exploded on the American food scene in the early 2000s. Unregulated tilapia farming in poor countries—where fish are crammed into cages—is worrisome to environmentalists, because fish waste pollutes the water and harms the ecosystem. While not your healthiest seafood choice, if you must eat it, go with tilapia that's tank farmed in the United States and Canada or comes from well-managed ponds in Ecuador.

CHAPTER 9

RECIPE HACKS—PREP NOW, USE LATER

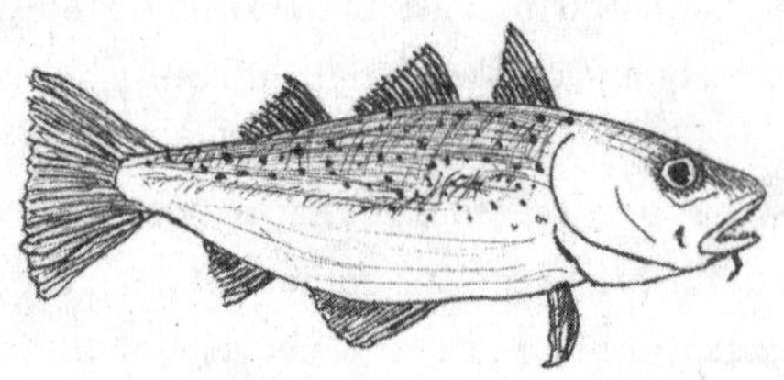

Next time you're catching up on your Netflix queue, why not busy your hands with our favorite quick-and-easy recipe hacks? Prepare them now and thank yourself later when all you do is grab from the freezer and go (just allow a few extra minutes of defrosting time when using in recipes).

THE MOTHER OF ALL TIPS

If we could give you only one tip, it would be this: Make lots of cashew cream in advance and stow it in the freezer. It will make the most decadent recipes that much simpler and quicker. Note that there are more than twenty mentions of cashew cream in this book. So blend now, cook later.

Carrots

- Pulse a large bag of peeled baby carrots in a food processor, toss into a plastic zip-top bag, and store in the freezer.

- To use: Bang the bag on the counter to loosen and remove what you need. Refreeze the remainder.

Cashew Cream

Amy usually buys 1 pound of cashews and makes the whole batch at once.

- Combine equal amounts of water and raw cashews (e.g., 1 cup of raw cashews with 1 cup of water).
- Purée the mixture in a high-powered food processor or blender until the texture is completely smooth (usually 3 to 5 minutes).
- Pour 1 tablespoon of cashew cream into each section of an ice-cube tray and freeze.
- Once cubes are frozen, toss the whole batch in a plastic zip-top bag and store in the freezer.

Fish

Raw fish freezes well. Buy extra when you see your favorites on sale.

- Air is your enemy, so wrap individual fillets tightly, or even better, vacuum-seal them.
- Fatty fish, like salmon and trout, should be frozen for no longer than three months; many other varieties last up to six months.
- Shrimp can be tossed frozen into recipes—just add extra cooking time for thawing.

Garlic

- Chop a tub of fresh, peeled garlic in the food processor, toss into a plastic bag, and freeze.
- To use: Bang the bag on the counter to loosen and remove what you need. Refreeze the remainder.

Ginger

- Buy a large head of ginger and peel. Snap small knobs for easy peeling of the larger head.
- Chop in a food processor, toss into a plastic zip-top bag, and freeze.
- To use: Bang the bag on the counter to loosen and remove what you need. Refreeze the remainder.

Onions

- Chop a bag of onions (peeled) in the food processor, toss into a plastic zip-top bag, and stow in the freezer.
- To use: Bang the bag on the counter to loosen and remove what you need. Refreeze the remainder.

Pasta

- Set aside leftover, unsauced al dente pasta (or intentionally make extra) and cool.
- Freeze in a plastic zip-top bag or a container.
- Add it to warm sauce in the pan to defrost.

CHAPTER 10

COOK'S TOOLKIT—KITCHEN ESSENTIALS

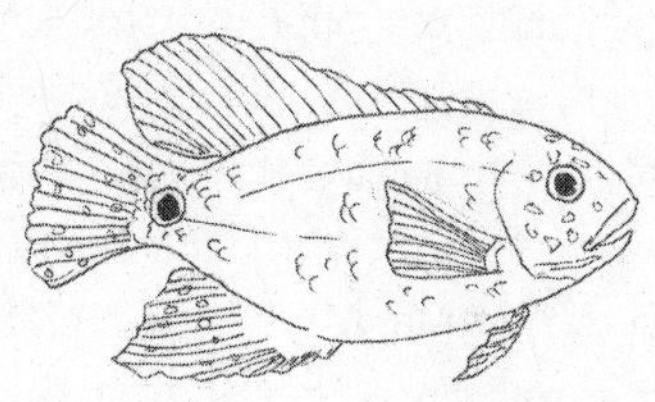

Stocking your kitchen with the right equipment leads to faster, easier cooking—and a happier chef. Here's a roundup of Amy's top picks.

Food Processor

My high-powered blender has taken over most of the jobs my old food processor used to do. But when I have to shred or thinly slice big batches of veggies, it's still king. For small batches, I prefer the mandoline, which involves less setup and cleanup.

Heavy, Dark Pot

Since all my cooking is oil-free, I go with my favorite old standby: a heavy, worn-in pot, which helps "caramelize" onions and veggies as I sauté them. Some people prefer cast iron. Others prefer nonstick. (Note: Nonstick pans are generally considered safe but can emit toxins at extremely high temperatures.)

High-Powered Blender

One of my daily go-to tools, the blender is on my counter at all times. I chose a model with a big blender attachment as well as an individual cup—the smaller container is ideal for chopping garlic and ginger, while I use the large one for making cashew cream. This is one appliance you shouldn't scrimp on—so if you can, splurge on one of the new high-powered blenders. (Mine is a Ninja, Lisa has the Vitamix.) A wimpy blender just can't handle big jobs, is not as sturdy, and will ultimately leave you frustrated.

Tip: When puréeing veggies and tofu, don't overblend to liquefy. Pulsing is usually your best choice.

Immersion/Stick Blender

After many years of cooking, I'm still in love with this versatile and inexpensive gadget. Use it to purée soups in the pot, make creamy sauces, whip up guacamole, cook up decadent desserts, and so much more.

Mandoline

I avoided buying a mandoline for years, thinking a fancy-named cooking instrument was too sophisticated for my basic style. Wow, was I wrong. I recently bought a small, simple mandoline (around $30), and have fallen head over heels in love. If you, too, want perfect, thinly sliced potatoes for chips, zucchini for lasagna, and carrots for salad, put the mandoline on your gotta-have-it list now.

Noodler or Vegetable Spiralizer

A "noodler" is a magic tool for under $20. I love to make zucchini noodles instead of pasta when I'm in the mood for a lighter meal. The great part is that the zucchini (raw) tricks you into thinking you're eating real pasta. Sometimes I mix it

50/50 with whole-wheat linguini. For a more elaborate—and expensive—gadget, try the spiralizer.

Easy, right? You probably have the other basic equipment—a good set of bowls, spoons, ladles, spatulas, baking dishes, and baking sheets—so you're all ready to begin your seagan cooking (and eating) adventure. Let's go!

CHAPTER 11

TWENTY-ONE DAYS OF SWOON-WORTHY SEAGAN MENUS

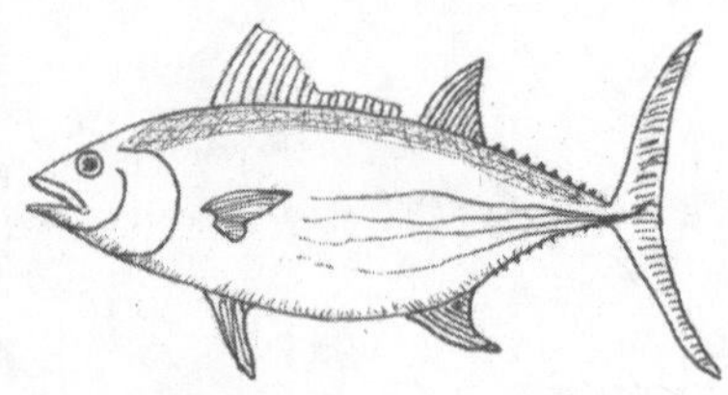

Tired of same old, same old? Need some meal inspiration? We've gathered three weeks' worth of seagan menus to take the guesswork out of eating well. You'll find a variety of healthful choices—with options for dining in or out—and we include fish and dessert (you're welcome) three times a week.

Feel free to tailor this to your own preferences by swapping out our recommendations for your personal faves. (Of course, if you have a health condition that requires you to severely restrict fats or sodium, please adjust accordingly.) Beef up the health factor by adding herbs and spices wherever, whenever you can. (Check out our Spicy Seventeen picks on pages 208 to 217.)

DAY 1

BREAKFAST: Mixed cereal bowl—raw oats, slivered almonds, fresh berries, almond milk ♦ **SNACK:** Fresh fruit ♦ **LUNCH:** *If you eat at home:* Salad topped with canned light tuna and veggies, topped with balsamic vinegar ♦ *If you go out:* Salad with fresh plain grilled salmon and veggies, topped with balsamic vinegar ♦ **SNACK:** Nondairy yogurt* and/or fresh fruit ♦ **DINNER:** Pasta Carbonara (recipe on page 102) ♦ **DESSERT:** Caramel Corn (recipe on page 142) or oil-free popcorn of your choice

 DAY 2

BREAKFAST: Quinoa topped with toasted coconut, almonds, chopped apple, ground cinnamon, and a splash of almond milk ♦ **SNACK:** Fresh fruit ♦ **LUNCH:** *If you eat at home:* Make a big bowl of layered greens, beans, and salsa ♦ *If you go out:* Head to Chipotle or another Mexican fast-food restaurant and order a bowl with black beans, brown rice, lettuce, salsa of choice, and guacamole ♦ **SNACK:** Fresh vegetables and low-fat, oil-free hummus or dip of choice (recipes on pages 125 to 128) ♦ **DINNER:** 10-Minute Flatbread Pizza (recipe on page 106) and salad with oil-free dressing (recipes on pages 125 to 128) ♦ **DESSERT:** Chocolate Chip–Banana Bread Pudding (recipe on page 134) and/or fresh fruit

 DAY 3

BREAKFAST: Simple oatmeal made with almond milk and topped with berries ♦ **SNACK:** Raw veggies with Ranch Dressing and Dip (recipe on page 127) ♦ **LUNCH:** *If you eat at home:* Whole-wheat wrap with oil-free hummus or avocado and fresh vegetables ♦ *If you go out:* Head to your local Italian restaurant and order whole-wheat pasta with marinara sauce (request low-oil, if

*Our preference is Greek-style coconut yogurt by SO Delicious.

available) and steamed broccoli ♦ **SNACK:** A handful of seeds or nuts ♦ **DINNER:** Big bowl of beans, brown rice, and chopped salad (dark-leaf lettuce, cucumbers, mandarin oranges, slivered almonds, and red onion) topped with oil-free dressing (recipes on pages 125 to 128)

DAY 4

BREAKFAST: Nondairy yogurt with nuts and fresh berries ♦ **SNACK:** Fresh vegetables and low-fat, oil-free hummus or dip of choice (recipes on pages 125 to 128) ♦ **LUNCH:** *If you eat at home:* Steamed vegetables, black beans, and brown rice or other grain ♦ *If you eat out:* Head to a Chinese restaurant and order steamed vegetables and brown rice ♦ **SNACK:** Fresh or dried fruit ♦ **DINNER:** Crab Mac and Cheese (recipe on page 65), salad, and oil-free dressing (recipes on pages 125 to 128)

DAY 5

BREAKFAST: Crunchy French Toast Casserole (recipe on page 130) ♦ **SNACK:** Apple, plain or with peanut or other nut butter ♦ **LUNCH:** *If you eat at home:* Veggie burger with tomato, wrapped in lettuce ♦ *If you go out:* Veggie burger with lettuce and tomato on whole-wheat bun ♦ **SNACK:** Vegan fruit-and-nut bar of choice or fresh fruit ♦ **DINNER:** BLT Sandwich (recipe on page 110) and side salad with dressing of choice (recipes on pages 125 to 128) or balsamic vinegar ♦ **DESSERT:** Three squares of dark chocolate ♦ *Before you go to bed: Prepare Banana Overnight Oatmeal (recipe on page 132) for tomorrow's breakfast*

DAY 6

BREAKFAST: Banana Overnight Oatmeal (recipe on page 132) ♦ **SNACK:** Fresh fruit ♦ **LUNCH:** *If you eat at home:* Farro salad with white beans, artichokes, and your choice of fresh veggies ♦ *If you go out:* Salad with grains and fresh veggies ♦ **SNACK:** Air-popped popcorn (to pop in microwave, see instructions on page 181) ♦ **DINNER:** Vegetable Pot Pie (recipe on page 107) and a side salad with dressing of choice (recipes on pages 125 to 128) or balsamic vinegar

DAY 7

BREAKFAST: Nondairy yogurt with nuts and fresh berries ♦ **SNACK:** Fresh fruit ♦ **LUNCH:** *If you eat at home:* Any fish in foil (so quick and easy with no real cleanup; see instructions on page 85) ♦ *If you go out:* Plain grilled fish and steamed veggies ♦ **SNACK:** Fresh vegetables and low-fat, oil-free hummus, or dip of choice (recipes pages 125 to 128) ♦ **DINNER:** Baked Ziti with Spinach (recipe on page 101)

DAY 8

BREAKFAST: 1 or 2 slices of toasted whole-grain bread topped with nut or apple butter and sliced bananas or apples ♦ **SNACK:** Handful of seeds or nuts ♦ **LUNCH:** *If you eat at home:* Steamed veggies and tofu with soy sauce and mirin (rice wine) ♦ *If you go out:* Vegetable sushi with brown rice ♦ **SNACK:** Fresh fruit ♦ **DINNER:** Black Cod Milanese (recipe on page 68)

DAY 9

BREAKFAST: Oatmeal made with almond milk instead of water, topped with ground nutmeg, fresh berries, and chia seeds ♦ **SNACK:** Fresh fruit ♦ **LUNCH:** *If you eat at home:* Steamed vegetables with baked sweet potato ♦ *If you go out:* Mixed salad with tons of veggies and beans, topped with a splash of balsamic vinegar ♦ **SNACK:** Air-popped popcorn (to pop in microwave, see instructions on page 181) ♦ **DINNER:** Eggplant Parmesan (recipe on page 105), side salad with oil-free dressing of choice (recipes on pages 125 to 128) or balsamic vinegar

DAY 10

BREAKFAST: Mixed cereal bowl—raw oats, a handful of walnuts, fresh berries, and almond milk ♦ **SNACK:** Fresh fruit ♦ **LUNCH:** *If you eat at home:* Large bowl of miso soup (just mix miso paste and water) with veggies and tofu cooked in soup while heating ♦ *If you go out:* Asian soba noodle soup bowl with veggies (check to make sure the broth is vegan) ♦ **SNACK:** Fruit-and-nut bar of choice ♦ **DINNER:** Spinach and Cheese Empanada (recipe on page 98)

DAY 11

BREAKFAST: Top a cooked grain—oats, quinoa, or amaranth—with a splash of almond milk, a sprinkle of ground cinnamon, and some seeds and berries ♦ **SNACK:** Handful of nuts ♦ **LUNCH:** *If you eat at home:* Lentils over brown rice with chopped tomatoes, onions, and cilantro and a dash of curry powder ♦ *If you go out:* Try your neighborhood Indian restaurant—request any vegetable dish made without dairy or ghee (clarified butter) that is very low in oil; I always like a side of mango chutney ♦ **SNACK:** Fresh fruit ♦ **DINNER:** Tuna Noodle Casserole (recipe on page 78) with mixed green salad and oil-free dressing (see recipes on pages 125 to 128) ♦ **DESSERT:** three squares of dark chocolate

DAY 12

BREAKFAST: Nondairy yogurt topped with berries, hemp seeds, and ground cinnamon ♦ **SNACK:** Fresh fruit ♦ **LUNCH:** *If you eat at home:* Lentils over brown rice with chopped peppers and tomatoes and a dash of curry powder ♦ *If you go out:* Hit your local salad bar and create a beautiful bowl of dark-green lettuces, fresh veggies, beans, fruit, seeds, and balsamic vinegar ♦ **SNACK:** Fresh vegetables and low-fat, oil-free hummus or dip of choice (recipes on pages 125 to 128) ♦ **DINNER:** 10-minute Flatbread Pizza (recipe on page 106)

DAY 13

BREAKFAST: Bowl of high-fiber, low-sugar cereal with almond milk, fresh berries, nuts, and/or seeds ♦ **SNACK:** Fresh fruit ♦ **LUNCH:** *If you eat at home:* Can of vegetarian chili over a baked sweet potato ♦ *If you go out:* Large bowl of dairy-free vegetarian soup with a hunk of whole-grain bread and a side salad dressed with balsamic vinegar ♦ **SNACK:** Air-popped popcorn (to pop in microwave, see instructions on page 181) ♦ **DINNER:** Fish Cakes (recipe on page 76) with a side of whole grains and steamed veggies ♦ **DESSERT:** Sorbet, frozen-fruit bar, or fresh fruit

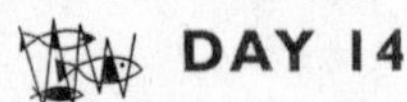

DAY 14

BREAKFAST: Low-sugar smoothie made with apple, pineapple, kale, coconut water, and a spritz of lemon juice ♦ **SNACK:** Fresh fruit ♦ **LUNCH:** *If you eat at home:* Giant salad (learn how to build the perfect salad on page 177), dressed with our oil-free dressing (recipes on pages 125 to 128) or balsamic vinegar ♦ *If you go out:* Hit your local salad bar and create a giant, healthful salad; drizzle with balsamic vinegar ♦ **SNACK:** Handful of seeds or nuts ♦ **DINNER:** Whole-wheat pasta topped with vodka sauce (mix jarred marinara with some cashew cream and a shot of vodka) with salad and oil-free dressing (recipes on pages 125 to 128) ♦ **DESSERT:** Three squares of dark chocolate

DAY 15

BREAKFAST: Quinoa topped with toasted coconut, almonds, chopped apple, ground cinnamon, and a splash of almond milk ♦ **SNACK:** Fresh fruit ♦ **LUNCH:** *If you eat at home:* Big bowl of layered greens, beans, salsa, and cilantro ♦ *If you go out:* Hit Chipotle or another Mexican fast-food restaurant and order a bowl with black beans, brown rice, lettuce, salsa of choice, and guacamole ♦ **SNACK:** Fresh vegetables and low-fat, oil-free hummus or dip of choice (recipes on pages 125 to 128) ♦ **DINNER:** Brazilian Fish Stew (recipe on page 80) ♦ **DESSERT:** Quick Tiramisu (recipe on page 135)

DAY 16

BREAKFAST: Breakfast parfait—layer nondairy yogurt, fresh berries, a spoonful of oats, a tablespoon of chia seeds, and a sprinkle of ground cinnamon ♦ **SNACK:** Fresh fruit ♦ **LUNCH:** *If you eat at home:* Whole-wheat wrap with oil-free hummus or avocado and fresh vegetables ♦ *If you go out:* Head to your local Chinese restaurant for steamed veggies, steamed tofu, and brown rice; request a side of any low-oil vegetarian sauce for dipping ♦ **SNACK:** Fruit-and-nut bar of choice ♦ **DINNER:** Thai Curry Haddock in Foil (follow recipe on page 92 but substitute slices of extra-firm tofu for the fish) with brown rice or other grain of choice

DAY 17

BREAKFAST: Mixed cereal bowl—raw oats, a handful of pecans, fresh berries, almond milk, a dash of ground cinnamon, and a sprinkling of hemp seeds ♦ **SNACK:** Nondairy yogurt or fresh fruit ♦ **LUNCH:** *If you eat at home:* Whole-wheat pasta with low-oil marinara sauce and steamed broccoli ♦ *If you go out:* Head to your local Italian restaurant for whole-wheat pasta with marinara sauce (oil-free, if possible) and steamed broccoli ♦ **SNACK:** Air-popped popcorn (to pop in microwave, see instructions on page 181) ♦ **DINNER:** Maple-Mustard–Glazed Salmon in Foil (follow recipe on page 89 but substitute slices of extra-firm tofu for the fish) with brown rice and steamed bok choy

DAY 18

BREAKFAST: Low-sugar smoothie made with water or coconut water, berries, half a banana, unsweetened nondairy yogurt, and flaxseed meal ♦ **SNACK:** Vegan fruit-and-nut bar of choice, or fresh fruit ♦ **LUNCH:** *If you eat at home:* Any fish in foil (so quick and easy with no real cleanup; see cooking instructions on page 85) with a side salad or steamed veggies ♦ *If you go out:* Plain grilled fish and steamed veggies ♦ **SNACK:** Fresh fruit ♦ **DINNER:** Lasagna (recipe on page 104) and tossed salad, topped with oil-free dressing of choice (recipes on pages 125 to 128) or balsamic vinegar

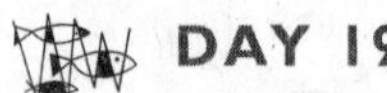

DAY 19

BREAKFAST: One or two slices of toasted whole-grain bread topped with nut or apple butter and sliced bananas or apples ♦ **SNACK:** Fresh fruit ♦ **LUNCH:** *If you eat at home:* Large bowl of miso soup (just mix miso paste and water) with veggies and tofu cooked in the soup while heating ♦ *If you go out:* Asian soba noodle soup bowl with veggies (make sure broth is vegan) ♦ **SNACK:** Fresh vegetables and oil-free, low-fat hummus or dip of choice (recipes on pages 125 to 128) ♦ **DINNER:** Crab-and-Spinach-Stuffed Portabella Mushrooms (see recipe on page 84 and substitute 1 cup of crumbled tempeh for the crabmeat) and salad with oil-free dressing (recipes on pages 125 to 128)

DAY 20

BREAKFAST: Amaranth porridge topped with almond milk, fresh berries, hempseeds, and a few cashews ♦ **SNACK:** Fresh fruit ♦ **LUNCH:** *If you eat at home:* Lentils over brown rice with chopped tomatoes and a dash of curry powder ♦ *If you go out:* Hit your local salad bar and create a beautiful bowl of dark-green lettuces, fresh veggies, beans, fruit, seeds, and balsamic vinegar ♦ **SNACK:** Air-popped popcorn (to pop in microwave, see instructions on page 181) ♦ **DINNER:** Have a picnic with Potato-Chip Pie in a Bag (recipe on page

109) or BLT Sandwiches (recipe on page 110), and Creamy Coleslaw (recipe on page 120) ♦ **DESSERT:** Caramel Corn (recipe on page 142) and/or fresh fruit

DAY 21

BREAKFAST: Low-sugar peach smoothie with light coconut milk, hemp seeds, a dash of vanilla extract, and a pinch of ground cinnamon ♦ **SNACK:** Fresh vegetables and oil-free hummus or dip of choice (recipes on pages 125 to 128) ♦ **LUNCH:** *If you eat at home:* Homemade quick pizza—whole-wheat tortilla topped with sliced tofu, chopped veggies, and a teaspoon of nutritional yeast, baked in a preheated oven at 425° for 3 to 5 minutes ♦ *If you go out:* Whole-wheat pizza topped with sauce and veggies, no cheese ♦ **SNACK:** Fresh fruit ♦ **DINNER:** Fettuccine Alfredo, without the shrimp (recipe on page 72), over: half noodled zucchini and half whole-wheat fettuccini ♦ **DESSERT:** Mocha-Coconut Almond Fudge Ice Cream (recipe on page 144) or store-bought vegan sorbet or ice cream

CHAPTER 12

DECADENT SEAGAN AND VEGAN RECIPES

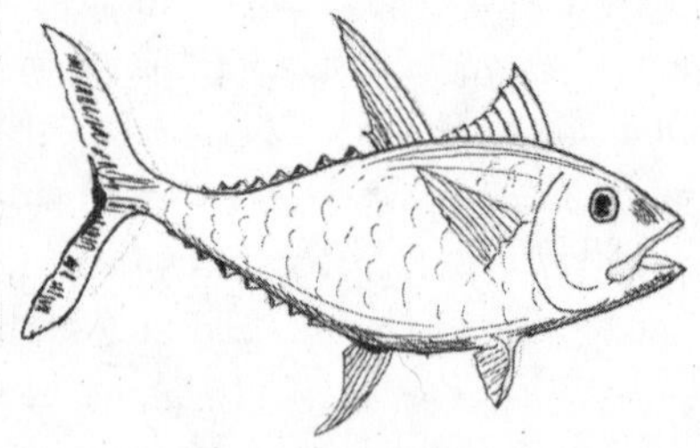

Amy has been cooking up a storm in her Boulder kitchen, tempting her family with achingly delicious aromas and fighting off their constant advances ("No, you *can't* eat that entire pan of brownies!") Here are her recipe superstars—all pretty easy, most *super easy*, and every single one a triumph in taste.

Note: When shopping for these recipes, be sure to consult our Seafood Buyers' Guide (page 22) and Good Catch, Bad Catch section (starting on page 36). Find more recipes at seaganeating.com.

RICH SEAFOOD DISHES

These lust-worthy meals only look sinful—dive in and enjoy with zero remorse.

Crab Mac and Cheese

SERVES 6

Let's rename this dish "The Most Decadent, Delicious Mac and Cheese on the Planet!" My teenage son, Cam, is the inspiration for this recipe, because he adores anything rich and creamy. Add the fabulousness of crab, and he is in nirvana—as is anyone else lucky enough to get a spoonful.

- 1 cup raw cashews
- 1 cup water
- 1 pound whole-wheat or gluten-free spiral or macaroni pasta
- 2 cups fresh cauliflower florets
- ½ cup peeled, chopped sweet potato
- 1 cup unsweetened plain almond milk
- 2½ tablespoons nutritional yeast
- 2½ teaspoons salt
- 1¼ teaspoons garlic powder
- ¼ teaspoon ground nutmeg
- 12 ounces fresh or canned crabmeat (picked and drained)
- ⅓ cup whole-wheat or gluten-free breadcrumbs (or 1 to 2 slices toast ground in a blender)

Preheat the oven to 425°.

In a blender or food processor, purée the cashews and water until smooth and creamy.

Cook the pasta 2 minutes less than instructed by the package directions. Drain and set aside.

Steam the cauliflower and sweet potato in a pot or in a microwave oven in 5-minute increments until tender.

With a food processor, blender, or immersion blender, purée the cauliflower, sweet potato, almond milk, nutritional yeast, salt, garlic powder, nutmeg, and cashew cream until smooth.

Add the crabmeat and pulse a few times until well incorporated. Stir the sauce into the pasta.

Pour into a 9- by 13-inch baking dish, top with the breadcrumbs, and bake, uncovered, for 20 minutes.

Serve quickly—so that ravenous 13-year-old boys (like my son) don't devour the entire thing before it hits the dinner table.

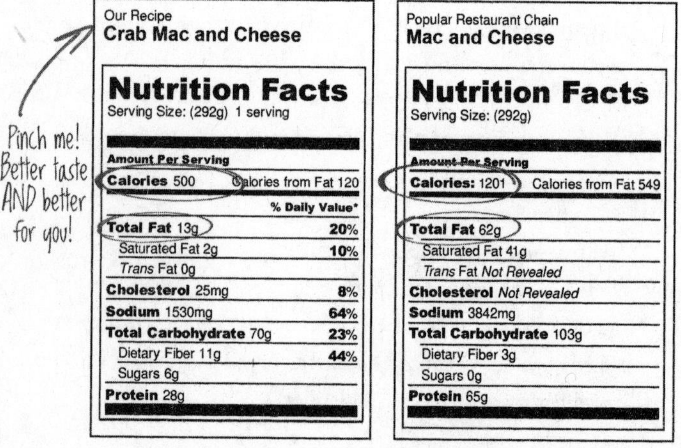

Pinch me!
Better taste
AND better
for you!

Our Recipe
Crab Mac and Cheese

Nutrition Facts
Serving Size: (292g) 1 serving

Amount Per Serving	
Calories 500	Calories from Fat 120
	% Daily Value*
Total Fat 13g	**20%**
Saturated Fat 2g	**10%**
Trans Fat 0g	
Cholesterol 25mg	**8%**
Sodium 1530mg	**64%**
Total Carbohydrate 70g	**23%**
Dietary Fiber 11g	**44%**
Sugars 6g	
Protein 28g	

Popular Restaurant Chain
Mac and Cheese

Nutrition Facts
Serving Size: (292g)

Amount Per Serving	
Calories: 1201	Calories from Fat 549
Total Fat 62g	
Saturated Fat 41g	
Trans Fat *Not Revealed*	
Cholesterol *Not Revealed*	
Sodium 3842mg	
Total Carbohydrate 103g	
Dietary Fiber 3g	
Sugars 0g	
Protein 65g	

Halibut à la Vodka

SERVES 4

This could not be easier or more delicious. For a fun time, add more vodka.

- ⅓ cup raw cashews
- ⅓ cup plus 2 tablespoons water
- 1½ cups fat-free marinara or other pasta sauce
- 2 to 4 tablespoons vodka (more makes it "spicier")
- 1 tablespoon nutritional yeast
- 4 Pacific halibut steaks, about 4 ounces each

In a small blender or food processor, purée the cashews and ⅓ cup water until smooth.

In a large frying pan, over low heat, combine the cashew cream, marinara sauce, vodka, remaining 2 tablespoons water, and nutritional yeast.

Add the halibut steaks to the pan in a single layer, skin-side down, and spoon the sauce over the fish.

Cover and cook until the fish is done, around 8 minutes.

Serve with whole-wheat pasta or over a bed of raw spinach (the heat from the sauce and fish should wilt the spinach).

NUTRITION (1 serving/249g): Calories 230, Calories from Fat 70, Total Fat 8g, Saturated Fat 1g, Trans Fat 0g, Cholesterol 55mg, Sodium 450mg, Total Carbohydrate 10g, Dietary Fiber 2g, Sugars 4g, Protein 24g

Black Cod Milanese

SERVES 4

My favorite meal in my carnivorous days was veal Milanese (it was also my signature dish). For fifteen vegan/seagan years, there was a big black hole in my diet—I longed for that perfect combination of warm and crispy topped with cold and crunchy. I wish I'd figured out this gem sooner. This one's for you, my dear husband of 25 years.

1 tablespoon ground flaxseed or flaxseed meal
3 tablespoons warm water
1 cup whole-wheat or gluten-free breadcrumbs (or 4 slices whole-grain toast ground in a blender)
1 teaspoon salt
1 teaspoon nutritional yeast
½ teaspoon ground dried thyme
½ teaspoon ground dried basil
¼ teaspoon garlic powder
4 black cod steaks, about 4 ounces each
3 cups finely chopped mixed lettuce of choice
¾ cup finely chopped fresh tomatoes
¼ teaspoon ground black pepper

Preheat the oven to 475°. Line a baking sheet with foil and set aside.

In a medium shallow bowl, combine the flaxseed and water and set aside for 5 minutes.

In a medium bowl, combine the breadcrumbs, ½ teaspoon of the salt, the nutritional yeast, thyme, basil, and garlic powder.

Dip the cod steaks in the flaxseed mixture, then dredge them in the breadcrumb mixture, using your hands to press the mixture and completely coat the fish.

Place the cod steaks on the prepared baking sheet and sprinkle with the remaining breadcrumb mixture.

Bake for 8 minutes (flipping the fish after 4 minutes, if desired), until the fish is cooked through.

In a medium bowl, combine the lettuce, tomatoes, remaining ½ teaspoon salt (to taste), and black pepper. Toss well.

Plate each piece of fish and top with a quarter of the salad mixture before serving.

NUTRITION (1 serving/206g): Calories 180, Calories from Fat 20, Total Fat 2g, Saturated Fat 0g, Trans Fat 0g, Cholesterol 55mg, Sodium 990mg, Total Carbohydrate 16g, Dietary Fiber 4g, Sugars 3g, Protein 23g

Shrimp Fried Rice

SERVES 4

This lighter take on a delicious (but greasy) classic is a cinch to make. With just a few minor revisions, a beloved Chinese dish is transformed into a healthy treat.

- 1 medium onion, diced
- 1 cup sliced mushrooms, any variety
- 2 cloves garlic, minced
- 1 cup bean sprouts
- 1 pound medium raw domestic shrimp, peeled and deveined
- 4 cups precooked brown rice
- 2 to 2½ tablespoons soy sauce to taste
- ¼ cup chopped scallion

In a heavy, dry pan, cook the onion and mushrooms over medium heat until the onion is translucent. If the ingredients begin to stick, add water, a few tablespoons at a time.

Add the garlic, bean sprouts, and shrimp. Sauté until the shrimp are cooked through, about 10 minutes.

Add the rice, soy sauce, and scallion and cook until the rice is well heated.

Serve alone or with a side of steamed veggies.

4x less fat and doubly delicious

Our Recipe
Shrimp Fried Rice

Nutrition Facts
Serving Size: (249g) 1 serving

Amount Per Serving	
Calories 330	Calories from Fat 25
	% Daily Value*
Total Fat 3g	**5%**
Saturated Fat 0.5g	**3%**
Trans Fat 0g	
Cholesterol 145mg	**48%**
Sodium 1210mg	**50%**
Total Carbohydrate 53g	**18%**
Dietary Fiber 5g	**20%**
Sugars 4g	
Protein 23g	

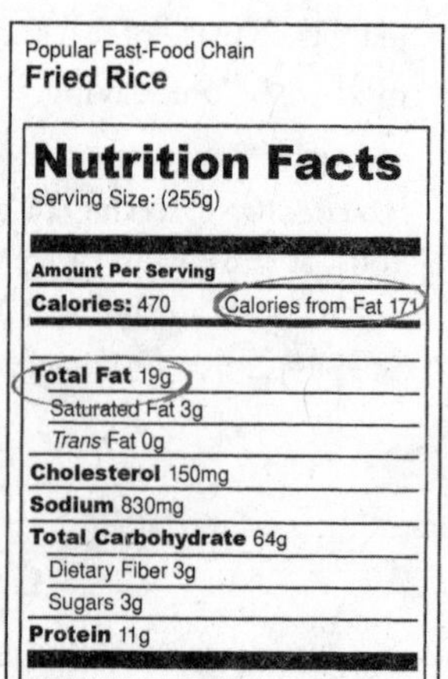

Popular Fast-Food Chain
Fried Rice

Nutrition Facts
Serving Size: (255g)

Amount Per Serving	
Calories: 470	Calories from Fat 171
Total Fat 19g	
Saturated Fat 3g	
Trans Fat 0g	
Cholesterol 150mg	
Sodium 830mg	
Total Carbohydrate 64g	
Dietary Fiber 3g	
Sugars 3g	
Protein 11g	

Coconut-Crusted Trout

SERVES 4

I salivate over coconut-crusted anything at restaurants but never order these dishes because they're usually deep-fried. Now I can enjoy my fantasy food without the morning-after guilt.

- 1 tablespoon ground flaxseed or flaxseed meal
- 3 tablespoons warm water
- ½ cup shredded coconut (unsweetened)
- ½ cup whole-wheat or gluten-free breadcrumbs (or 2 slices whole-grain toast ground in a blender)
- ½ teaspoon salt

¼ teaspoon ground black pepper

4 rainbow trout fillets, about 4 ounces each

Preheat the oven to 450°.

In a shallow medium bowl, combine the flaxseed and water, and set aside for 5 minutes.

In a medium bowl, combine the coconut, breadcrumbs, salt, and pepper.

Dip the fish fillets in the flax mixture, then dredge them in the coconut mixture, using your hands to press the coconut mixture onto the fish.

Place the fish on a foil-lined baking sheet. Surround with a single layer of extra coconut-breadcrumb mixture.

Bake for 8 to 10 minutes, flipping the fillets halfway through if desired, until the fish is cooked through.

Top with extra toasted-coconut mixture and serve. Optional: Add an Asian sweet chili sauce for dipping.

NUTRITION (1 serving/150g): Calories 270, Calories from Fat 130, Total Fat 15g, Saturated Fat 8g, Trans Fat 0g, Cholesterol 65mg, Sodium 400mg, Total Carbohydrate 9g, Dietary Fiber 3g, Sugars 1g, Protein 25g

Trout Piccata

SERVES 4

This light, super-flavorful rendition of the butter-and-oil-infused classic is perfect for summer evenings or even a special lunch.

1½ cups dry white wine

4 tablespoons capers

3 tablespoons fresh-squeezed lemon juice
3 cloves garlic, chopped
4 rainbow trout fillets, about 4 ounces each
Salt to taste

In a large heavy, dry pan, heat the wine, capers, lemon juice, and garlic over medium heat for 2 minutes.

Reduce heat to low, add the fish to the pan in a single layer, flesh side down, and cover the pan.

Poach for 6 to 8 minutes, or until the fish is cooked through. Add salt to taste and serve alone or over brown rice.

NUTRITION (1 serving/222g): Calories 240, Calories from Fat 60, Total Fat 7g, Saturated Fat 1.5g, Trans Fat 0g, Cholesterol 65mg, Sodium 300mg, Total Carbohydrate 4g, Dietary Fiber 0g, Sugars 1g, Protein 23g

Fettuccine Alfredo with Shrimp

SERVES 4

One of my fondest childhood memories is skiing with my parents in Massachusetts and ordering fettuccine Alfredo after a long day on the slopes. One of my worst childhood memories is my ski pants being so tight and unyielding the next day that I hated to ski. Well, now I can have it all: rich and creamy Alfredo sauce with my slim and comfortable ski pants.

12 ounces whole-wheat or gluten-free fettuccine pasta
¾ cup raw cashews
¾ cup water
1¼ pounds medium domestic shrimp, peeled and deveined
1 tablespoon (3 to 4 cloves) minced garlic

4 tablespoons nutritional yeast
Salt to taste
Cracked black pepper to taste

Cook the pasta according to the package directions. Drain and set aside.

In a blender or food processor, purée the cashews and ¾ cup water until smooth and creamy.

In a heavy dry pan, sauté the shrimp and garlic over low heat for 2 to 3 minutes.

Add the cashew cream, nutritional yeast, salt, pepper, and ¼ cup water. Stir well. If the sauce is too thick, add more water.

Cover and simmer for 6 to 8 minutes, until the shrimp are cooked through.

Toss the pasta in the pan with the sauce and serve with an excellent glass of chardonnay.

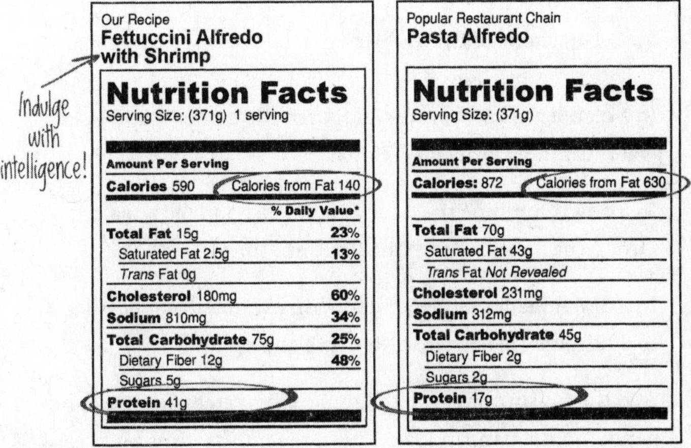
Indulge with intelligence!

Our Recipe
Fettuccini Alfredo with Shrimp

Nutrition Facts	
Serving Size: (371g) 1 serving	
Amount Per Serving	
Calories 590	Calories from Fat 140
	% Daily Value*
Total Fat 15g	**23%**
Saturated Fat 2.5g	**13%**
Trans Fat 0g	
Cholesterol 180mg	**60%**
Sodium 810mg	**34%**
Total Carbohydrate 75g	**25%**
Dietary Fiber 12g	**48%**
Sugars 5g	
Protein 41g	

Popular Restaurant Chain
Pasta Alfredo

Nutrition Facts	
Serving Size: (371g)	
Amount Per Serving	
Calories: 872	Calories from Fat 630
Total Fat 70g	
Saturated Fat 43g	
Trans Fat *Not Revealed*	
Cholesterol 231mg	
Sodium 312mg	
Total Carbohydrate 45g	
Dietary Fiber 2g	
Sugars 2g	
Protein 17g	

Trout Marsala

SERVES 4

When I first met my husband, Ken, he made me delicious chicken Marsala. I believe they call it "false advertising," since he has yet to cook for me since. However, he still loves to eat this classic, redone—and I still love him. (Newsflash! Since writing this, Ken made me dinner for Mother's Day: whole-wheat pasta marinara and some cashew cream that he found in the freezer. It was divine.)

⅓ cup raw cashews
⅓ cup plus 2 tablespoons water
2 tablespoons white whole-wheat flour, or whole-wheat pastry flour
½ teaspoon salt
4 rainbow trout fillets, about 4 ounces each
8 ounces cremini or baby bella mushrooms, stemmed and sliced
¼ to ½ teaspoon cracked black pepper to taste
1 cup Marsala wine
¼ cup chopped flat-leaf parsley

In a blender or food processor, purée the cashews and ⅓ cup water until smooth and creamy.

In a bowl, combine the flour and ¼ teaspoon of the salt. Dredge each fish fillet in the flour mixture.

In a dry, nonstick skillet, fry the fish over medium heat for 2 to 3 minutes on each side. Remove and set aside.

Add the mushrooms and the remaining ¼ teaspoon salt and pepper to the pan, and sauté until the mushrooms are tender.

Add the wine and the remaining 2 tablespoons of water and simmer over medium heat for 1 to 2 minutes.

Reduce heat to low and stir in the cashew cream. Add the fish fillets back to the pan, spoon sauce over the fish, and heat through.

Top with parsley and serve. I love this over whole-wheat pasta or fresh spinach.

NUTRITION (1 serving/243g): Calories 340, Calories from Fat 110, Total Fat 12g, Saturated Fat 2.5g, Trans Fat 0g, Cholesterol 65mg, Sodium 330mg, Total Carbohydrate 16g, Dietary Fiber 1g, Sugars 6g, Protein 27g

Black Cod Curry

SERVES 4

I struggled for years to make a good curry. I finally realized that less is more when it comes to balanced flavor.

- 1 medium onion, diced
- 1 (15-ounce) can chopped tomatoes in juice
- 1 tablespoon curry powder
- ½ cup canned light coconut milk
- ¼ cup water
- ½ teaspoon salt
- 4 black cod fillets, about 4 ounces each

In a heavy, dry pan, sauté the onion over medium heat until light brown. Add the tomatoes, curry powder, coconut milk, water, and salt to the pan and cook for 10 minutes.

Reduce heat to low, add the fish to the pan, and spoon the sauce over each fillet to coat.

Cover the pan and simmer for 6 to 8 minutes, or until the fish is cooked through.

Serve alone or over brown rice.

NUTRITION (1 serving/180g): Calories 130, Calories from Fat 25, Total Fat 3g, Saturated Fat 2, Trans Fat 0g, Cholesterol 55mg, Sodium 630mg, Total Carbohydrate 8g, Dietary Fiber 2g, Sugars 4g, Protein 19g

Fish Cakes

SERVES 4

Prior to creating this dish, the last time I'd eaten a fish cake was as a child. My mammar (grandma) used to make them en masse and freeze the leftovers. This healthy adaptation is perfect for a small family dinner—or make ahead and freeze for large gatherings. Mammar would approve.

2 cups peeled, diced russet potatoes
8 ounces cooked fish of choice (any leftover cooked salmon, cod, or halibut)
¼ cup unsweetened almond milk
¾ cup whole-wheat or gluten-free breadcrumbs (or 3 slices whole-grain toast ground in a blender)
2 tablespoons finely chopped flat-leaf parsley
1 teaspoon salt
¼ teaspoon ground black pepper
1 lemon, cut into wedges

Preheat the oven to 475°.

Steam the potatoes in a pot or in a microwave oven in 5-minute increments until very tender.

Using a fork, flake the fish into small pieces. In a separate bowl, mash the potatoes with the almond milk.

In a large bowl, combine the fish, potatoes, breadcrumbs, parsley, salt, and pepper. Use your hands to work all the ingredients together. Form the mixture into 8 to 10 patties, each 2 inches in diameter.

Bake on a baking sheet for 6 minutes. Flip and cook for another 6 minutes, or until the cakes are light golden brown.

Serve with lemon or marinara. Add a side of pasta marinara like my mammar did.

NUTRITION (1 cake/208g): Calories 230, Calories from Fat 15, Total Fat 2g, Saturated Fat 0g, Trans Fat 0g, Cholesterol 30mg, Sodium 730mg, Total Carbohydrate 37g, Dietary Fiber 4g, Sugars 3g, Protein 16g

Mexican Fish Casserole

SERVES 4

Bring on some serious flavor with this easy-to-make crowd pleaser. It's perfect for when you're low on fresh veggies, as most of the ingredients are pantry staples.

1 (15-ounce) can chopped tomatoes, undrained
1 (15-ounce) can pitted black olives, drained and chopped
3 tablespoons fresh lime juice
2 cloves garlic, minced
1 teaspoon ground cumin
1 teaspoon salt
4 Alaskan salmon fillets or fish of choice, about 4 ounces each
½ cup chopped fresh cilantro

Preheat the oven to 375°.

In a medium bowl, mix the tomatoes, olives, lime juice, garlic, cumin, and salt.

Place the fish in a 9-by-9-inch baking dish. Pour the sauce over the fish.

Cover with foil and bake for 25 minutes.

Garnish with cilantro to serve. For a fuller meal, add a side of brown rice and black beans.

NUTRITION (1 serving/313g): Calories 290, Calories from Fat 150, Total Fat 17g, Saturated Fat 3g, Trans Fat 0g, Cholesterol 60mg, Sodium 1390mg, Total Carbohydrate 11g, Dietary Fiber 4g, Sugars 2g, Protein 26g

Tuna Noodle Casserole

SERVES 8

Cook's confession—until writing this book, I'd never tried tuna noodle casserole (isn't that un-American?). It just seemed so unappetizing. Well, I stand corrected. This is truly one of my new recipe favorites, and makes a perfect family dish.

1 large onion, diced
8 ounces white or brown mushrooms, diced (optional)
16 ounces whole-wheat or gluten-free short pasta, cooked according to the package directions
1½ cups fresh or frozen green peas
3 (5-ounce) cans light tuna in water, drained
2 (6-ounce) containers plain nondairy yogurt
¾ cup unsweetened almond milk
¼ cup plus 2 tablespoons nutritional yeast
1½ teaspoons salt, or more to taste
½ teaspoon ground black pepper

Preheat the oven to 375°.

In a heavy, dry pan, sauté the onion and mushrooms over medium heat until the onion is translucent. If the ingredients begin to stick, add water, 2 tablespoons at a time.

In a large bowl, combine the noodles, onion, mushrooms, peas, tuna, yogurt, almond milk, ¼ cup nutritional yeast, salt, and pepper.

Pour into a 9-by-13-inch casserole pan. Top with the remaining 2 tablespoons of nutritional yeast. Cover with foil and bake for 25 to 30 minutes.

Serve as quickly as possible, or your family will devour it on the countertop.

NUTRITION (1 serving/258g): Calories 350, Calories from Fat 40, Total Fat 4.5g, Saturated Fat 1.5g, Trans Fat 0g, Cholesterol 15mg, Sodium 610mg, Total Carbohydrate 56g, Dietary Fiber 10g, Sugars 9g, Protein 22g

Seafood Newburg

SERVES 6

Thanks to its unhealthy reputation, this ultra-rich dish—traditionally made with a stick of butter and two cups of cream—is almost obsolete. With these healthy twists, we can happily say, "Welcome back, Newburg!"

1 cup raw cashews
1 cup water
½ cup dry sherry
1 teaspoon salt
½ teaspoon paprika
½ teaspoon coarse ground black pepper to taste

Pinch ground nutmeg
1 pound medium domestic shrimp, peeled, deveined, and chopped
½ pound Pacific cod, skinned and cut into 1½-inch chunks
½ pound flaked crabmeat, fresh or canned (picked and drained)

In a blender or food processor, purée the cashews and water until smooth and creamy.

In a heavy, dry pan, mix the cashew cream, sherry, salt, paprika, pepper, and nutmeg over low heat. Add water to thin out the sauce if needed.

Add the seafood to the pan and spoon the sauce on top.

Cover and heat for 10 to 12 minutes, or until the seafood is cooked through.

Serve over a whole grain, such as brown rice, to absorb the outrageous sauce.

NUTRITION (1 serving/250g): Calories 240, Calories from Fat 90, Total Fat 11g, Saturated Fat 2g, Trans Fat 0g, Cholesterol 130mg, Sodium 1360mg, Total Carbohydrate 10g, Dietary Fiber less than 1g, Sugars 1g, Protein 26g

Brazilian Fish Stew

SERVES 4

This is an adaption of The Vegan Cheat Sheet*'s Brazilian Vegetable Stew. I loved it then, but the addition of seafood has shown me the meaning of a deeper love.*

1 cup chopped onion
2 cloves garlic, chopped

1 tablespoon finely chopped ginger
1 (28-ounce) can diced plum tomatoes
1 large yam or sweet potato, peeled and cut into ½-inch cubes
½ teaspoon salt
½ teaspoon saffron, soaked in 2 tablespoons hot water to bloom
¾ pound medium raw domestic shrimp, peeled and deveined
¾ pound wild-caught Alaskan salmon or fish of choice, cut into 1½-inch chunks
¾ cup canned light coconut milk

In a heavy, dry pan, sauté the onion over medium heat until light brown. Add the garlic and ginger and cook for 3 minutes. If the ingredients begin to stick, add water, a few tablespoons at a time.

Add the tomatoes and yams and cook for 10 to 15 minutes, or until the potatoes are tender.

Add the salt, saffron, shrimp, and salmon and cook, covered, over medium heat until the fish is cooked through, about 10 to 15 minutes.

Add the coconut milk and heat through.

Serve alone in a big soup bowl or plate smaller portions with rice and black beans.

NUTRITION (1 serving/488g): Calories 290, Calories from Fat 80, Total Fat 9g, Saturated Fat 3.5g, Trans Fat 0g, Cholesterol 150mg, Sodium 900mg, Total Carbohydrate 19g, Dietary Fiber 4g, Sugars 8g, Protein 32g

10-Minute Shrimp-and-Spinach Risotto

SERVES 4

Do you (like me) have a wonderful spouse who comes home from work hungry, with a forlorn, "What, you haven't started dinner yet?" look in his or her eyes? Fear not, your feast will be ready in minutes.

4 cups precooked brown rice or rice blend
3 cloves garlic, minced
½ cup dry sherry
1 pound medium raw domestic shrimp, peeled and deveined
2 teaspoons nutritional yeast
5 ounces fresh baby spinach or escarole
½ teaspoon salt or to taste
¼ teaspoon black pepper or to taste

Heat a medium pan over medium heat and add all of the ingredients. Cook, stirring continuously, until the shrimp is done and the spinach is wilted, 5 to 10 minutes.

Serve and enjoy. (See, I told you that was fast!)

NUTRITION (1 serving/380g): Calories 350, Calories from Fat 30, Total Fat 3g, Saturated Fat 0.5g, Trans Fat 0g, Cholesterol 145mg, Sodium 1150mg, Total Carbohydrate 54g, Dietary Fiber 7g, Sugars 1g, Protein 25g

Simple Crab-and-Spinach Calzones

SERVES 4 FOR DINNER OR 8 FOR APPETIZERS

Seriously, this is really easy and looks so impressive. It's the perfect dish to make before you ask your kids or friends for a huge favor. Since they'll think you slaved for hours in the kitchen to impress them, they are sure to comply.

- 1 (12-ounce) box silken extra-firm tofu, drained
- 1 pound fresh baby spinach, steamed to wilt, and squeezed to remove all excess water (or frozen, defrosted, and squeezed)
- 1 tablespoon sweet sherry
- 1 teaspoon salt
- 10 ounces flaked crabmeat, fresh or canned (picked and drained)
- 6 to 8 (8-inch) whole-wheat tortillas

Preheat the oven to 400°. If you do not have a nonstick baking sheet, line a baking sheet with parchment paper and set aside.

Pulse the tofu, spinach, sherry, and salt in a food processor or with an immersion blender until just blended, or mash together with a fork. Fold in the flaked crabmeat.

Lay the tortillas on a flat surface. Spoon ⅓ to ½ cup of the crab mixture into the center of each tortilla. Fold the bottom half of the tortilla up to the center of the mixture. Fold each side into the center. Fold the bottom up to the top to form a square.

Place each packet on the prepared baking sheet.

Bake for 15 minutes or until the tortillas begin to crisp.

These don't need sauce; however, for a treat, make a dipping sauce by mixing cashew cream and Sriracha or lemon juice.

NUTRITION (1 dinner serving/359g): Calories 390, Calories from Fat 90, Total Fat 10g, Saturated Fat 0g, Trans Fat 0g, Cholesterol 30mg, Sodium 1820mg, Total Carbohydrate 45g, Dietary Fiber 6g, Sugars 2g, Protein 29g

Crab-and-Spinach-Stuffed Portabella Mushrooms

SERVES 4 FOR DINNER OR 8 FOR A SIDE DISH

This makes a special dinner or accompaniment—or use small mushrooms to create fancy hors d'oeuvres. This one is for my lovely crustacean-loving sister, Liz.

- ⅓ cup raw cashews
- 3 tablespoons water
- 2½ tablespoons dry sherry
- 1 pound fresh baby spinach, steamed to wilt, and squeezed to remove excess water (or frozen, defrosted, and squeezed)
- 1 tablespoon nutritional yeast
- 1½ teaspoons salt
- 6 ounces flaked crabmeat, fresh or canned (picked and drained)
- 2 tablespoons whole-wheat or gluten-free breadcrumbs (or ½ slice whole-wheat toast ground in a blender)
- 8 large portabella mushroom caps, stems removed

Preheat the oven to 375°.

In a blender or food processor, purée the cashews, water, and sherry until smooth. Add the spinach, nutritional yeast, and salt and pulse until blended.

In a bowl, combine the crabmeat, spinach mixture, and breadcrumbs. Scoop one-quarter of the mixture on top of each mushroom cap.

Place the stuffed mushrooms on a baking sheet. Bake for 30 minutes.

Serve whole, or cut in half for a side dish.

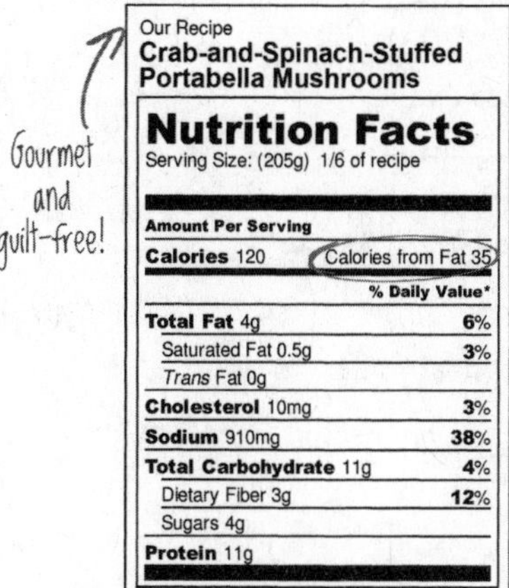

Our Recipe
Crab-and-Spinach-Stuffed Portabella Mushrooms

Nutrition Facts
Serving Size: (205g) 1/6 of recipe

Amount Per Serving	
Calories 120	Calories from Fat 35
	% Daily Value*
Total Fat 4g	**6%**
Saturated Fat 0.5g	**3%**
Trans Fat 0g	
Cholesterol 10mg	**3%**
Sodium 910mg	**38%**
Total Carbohydrate 11g	**4%**
Dietary Fiber 3g	**12%**
Sugars 4g	
Protein 11g	

Popular Restaurant Chain
Shrimp-Stuffed Mushrooms

Nutrition Facts
Serving Size: (205g)

Amount Per Serving	
Calories: 245	Calories from Fat 175
Total Fat 19g	
Saturated Fat g	
Trans Fat Not Revealed	
Cholesterol mg	
Sodium 578mg	
Total Carbohydrate 7g	
Dietary Fiber 2g	
Sugars 5g	
Protein 13g	

SIMPLY PERFECT FISH IN FOIL —EIGHT VARIATIONS

Nothing—and I mean nothing—is easier than preparing fish in foil. The variations of this dish are endless. And best of all, there's no cleanup.

If you'd rather serve the foiled fish on top of a grain or green, you can flip the order of the recipe so that toppings go in the foil first, followed by the fish, skin-side up.

Salmon with Dill in Foil

SERVES 4

The fresh herbs make this a tasty light meal, perfect with a glass of chardonnay while watching the sunset.

- 4 wild-caught Alaskan salmon fillets, about 4 ounces each
- ½ cup white wine
- 1 tablespoon chopped fresh dill
- 1 tablespoon chopped scallions
- 1 tablespoon chopped fresh flat-leaf parsley
- ½ teaspoon salt

Preheat the oven to 425°.

Place each fillet in the center of a 9-by-12-inch piece of foil. Scrunch the foil around the fish, making it into a package with high sides.

In a small bowl, combine the wine, dill, scallions, parsley, and salt. Spoon the wine mixture over each fillet and close the foil on top to make a loose package.

Place each package on a baking sheet and cook for 15 minutes.

Serve in foil for a fun presentation.

NUTRITION (1 serving/153g): Calories 190, Calories from Fat 60, Total Fat 6g, Saturated Fat 1.5g, Trans Fat 0g, Cholesterol 60mg, Sodium 400mg, Total Carbohydrate 1g, Dietary Fiber 0g, Sugars 0g, Protein 24g

Arctic Char Puttanesca in Foil

SERVES 4

Full-bodied flavor in no time with zero mess.

4 Arctic char fillets, about 4 ounces each
2 to 3 cloves garlic, minced
1 large (¾ cup) tomato, chopped
¼ cup chopped pitted black olives
2 tablespoons capers
¼ cup water

Preheat the oven to 425°.

Place each fillet in the center of a 9-by-12-inch piece of foil. Scrunch the foil around the fish, making it into a package with high sides.

In a small bowl, combine the garlic, tomatoes, olives, capers, and water. Spoon this mixture over the fillets. Close the foil on top to make a loose package.

Place each package on a baking sheet and cook for 15 minutes.

To serve, pour over a bed of brown rice or other grain.

NUTRITION (1 serving/203g): Calories 180, Calories from Fat 70, Total Fat 7g, Saturated Fat 1.5g, Trans Fat 0g, Cholesterol 60mg, Sodium 310mg, Total Carbohydrate 3g, Dietary Fiber less than 1g, Sugars 1g, Protein 25g

White Wine–Tarragon Catfish in Foil

SERVES 4

Going, going, gone. This dish is so quick and delicious. I dedicate the asparagus in this recipe to my dear friend and asparagus-crazy coauthor, Lisa. I despise those stalky spears and substitute broccolini (baby broccoli) when I make this dish.

4 catfish fillets, about 4 ounces each
½ cup white wine
2 teaspoons dried tarragon
½ teaspoon salt
1½ cups chopped asparagus

Preheat the oven to 425°.

Place each fillet in the center of a 9-by-12-inch piece of foil. Scrunch the foil around the fish, making it into a package with high sides.

In a small bowl, combine the wine, tarragon, and salt. Top each fillet with the wine mixture, then the asparagus. Close the foil on top to make a loose package.

Place each package on a baking sheet and cook for 15 minutes.

Serve in foil for a creative touch.

NUTRITION (1 serving/194g): Calories 140, Calories from Fat 30, Total Fat 3.5g, Saturated Fat 1g, Trans Fat 0g, Cholesterol 65mg, Sodium 310mg, Total Carbohydrate 3g, Dietary Fiber 1g, Sugars 1g, Protein 20g

Maple-Mustard–Glazed Salmon in Foil

SERVES 4

How can something so fast taste so good?

- 4 wild-caught Alaskan salmon fillets, about 4 ounces each
- ¼ cup maple syrup
- 2 tablespoons stone-ground mustard
- ¼ teaspoon salt
- 1 cup sliced mushrooms

Preheat the oven to 425°.

Place each fillet in the center of a 9-by-12-inch piece of foil. Scrunch the foil around the fish, making it into a package with high sides.

In a small bowl, combine the maple syrup, mustard, and salt. Top each fillet with the maple syrup mixture, then the mushrooms. Close the foil on top to make a loose package.

Place each package on a baking sheet and cook for 15 minutes.

Serve in foil, or remove and add a side of your favorite grain.

NUTRITION (1 serving/158g): Calories 230, Calories from Fat 60, Total Fat 7g, Saturated Fat 1.5g, Trans Fat 0g, Cholesterol 60mg, Total Carbohydrate 15g, Dietary Fiber less than 1g, Sugars 14g, Protein 25g

Southwestern Halibut in Foil

SERVES 4

Done before you can say olé!

- 4 Pacific halibut fillets, about 4 ounces each
- 1½ cups chopped fresh tomatoes
- ¾ cup canned black beans, drained and rinsed
- ¾ cup canned corn, drained
- ½ cup chopped fresh cilantro
- ½ teaspoon salt

Preheat the oven to 425°.

Place each fillet in the center of a 9-by-12-inch piece of foil. Scrunch the foil around the fish, making it into a package with high sides.

In a small bowl, combine the tomatoes, beans, corn, cilantro, and salt. Spoon the tomato mixture over each fish fillet. Close the foil on top to make a loose package.

Place each package on a baking sheet and cook for 15 minutes.

Place a mound of brown rice on each dinner plate. Pour each fish packet over the rice.

NUTRITION (1 serving/263g): Calories 180, Calories from Fat 20, Total Fat 2.5g, Saturated Fat 0g, Trans Fat 0g, Cholesterol 55mg, Sodium 410mg, Total Carbohydrate 15g, Dietary Fiber 4g, Sugars 3g, Protein 25g

Soy-Ginger Halibut with Bok Choy in Foil

SERVES 4

With its medley of flavors, this dish will kick dinner up a notch (or several).

4 Pacific halibut fillets, about 4 ounces each
2 cups chopped bok choy
1 cup sliced white mushrooms
¼ cup soy sauce
2 tablespoons seasoned mirin (rice wine)
2 teaspoons minced fresh garlic
2 teaspoons fresh minced ginger

Preheat the oven to 425°.

Place each fillet in the center of a 9-by-12-inch piece of foil. Scrunch the foil around the fish, making it into a package with high sides. Top with the bok choy and mushrooms.

In a small bowl, combine the soy sauce, mirin, garlic, and ginger. Top each fillet with the soy mixture. Close the foil on top to make a loose package.

Place each package on a baking sheet and cook for 15 minutes.

Serve in foil or pour over brown rice or rice noodles.

NUTRITION (1 serving/185g): Calories 140, Calories from Fat 15, Total Fat 1.5g, Saturated Fat 0g, Trans Fat 0g, Cholesterol 55mg, Sodium 650mg, Total Carbohydrate 6g, Dietary Fiber less than 1g, Sugars 4g, Protein 23g

Thai Curry Haddock in Foil

SERVES 4

The quickest curry in town!

4 haddock fillets, about 4 ounces each
½ cup canned light coconut milk
2 tablespoons Thai green curry paste
1 cup chopped fresh tomatoes
1 cup sliced white mushrooms
4 scallions, diced

Preheat the oven to 425°.

Place each fillet in the center of a 9-by-12-inch piece of foil. Scrunch the foil around the fish, making it into a package with high sides.

In a medium bowl, combine the coconut milk and curry paste and blend well. Stir in the tomatoes, mushrooms, and scallions.

Spoon the coconut milk mixture over each fish fillet. Close the foil on top to make a loose package.

Place each package on a baking sheet and cook for 15 minutes.

Remove the fish from the foil and serve over brown rice or keep in foil for easy eating and cleanup.

NUTRITION (1 serving/225g): Calories 130, Calories from Fat 25, Total Fat 2.5g, Saturated Fat 1.5g, Trans Fat 0g, Cholesterol 60mg, Sodium 430mg, Total Carbohydrate 5g, Dietary Fiber 1g, Sugars 3g, Protein 20g

Catfish with Mango Salsa in Foil

SERVES 4

Catfish got your tongue? It will now in this delicious recipe.

4 catfish fillets, about 4 ounces each
2 cups cubed frozen or fresh mango
¼ cup chopped red onion
¼ cup chopped fresh cilantro
2 tablespoons fresh lime juice
1 teaspoon ground cumin
1 teaspoon salt

Preheat the oven to 425°.

Place each fillet in the center of a 9-by-12-inch piece of foil. Scrunch the foil around the fish, making it into a package with high sides.

In a small bowl, combine the mango, onion, cilantro, lime juice, cumin, and salt. Spoon the mango mixture over each fish fillet. Close the foil on top to make a loose package.

Place each package on a baking sheet and cook for 15 minutes.

Remove from the foil and serve with a fresh green salad.

NUTRITION (1 serving/226g): Calories 210, Calories from Fat 60, Total Fat 7g, Saturated Fat 1.5g, Trans Fat 0g, Cholesterol 60mg, Sodium 640mg, Total Carbohydrate 17g, Dietary Fiber 2g, Sugars 14g, Protein 18g

CREAMY SOUPS OF THE SEA

A healthy new take on some comforting classics.

Creamy Shrimp and Corn Chowder

SERVES 4

This is a simple adaptation of my luscious vegan corn chowder from The Vegan Cheat Sheet. *Now it's a complete perfect meal.*

½ cup chopped onion
½ cup cored, seeded, and chopped red bell pepper
¼ cup diced celery
1 cup peeled and diced potato
½ teaspoon salt
1 to 2 teaspoons Sriracha
2 (15-ounce) cans corn, drained, with liquid reserved
Water
½ cup unsweetened plain almond milk
1 pound medium raw domestic shrimp, peeled and deveined

In a heavy, dry pan, sauté the onion, pepper, and celery over medium heat until the onion begins to brown. If the ingredients begin to stick, add water, a few tablespoons at a time.

Add the potatoes, salt, Sriracha, and all the liquid from the canned corn. Add water until the potatoes is just covered. Cover and cook until just tender, 8 to 10 minutes, and set aside.

In a blender, mix half the corn and the almond milk and blend until creamy. Pour over the potato mixture, and add the remaining corn and the shrimp.

Heat for 10 minutes, or until the shrimp are cooked through.

Serve with a hunk of whole-wheat bread.

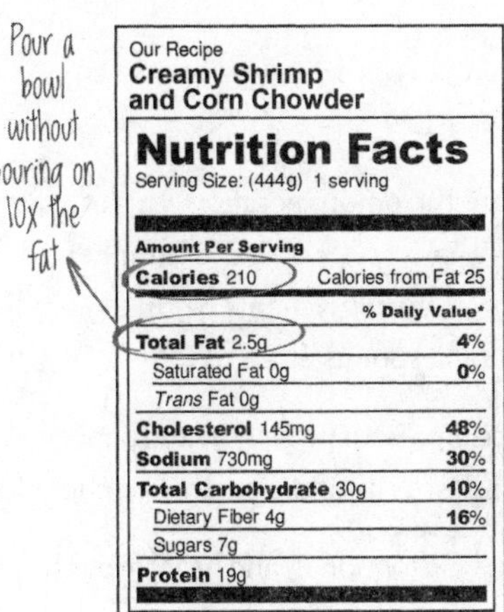

Pour a bowl without pouring on 10x the fat

Our Recipe
Creamy Shrimp and Corn Chowder

Nutrition Facts
Serving Size: (444g) 1 serving

Amount Per Serving	
Calories 210	Calories from Fat 25
	% Daily Value*
Total Fat 2.5g	**4%**
Saturated Fat 0g	**0%**
Trans Fat 0g	
Cholesterol 145mg	**48%**
Sodium 730mg	**30%**
Total Carbohydrate 30g	**10%**
Dietary Fiber 4g	**16%**
Sugars 7g	
Protein 19g	

Popular Restaurant Chain
Corn Chowder

Nutrition Facts
Serving Size: (444g)

Amount Per Serving	
Calories: 449	Calories from Fat 215
Total Fat 25g	
Saturated Fat 12g	
Trans Fat 0g	
Cholesterol 59mg	
Sodium 1485mg	
Total Carbohydrate 55g	
Dietary Fiber 4g	
Sugars 12g	
Protein 12g	

New England Clam Chowder

MAKES 6 BOWLS OR 10 CUPS

My childhood self would order clam chowder at every single restaurant—the creamier the better. As I got older and wiser, I deleted this heavy cream–infused favorite from my menu. Now it's back, in my just-as-delicious-but-good-for-you version.

- 2 cups raw cashews
- 2 cups, plus ½ cup water
- 3 cups chopped yellow onion
- 2 cups peeled and diced russet potato
- 1½ cups peeled and chopped carrot

1½ cups chopped celery
5 to 6 cloves garlic, minced
4 cups plain unsweetened almond milk
4 (6.5-ounce) cans minced clams with juice
2 teaspoons salt or to taste
1½ teaspoons ground black pepper or to taste
½ cup white wine (optional for a grown-up taste)

In a blender or food processor, purée the cashews and 2 cups of the water until smooth. Set aside.

In a heavy, dry soup pot, sauté the onion, potatoes, carrot, and celery in the remaining ½ cup water over medium heat until the onion is translucent. If the ingredients begin to stick, add more water, a few tablespoons at a time.

Add the garlic, almond milk, clams with juice, salt, and pepper. Cover and simmer for 10 minutes, or until the potato is tender.

Stir in the cashew cream and wine (optional) and heat through.

Serve in cups for an appetizer or in big bowls for dinner.

This creams the competition!

Our Recipe
New England Clam Chowder

Nutrition Facts
Serving Size: (299g) 1 cup

Amount Per Serving	
Calories 220	Calories from Fat 110
	% Daily Value*
Total Fat 13g	**20%**
Saturated Fat 2g	**10%**
Trans Fat 0g	
Cholesterol 0mg	**0%**
Sodium 640mg	**27%**
Total Carbohydrate 22g	**7%**
Dietary Fiber 4g	**16%**
Sugars 5g	
Protein 7g	

Popular Restaurant Chain
New England Clam Chowder

Nutrition Facts
Serving Size: 1 cup

Amount Per Serving	
Calories: 480	Calories from Fat 378
Total Fat 42g	
Saturated Fat 27g	
Trans Fat 1g	
Cholesterol 105mg	
Sodium 68mg	
Total Carbohydrate 21g	
Dietary Fiber 2g	
Sugars 1g	
Protein 6g	

Shrimp Bisque

MAKES 4 BOWLS OR 8 CUPS

Shrimp, lobster, or crab—try your favorite in this bisque. My teenage son, Cam, adores this recipe, and so do I.

- 1½ cups raw cashews
- 1½ cups water
- 1 cup chopped onion
- 1 cup chopped carrot
- ½ cup chopped celery
- 2 cups fish or vegetable stock
- 1½ pounds medium raw domestic shrimp, peeled and deveined
- ½ teaspoon salt
- ¼ teaspoon cayenne pepper
- ⅔ cup sweet sherry

In a blender or food processor, purée the cashews and water until smooth and creamy. Set aside.

In a heavy, dry pan, sauté the onion, carrot, and celery over medium heat until the carrot is tender. If the ingredients begin to stick, add water, 2 tablespoons at a time.

Add the stock, shrimp, salt, and cayenne pepper to the pan, and heat until the shrimp are pink and cooked through.

Pour the entire mixture into a blender or food processor and purée with the cashew cream until smooth.

Pour the mixture back in the pan, add the sherry, and heat through.

Make sure to subtly pour extra bisque into your own bowl. It's so good, there will be no leftovers.

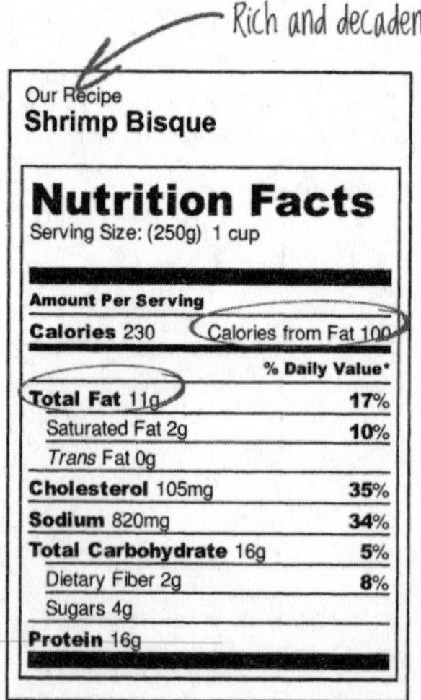
Rich and decadent with half the fat

Our Recipe
Shrimp Bisque

Nutrition Facts
Serving Size: (250g) 1 cup

Amount Per Serving	
Calories 230	Calories from Fat 100
	% Daily Value*
Total Fat 11g	**17%**
Saturated Fat 2g	**10%**
Trans Fat 0g	
Cholesterol 105mg	**35%**
Sodium 820mg	**34%**
Total Carbohydrate 16g	**5%**
Dietary Fiber 2g	**8%**
Sugars 4g	
Protein 16g	

Popular Restaurant Chain
Lobster Bisque

Nutrition Facts
Serving Size: 1 cup

Amount Per Serving	
Calories: 290	Calories from Fat 207
Total Fat 23g	
Saturated Fat 13g	
Trans Fat 0g	
Cholesterol 65mg	
Sodium 820mg	
Total Carbohydrate 15g	
Dietary Fiber 1g	
Sugars 2g	
Protein 6g	

HOMESTYLE CLASSICS AND COMFORT FOOD

These vegan reboots of America's favorite decadent dishes aren't even the tiniest bit naughty.

Spinach and Cheese Empanada

SERVES 4 FOR DINNER OR 12 FOR APPETIZERS

Warning: If you make this for your family once, they'll never stop begging you to make it again. It's great to prepare in advance and freeze. Or make extra dough and freeze it for another recipe.

DOUGH INGREDIENTS:

Timesaver: Use whole-wheat tortillas instead of dough—(see instructions from Simple Crab-and-Spinach Calzones on page 83).

¼ cup cashews
¾ cup water
2 cups white whole-wheat flour or whole-wheat pastry flour
½ teaspoon salt

FILLING INGREDIENTS:

2 cups fresh cauliflower florets
1 (12-ounce) box silken light tofu, drained
1½ teaspoons salt
1 teaspoon nutritional yeast
Dash nutmeg
1 pound fresh baby spinach, steamed to wilt, and squeezed to remove excess water (or frozen, defrosted, and squeezed)

DOUGH PREP:

In a small blender or food processor, purée the cashews and water until smooth and creamy.

Combine the flour and salt in a mixing bowl. Add half the cashew cream to the flour mixture and blend with your hands. Gradually add the remaining cashew cream and blend/knead for 5 minutes until a smooth dough forms. If the dough is too dry, add a bit of water; if too sticky, add a tad more flour.

Lightly flour a smooth surface. (I use my granite countertop). Divide the dough in half and begin to roll. Regularly dust the rolling pin and dough with flour to prevent sticking. Flip the dough and roll in four directions. Continue to flip and roll dough until it forms a 1/8-inch-thick sheet. Repeat with other dough ball.

With a biscuit cutter or upside-down water glass, cut the dough into 2½-inch-diameter circles. Afterward, reroll each circle to expand it and make it thinner (but not so thin that you can see through it).

FILLING:

Steam the cauliflower in a pot or in a microwave oven in 5-minute increments until tender.

With a food processor, blender, or immersion blender, purée the cauliflower, tofu, salt, nutritional yeast, and nutmeg until smooth. Add the spinach and pulse a few times to blend.

PREPARE:

Preheat the oven to 425°. Line a baking sheet with foil and set aside.

Prepare a small bowl with ¼ cup room-temperature water.

Place 1 tablespoon of filling in the center of each dough circle.

Dip a finger in the water and moisten the outer edges of each dough circle. Fold in half and press the edges together. Press a fork flat around the edges to seal it and give it a homemade look.

Place the empanadas on the prepared baking sheet. Bake for 15 minutes. Or place in boiling water and cook until the empanadas float to the top, 5 to 7 minutes.

Serve as is or top with your favorite salsa.

NUTRITION (1 dinner portion/323g): Calories 340, Calories from Fat 50, Total Fat 6g, Saturated Fat 1g, Trans Fat 0g, Cholesterol 0mg, Sodium 1310mg, Total Carbohydrate 57g, Dietary Fiber 12g, Sugars 2g, Protein 17g

Baked Ziti with Spinach

SERVES 6

My not-picky (yeah, right!) super-duper, kind, wonderful daughter, Cai, loves this simple family classic.

½ cup raw cashews
½ cup water
1 pound whole-wheat or gluten-free spirals or macaroni pasta
2 cups fresh cauliflower florets
1 (12-ounce) box silken light tofu, drained
1½ teaspoons salt
2 teaspoons nutritional yeast
10 ounces fresh baby spinach, steamed to wilt, and squeezed to remove excess water (or frozen, defrosted and squeezed)
1 (24-ounce) jar fat-free marinara or pasta sauce

Preheat the oven to 425°.

In a blender or food processor, purée the cashews and water until smooth and creamy and set aside.

Cook the pasta 2 minutes less than called for in the package directions. Drain and set aside.

Steam the cauliflower in a pot or in a microwave in 5-minute increments until tender.

With a food processor, blender, or immersion blender, purée the cauliflower, tofu, salt, and nutritional yeast. Add the spinach and pulse several times to blend.

Stir together the cashew cream and marinara.

Pour the pasta into a 9-by-11-inch baking dish. Stir in the marinara mixture. Spoon the cauliflower mixture over the pasta, and swirl in, trying not to blend completely.

Cover with foil and bake for 20 minutes. Uncover and bake for 10 more minutes.

Serve quickly before little hands start picking at it right from the dish.

NUTRITION (1 serving/341g): Calories 430, Calories from Fat 80, Total Fat 9g, Saturated Fat 1g, Trans Fat 0g, Cholesterol 0mg, Sodium 1130mg, Total Carbohydrate 71g, Dietary Fiber 12g, Sugars 9g, Protein 19g

Pasta Carbonara

SERVES 6

I cannot believe the word bacon *has made it into one of my recipes. It's worth it!*

Timesaver: Buy smoked tempeh strips and go directly to the sauce section.

"BACON" INGREDIENTS:

1 (12-ounce) package extra-firm tofu

¾ cup water

½ cup soy sauce or tamari

2 tablespoons tomato paste

1½ tablespoons maple syrup

1 tablespoon smoked paprika

1 tablespoon nutritional yeast

SAUCE AND PASTA INGREDIENTS:

1 pound whole-wheat or gluten-free spiral or macaroni pasta
¾ cup raw cashews
¾ cup water
1 tablespoon (3 to 4 cloves) minced garlic
4 tablespoons nutritional yeast
1 teaspoon salt
½ teaspoon ground nutmeg
Cracked black pepper to taste
¼ to 1 cup water, as needed
¾ cup chopped flat-leaf parsley

BACON PREP:

Freeze the tofu for easier slicing and slice to the desired thickness. (I like my slices 1/8 inch thick.)

In a medium shallow bowl, combine the water, soy sauce, tomato paste, maple syrup, smoked paprika, and nutritional yeast.

Add the tofu to the bowl and cover all of the slices completely with marinade. If necessary, transfer to a small baking dish to submerge all of the slices. Marinate for at least 1 hour.

Preheat the oven to 400°.

Line a baking sheet with parchment paper. Lay the tofu slices out in a single layer. Bake for 15 minutes, flipping them after 8 minutes. For thicker slices, you may have to bake longer for crispiness.

SAUCE AND PASTA PREP:

Cook the pasta according to the package directions. Drain and set aside.

In a blender or food processor, purée the cashews and water until smooth and creamy.

In a heavy, dry pan, sauté the garlic over low heat for 2 minutes. Add the cashew cream, nutritional yeast, salt, nutmeg, pepper, and ¼ cup of water. Stir well. If the sauce is too thick, add more water.

Add the tofu bacon and cook until heated through. Toss the pasta in the pan with the sauce.

Top with parsley and serve.

NUTRITION (1 serving/213g): Calories 420, Calories from Fat 90, Total Fat 10g, Saturated Fat 1.5g, Trans Fat 0g, Cholesterol 0mg, Sodium 840mg, Total Carbohydrate 66g, Dietary Fiber 11g, Sugars 5g, Protein 20g

Lasagna

SERVES 6

This recipe runs circles around other lasagnas. The "cheese" adds a truly decadent touch.

1 cup raw cashews
1 cup water
2 cups fresh cauliflower florets
1 (12-ounce) box silken light tofu, drained
1 teaspoon salt
1 tablespoon nutritional yeast
1 (24-ounce) jar fat-free marinara or pasta sauce
1 (9-ounce) box whole-wheat or gluten-free lasagna noodles
1½ cups crumbled tempeh (optional)
1 cup shredded vegan mozzarella cheese (optional)

Preheat the oven to 375°.

In a blender or food processor, purée the cashews and water until smooth; set aside.

Steam the cauliflower in a pot or in a microwave oven in 5-minute increments until tender.

With a food processor, blender, or immersion blender, purée the cauliflower, tofu, salt, and nutritional yeast.

Stir together the cashew cream and marinara.

Layer a 9-by-13-inch baking dish as follows: a third of the marinara mixture (enough to coat the bottom of the dish), a third of the uncooked pasta, half the cauliflower mixture, half the tempeh, if using, a third of the pasta, a third of the marinara mixture, half the cauliflower mixture, half the tempeh, a third of the pasta, and a third of the marinara mixture. Top with cheese, if using.

Cover with foil and bake for 30 minutes. Uncover and bake for 10 to 15 more minutes.

Serve piping hot.

NUTRITION (1 serving/350g, with tempeh and cheese): Calories 480, Calories from Fat 210, Total Fat 23g, Saturated Fat 5g, Trans Fat 0g, Cholesterol 0mg, Sodium 1010mg, Total Carbohydrate 51g, Dietary Fiber 11g, Sugars 9g, Protein 23g

Eggplant Parmesan

SERVES 4 TO 6

I probably make this dish more than any other in my repertoire, because it's so quick to assemble and bake. Plus, it's loaded with veggies and protein. Even eggplant-hating Lisa loves it.

¾ cup raw cashews
¾ cup water
1 (25-ounce) jar fat-free marinara
¾ cup whole-wheat or gluten-free breadcrumbs (or 3 slices whole-grain toast ground in a blender)
¼ cup nutritional yeast
1 large eggplant, cut in ¼-inch-thick slices

Preheat the oven to 400°.

In a blender or food processor, purée the cashews and water until smooth and creamy. Add the marinara sauce, blend, and set aside.

Mix the breadcrumbs with the nutritional yeast.

Coat the bottom of a lasagna pan with sauce, then layer eggplant, breadcrumb mixture, and sauce, repeating until all of the ingredients are used. End with sauce.

Bake, covered, for 45 minutes or until the eggplant is tender.

Serve with a side salad.

NUTRITION (1/5 recipe/286g): Calories 270, Calories from Fat 110, Total Fat 12g, Saturated Fat 1.5g, Trans Fat 0g, Cholesterol 0mg, Sodium 620mg, Total Carbohydrate 32g, Dietary Fiber 9g, Sugars 11g, Protein 12g

10-Minute Flatbread Pizza

SERVES 2

This quickie makes a perfect lunch, snack, or light dinner.

2 large (8-inch) whole-wheat tortillas
¼ cup marinara sauce

- 8 thin slices firm tofu (about half of 12-ounce block)
- ½ cup seeded and chopped bell pepper
- 1 tablespoon nutritional yeast

Preheat the oven to 400°. Line a baking sheet with parchment paper.

Place the tortillas on the prepared baking sheet.

Top tortillas with the marinara sauce, tofu slices, chopped pepper, and nutritional yeast.

Bake for 5 to 10 minutes, or until heated through. Use a large spatula to transfer pizzas to a plate.

Slice like a pizza and enjoy.

NUTRITION (1 serving/192g): Calories 220, Calories from Fat 70, Total Fat 7g, Saturated Fat 0.5g, Trans Fat 0g, Cholesterol 0mg, Sodium 460mg, Total Carbohydrate 29g, Dietary Fiber 6g, Sugars 3g, Protein 14g

Vegetable Pot Pie

SERVES 4

Who in the world decided that a pie should be eaten for a meal? Perhaps it was my awesome middle child, Liv. This one's for you—without the bad stuff.

- 1 cup chopped onion
- ¾ cup diced carrot
- ½ cup diced celery
- 2 medium russet potatoes, peeled and diced
- 2 cups vegetable stock
- ¼ cup nutritional yeast
- ¾ cup frozen peas

- 2 tablespoons tomato paste
- 1 to 1½ teaspoons salt to taste
- ½ teaspoon ground black pepper
- 1 tablespoon dried rosemary
- 1 tablespoon dried thyme
- ¼ cup or more white whole-wheat flour
- 4 large or 8 small whole-wheat tortillas (depending on the size of the ramekins)

Preheat the oven to 400°.

In a heavy, dry pan, sauté the onion, carrot, and celery over medium heat until the onion is translucent. If the ingredients begin to stick, add water, a few tablespoons at a time.

Add the potatoes and ½ cup of the vegetable stock, stir, and cook for 5 minutes. Add the nutritional yeast, peas, tomato paste, salt, pepper, rosemary, and thyme to the pan, stir, and cook for 5 more minutes.

Remove half the hot liquid from the pan and mix it with the flour in a large bowl to form a slurry. Add the flour mixture back to the pan to thicken the sauce. Repeat the slurry steps, adding more flour if a thicker gravy is desired.

Line 4 ramekins each with one tortilla, leaving the edges to flap evenly over the sides. Fill each tortilla with the veggie mixture. Fold the tortilla flaps over the top, then tuck them into the sides to cover.

Bake for 15 minutes, or until the tortillas are crispy.

Place hot ramekins on individual plates to serve.

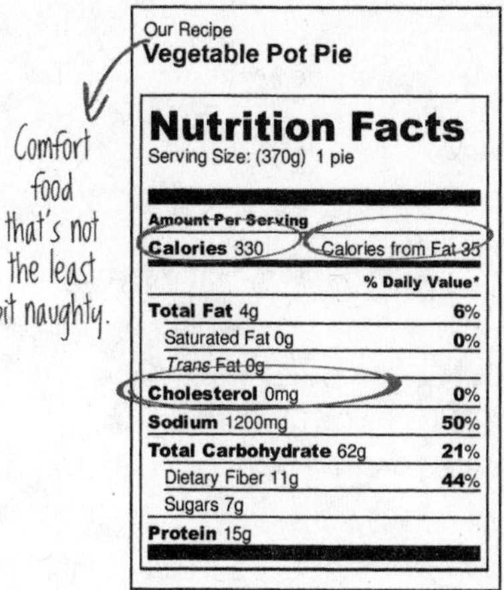

Comfort food that's not the least bit naughty.

Our Recipe
Vegetable Pot Pie

Nutrition Facts
Serving Size: (370g) 1 pie

Amount Per Serving	
Calories 330	Calories from Fat 35
	% Daily Value*
Total Fat 4g	**6%**
Saturated Fat 0g	**0%**
Trans Fat 0g	
Cholesterol 0mg	**0%**
Sodium 1200mg	**50%**
Total Carbohydrate 62g	**21%**
Dietary Fiber 11g	**44%**
Sugars 7g	
Protein 15g	

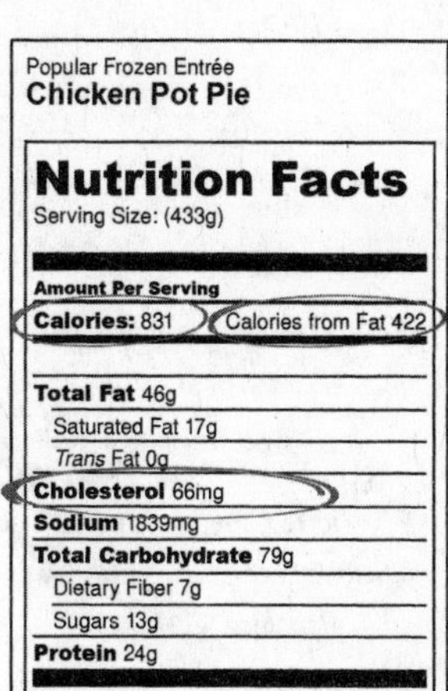

Popular Frozen Entrée
Chicken Pot Pie

Nutrition Facts
Serving Size: (433g)

Amount Per Serving	
Calories: 831	Calories from Fat 422
Total Fat 46g	
Saturated Fat 17g	
Trans Fat 0g	
Cholesterol 66mg	
Sodium 1839mg	
Total Carbohydrate 79g	
Dietary Fiber 7g	
Sugars 13g	
Protein 24g	

Potato-Chip Pie in a Bag

SERVES 4

My kitchen staff rolled their eyes when I shared this recipe idea. Well, they rubbed their satisfied tummies after trying it. This is fantastic for a quick, on-the-go dinner or a fun, entertaining novelty. Kids flip for it.

1 (12-ounce) can baked beans or chili beans, lightly drained
4 individual-size bags baked potato chips (I like Baked Lays®)
1 cup chopped tomatoes
1 ripe avocado, diced
1 (4-ounce) can diced green chilies, drained
¼ cup fresh chopped cilantro
¼ cup chopped onion (optional)

In a small pan over medium heat, heat the beans through.

Open each bag of chips, and evenly divide beans, tomatoes, avocado, chilies, cilantro, and onion, if using, among them.

Serve in the bag with a fork.

For picky (or creative) eaters, have them stuff their own bags.

NUTRITION (1 bag/238g): Calories 320, Calories from Fat 140, Total Fat 15g, Saturated Fat 3g, Trans Fat 0g, Cholesterol 0mg, Sodium 610mg, Total Carbohydrate 43g, Dietary Fiber 9g, Sugars 8g, Protein 7g

BLT Sandwich

SERVES 4

This is the second mention of bacon in my recipes. I guess I'm a "pleaser," at least according to my son, Cam, whose childhood nickname is "bacon boy."

Timesaver: Buy smoked tempeh strips and go directly to the sandwich section.

"BACON" INGREDIENTS:

1 (12-ounce) package extra firm tofu
¾ cup water
½ cup soy sauce or tamari
2 tablespoons tomato paste
1½ tablespoons maple syrup
1 tablespoon smoked paprika
1 tablespoon nutritional yeast

SANDWICH FIXINGS:

8 slices whole-wheat or gluten-free bread, toasted
1 ripe avocado, mashed

4 sandwich-size pieces lettuce of choice

1 large tomato, sliced

Preheat the oven to 400°. Line a baking sheet with parchment paper and set aside.

Freeze the tofu for easier slicing and slice to the desired thickness. (I prefer ⅛-inch-thick slices.)

In a shallow medium bowl, combine the water, soy sauce, tomato paste, maple syrup, smoked paprika, and nutritional yeast. Add the tofu to the bowl and cover all of the slices completely with marinade. If necessary, transfer to a small baking dish to submerge all the slices. Marinate for at least 1 hour.

Remove the tofu slices from the marinade, and lay them on the prepared baking sheet in a single layer. Bake for 15 minutes, flipping them after 8 minutes. For thicker slices, you may have to bake longer for crispiness.

Spread each slice of toast with mashed avocado. Layer the tofu bacon, lettuce, and tomato on 4 slices of toast. Top with remaining pieces of toast, grab a beer, and serve.

Our Recipe
BLT

Nutrition Facts
Serving Size: (254g) 1 sandwich

Amount Per Serving	
Calories 290	Calories from Fat 90
	% Daily Value*
Total Fat 10g	**15%**
Saturated Fat 1.5g	**8%**
Trans Fat 0.5g	
Cholesterol 0mg	**0%**
Sodium 580mg	**24%**
Total Carbohydrate 36g	**12%**
Dietary Fiber 9g	**36%**
Sugars 7g	
Protein 16g	

Classic Recipe
BLT

Nutrition Facts
Serving Size: (218g)

Amount Per Serving	
Calories 560	Calories from Fat 360
	% Daily Value*
Total Fat 40g	**62%**
Saturated Fat 9g	**45%**
Trans Fat 2g	
Cholesterol 65mg	**22%**
Sodium 1350mg	**56%**
Total Carbohydrate 30g	**10%**
Dietary Fiber 3g	**12%**
Sugars 4g	
Protein 21g	

Spanakopita (Spinach Pie)

SERVES 4

I'm floored by the simplicity and deliciousness of these individual spinach pies. The fresh spices make for a truly authentic flavor.

- 1 (12-ounce) package firm tofu, drained
- 1 (10-ounce) package frozen chopped spinach (defrosted and squeezed)
- 4 scallions, finely chopped
- ¼ cup finely chopped fresh dill
- 2 tablespoons finely chopped flat-leaf parsley
- 1 teaspoon salt
- ⅛ teaspoon ground nutmeg
- 4 (8-inch) whole-wheat tortillas

Preheat the oven to 400°. If you do not have a nonstick baking sheet, line a baking sheet with parchment paper and set aside.

In a small bowl, crumble the tofu. Add the spinach, scallion, dill, parsley, salt, and nutmeg and stir until well mixed.

Lay each tortilla on a flat surface. Spoon ½ cup of the spinach mixture into the center of each tortilla. Fold the bottom half of the tortilla up to the center of the mixture. Fold each side into the center. Fold the bottom up to the top to form a square.

Place each packet on the prepared baking sheet. Bake for 15 minutes, or until the tortillas begin to crisp.

Say "Opa!" and serve.

NUTRITION (1 pie/280g): Calories 410, Calories from Fat 110, Total Fat 12g, Saturated Fat 0g, Trans Fat 0g, Cholesterol 0mg, Sodium 1250mg, Total Carbohydrate 56g, Dietary Fiber 7g, Sugars 2g, Protein 18g

SUMPTUOUS SIDES AND SNACKS

Guaranteed to keep meal- and between-mealtime tantalizing.

Twice-Baked Potatoes

SERVES 4

These are so delicious, you'll wonder why you ever bothered with their fat-laden fraternal twin.

4 large russet potatoes, scrubbed clean
½ cup unsweetened plain almond milk
¼ teaspoon salt
¼ teaspoon garlic powder
⅓ cup chopped smoked tempeh
½ cup shredded vegan cheddar cheese (optional)

Preheat the oven to 400°.

Poke several holes in the potatoes with a fork and cook in a microwave oven in 8-minute increments until tender.

Slice the potatoes lengthwise three-quarters of the way through the top. Using a dishtowel, gently squeeze the ends of each potato together to create an opening.

Spoon the majority of the insides out into a large bowl, leaving the skin intact. (I sometimes use a butter knife to carefully loosen the flesh.)

Beat the potatoes with a hand mixer until no lumps remain. Add the almond milk, salt, and garlic powder, and mix until blended. For creamier potatoes, add more almond milk.

Add the tempeh to the mixture and stir in with a spoon.

Carefully restuff the potatoes with the filling. Top with vegan cheese, if desired.

Bake for 12 to 15 minutes.

These are hearty enough to serve as a main course with a side salad.

NUTRITION (1 potato/261g): Calories 290, Calories from Fat 45, Total Fat 5g, Saturated Fat 1.5g, Trans Fat 0g, Cholesterol 0mg, Sodium 420mg, Total Carbohydrate 55g, Dietary Fiber 6g, Sugars 5g, Protein 8g

Sweet Potato Pie

SERVES 5 TO 6

My awesome mother-in-law would not set a holiday table without sweet potatoes. This holiday classic is a year-round treat in my house. It makes a scrumptious side with simple grilled-fish dishes.

2 pounds sweet potatoes, peeled and chopped
½ cup unsweetened plain almond milk
2 tablespoons pure maple syrup
¼ teaspoon ground cinnamon
¼ teaspoon salt
12 to 15 standard-size vegan marshmallows

Preheat the oven to 425°.

Steam the sweet potatoes in a pot or in a microwave oven in 7-minute increments until very tender.

In a large bowl, purée the potatoes with an electric hand mixer until smooth. Add the almond milk, maple syrup, cinnamon, and salt and beat until smooth and creamy.

Spoon the mixture into an 8-by-8-inch casserole dish. Cover with foil and bake for 20 minutes, until hot.

Remove the casserole from the oven, cover the top of it with marshmallows, and return it to the oven. Cook until the marshmallows begin to brown, around 5 minutes.

Spoon the gooey goodness onto each dinner plate and watch your diners swoon.

Healthy holidays are here again!

Our Recipe
Sweet Potato Pie

Nutrition Facts
Serving Size: (212g) 1 serving

Amount Per Serving	
Calories 230	Calories from Fat 5
	% Daily Value*
Total Fat 0.5g	**1%**
Saturated Fat 0g	**0%**
Trans Fat 0g	
Cholesterol 0mg	**0%**
Sodium 190mg	**8%**
Total Carbohydrate 54g	**18%**
Dietary Fiber 6g	**24%**
Sugars 26g	
Protein 4g	

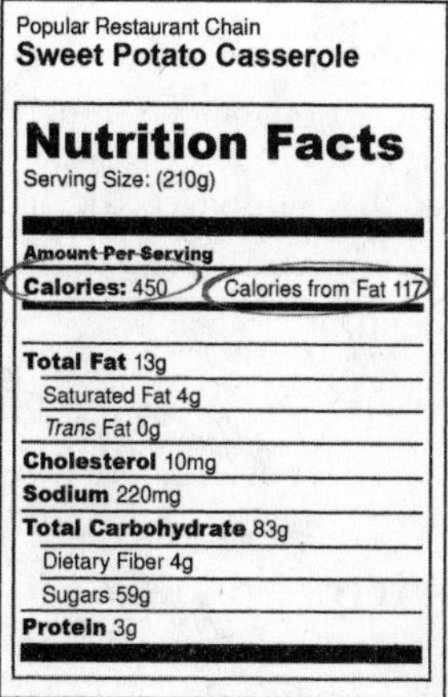

Popular Restaurant Chain
Sweet Potato Casserole

Nutrition Facts
Serving Size: (210g)

Amount Per Serving	
Calories: 450	Calories from Fat 117
Total Fat 13g	
Saturated Fat 4g	
Trans Fat 0g	
Cholesterol 10mg	
Sodium 220mg	
Total Carbohydrate 83g	
Dietary Fiber 4g	
Sugars 59g	
Protein 3g	

Creamy Cauliflower Mash

SERVES 4 TO 6

I could eat the whole batch myself—but I'd have to fight with Lisa's dad, Ed, who loves this dish as much as I do. For the veggie-phobic, you could even pass these off as mashed potatoes (shhh).

¼ cup raw cashews
¼ cup water
4 cups fresh cauliflower florets
1 teaspoon salt
1 teaspoon nutritional yeast

In a blender or food processor, purée the cashews and water until smooth and set aside.

Steam the cauliflower in a pot or in a microwave oven in 5-minute increments until tender.

Add the cauliflower, salt, and nutritional yeast to a blender or food processor and purée with the cashew cream until smooth.

If the mixture has cooled down, heat it in a pot or microwave oven before serving.

NUTRITION (1/5 recipe/105g): Calories 60, Calories from Fat 30, Total Fat 3g, Saturated Fat 0.5g, Trans Fat 0g, Cholesterol 0mg, Sodium 450mg, Total Carbohydrate 6g, Dietary Fiber 2g, Sugars 2g, Protein 3g

Mushroom Gravy

SERVES 8 TO 10

Gravy? For what? On special occasions like my monthly Thanksgiving feast, I may grab a healthy faux-turkey product—which, like the real bird, requires ample servings of delicious gravy. But top anything with this special sauce, and nirvana will be on the tip of your tongue.

⅓ cup raw cashews
⅓ cup water
2½ cups coarsely chopped cremini or baby bella mushrooms
¼ cup minced shallot
1 cup port wine
½ teaspoon salt
¼ teaspoon ground black pepper

In a blender or food processor, purée the cashews and water until smooth and set aside.

In a heavy, dry saucepan, sauté the mushrooms and shallot over medium heat for 3 minutes.

Add the port and cook until the mushrooms are tender.

Add the salt, pepper, and cashew cream to the pan and simmer until the gravy reaches the desired thickness. For thinner gravy, add a bit of water or more port.

This thick, creamy delight is best served in a bowl with a small ladle.

NUTRITION (1/9 recipe/64g): Calories 70, Calories from Fat 20, Total Fat 2g, Saturated Fat 0g, Trans Fat 0g, Cholesterol 0mg, Sodium 120mg, Total Carbohydrate 6g, Dietary Fiber 0g, Sugars 3g, Protein 1g

Scalloped Potatoes

SERVES 6

I always thought scalloped potatoes were a decadent treat that only "others" got to enjoy, but this healthful take on a comforting classic is pure bliss.

½ cup raw cashews
½ cup water
¼ cup chopped shallots
¾ cup unsweetened plain almond milk
2 tablespoons nutritional yeast
1½ teaspoons salt
½ teaspoon ground black pepper
4 to 5 medium russet potatoes, peeled and sliced very thin (I use a mandoline)

Preheat the oven to 375°.

In a blender or food processor, purée the cashews and water until smooth and creamy.

In a small bowl, combine the cashew cream, shallots, almond milk, nutritional yeast, salt, and pepper.

In a 6-by-6-inch casserole dish, layer a third of the potatoes and a third of the sauce and repeat twice, ending with sauce.

Bake, covered, about 45 minutes, or until the potatoes are tender.

Remove the cover and broil for 2 to 3 minutes, until golden brown. (Use a timer and check after each minute.)

Serve steaming hot.

NUTRITION (1 serving/186g): Calories 190, Calories from Fat 50, Total Fat 5g, Saturated Fat 1g, Trans Fat 0g, Cholesterol 0mg, Sodium 610mg, Total Carbohydrate 31g, Dietary Fiber 4g, Sugars 2g, Protein 6g

Green Bean Casserole

SERVES 6 TO 8

As Alicia, Lisa's mom, would say: "What's a holiday table without this all-time classic?" My version duplicates the flavor of the fat-laden original and is so good, even Alicia gives it the thumbs-up.

- ⅓ cup raw cashews
- ⅓ cup water
- ¼ cup whole-wheat or gluten-free breadcrumbs (or 1 slice whole-grain toast ground in a blender)
- ¼ cup white whole-wheat flour, whole-wheat pastry flour, or gluten-free flour
- 1½ teaspoons salt
- 1 large onion, halved and sliced thin
- ¼ cup chopped shallots
- 1 (8-ounce) package cremini or baby bella mushrooms, sliced
- 3 tablespoons vegetable stock
- 1 pound green beans, trimmed and cut in half
- 3 tablespoons plain, unsweetened almond milk

Preheat the oven to 475°.

In a blender or food processor, purée the cashews and water until smooth and creamy. Set aside.

In a plastic zip-top bag, mix the breadcrumbs, flour, and ½ teaspoon salt. Toss in the onion slices until all are well coated.

Lay the onion slices flat on a baking sheet, and bake for 25 minutes, tossing halfway through to cook evenly. Set aside.

Lower the oven temperature to 350°.

In a heavy, dry pan, sauté the shallots and mushrooms in the vegetable stock over medium heat for 5 minutes. Add the green beans and remaining 1 teaspoon of salt and cook for another 2 minutes. Stir in the cashew cream and almond milk.

Transfer the green bean mixture to an 8-by-8-inch casserole dish and stir in half the onion slices.

Top with the remaining breaded onion slices. Bake for 20 minutes and serve.

NUTRITION (1/7 recipe/160g): Calories 100, Calories from Fat 30, Total Fat 3g, Saturated Fat 0.5g, Trans Fat 0g, Cholesterol 0mg, Sodium 530mg, Total Carbohydrate 16g, Dietary Fiber 4g, Sugars 5g, Protein 5g

Creamy Coleslaw

SERVES 6 TO 8

Growing up, my wonderful mom made her famous coleslaw for every holiday meal, and it was one of my favorite sides. I made a few healthy swaps (bye-bye, mayo) and was blown away. What do you think, Ma?

⅓ cup raw cashews
⅓ cup water
3 tablespoons white vinegar
1½ tablespoons organic sugar or vegan cane sugar
½ teaspoon sea salt
1 pound bagged coleslaw mix (or improvise your own by shredding green and purple cabbage and carrots)

In a blender or food processor, purée the cashews, water, vinegar, sugar, and salt until smooth.

Mix with the coleslaw.

Refrigerate overnight or serve immediately.

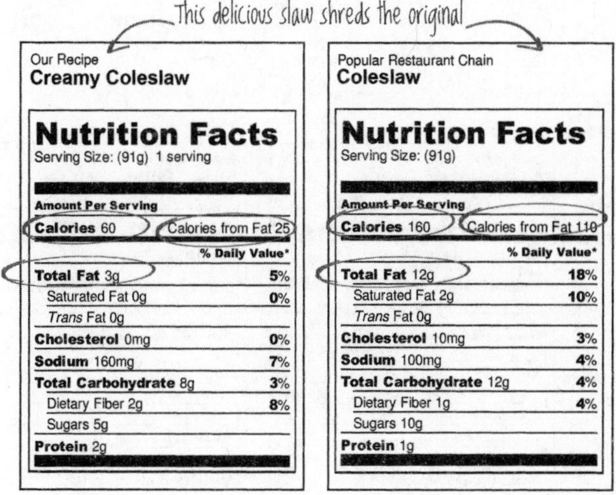
This delicious slaw shreds the original

Our Recipe
Creamy Coleslaw

Nutrition Facts	
Serving Size: (91g) 1 serving	
Amount Per Serving	
Calories 60	Calories from Fat 25
	% Daily Value*
Total Fat 3g	**5%**
Saturated Fat 0g	**0%**
Trans Fat 0g	
Cholesterol 0mg	**0%**
Sodium 160mg	**7%**
Total Carbohydrate 8g	**3%**
Dietary Fiber 2g	**8%**
Sugars 5g	
Protein 2g	

Popular Restaurant Chain
Coleslaw

Nutrition Facts	
Serving Size: (91g)	
Amount Per Serving	
Calories 160	Calories from Fat 110
	% Daily Value*
Total Fat 12g	**18%**
Saturated Fat 2g	**10%**
Trans Fat 0g	
Cholesterol 10mg	**3%**
Sodium 100mg	**4%**
Total Carbohydrate 12g	**4%**
Dietary Fiber 1g	**4%**
Sugars 10g	
Protein 1g	

Sweet Potato Chips

SERVES 4

Try this with your favorite root vegetables—beets, potatoes, and parsnips—to make a rainbow of chips.

1 large sweet potato, peeled (and/or other root vegetables of your choice)
½ teaspoon salt
¼ teaspoon ground black pepper

Preheat the oven to 200°. Line two baking sheets with parchment paper and set aside.

Slice the potatoes into thin chips, using a sharp knife or mandoline.

Arrange the slices on the prepared baking sheets so that the chips don't touch.

Sprinkle with salt and pepper.

Bake for 55 to 65 minutes, or until just crisp. Remove from the oven—they'll crisp more when cooled.

Our Recipe
Sweet Potato Chips

Nutrition Facts
Serving Size: (46g) 1 serving

Amount Per Serving	
Calories 40	Calories from Fat 0
	% Daily Value*
Total Fat 0g	**0%**
Saturated Fat 0g	**0%**
Trans Fat 0g	
Cholesterol 0mg	**0%**
Sodium 280mg	**12%**
Total Carbohydrate 9g	**3%**
Dietary Fiber 2g	**8%**
Sugars 3g	
Protein 1g	

Popular Brand
Sweet Potato Chips

Nutrition Facts
Serving Size: (46g)

Amount Per Serving	
Calories 230	Calories from Fat 100
	% Daily Value*
Total Fat 11g	**17%**
Saturated Fat 1g	**5%**
Trans Fat 0.5g	
Cholesterol 0mg	**0%**
Sodium 15mg	**1%**
Total Carbohydrate 30g	**10%**
Dietary Fiber 2g	**8%**
Sugars 3g	
Protein 2g	

One-Minute Tortilla Chips

SERVES 6

Necessity breeds ingenuity. After making a huge bowl of guacamole for my kids, I (gasp!) ran out of chips and quickly whipped up these substitutes. The next week, with store-bought chips in hand, the kids pleaded for the homemade (healthy) ones. Score!

12 small corn tortillas
1 teaspoon salt or to taste

In a standard toaster, place 1 tortilla in each slot on medium heat.

Toast, spinning the tortilla once if it's not completely inside the toaster.

Stack each batch. Slice into pie-shaped quarters immediately.

Salt and serve.

Our Recipe
Tortilla Chips

Nutrition Facts
Serving Size: (43g) 1 serving

Amount Per Serving	
Calories 90	Calories from Fat 10
	% Daily Value*
Total Fat 1g	**2%**
Saturated Fat 0g	**0%**
Trans Fat 0g	
Cholesterol 0mg	**0%**
Sodium 410mg	**17%**
Total Carbohydrate 19g	**6%**
Dietary Fiber 3g	**12%**
Sugars 0g	
Protein 2g	

Popular Brand
Tortilla Chips

Nutrition Facts
Serving Size: (43g)

Amount Per Serving	
Calories 210	Calories from Fat 90
	% Daily Value*
Total Fat 10g	**15%**
Saturated Fat 1g	**5%**
Trans Fat 0g	
Cholesterol 0mg	**0%**
Sodium 135mg	**6%**
Total Carbohydrate 29g	**10%**
Dietary Fiber 2g	**8%**
Sugars less than 1g	
Protein 3g	

Power Crackers

SERVES 8 TO 12 (20 TO 30 CRACKERS)

Lisa's good friend Wendy Bright-Fallon, wellness coach, and coauthor of the fabulous cookbook Nourish, *made crackers similar to these at one of her parties. After trying them again (and again and again), Lisa walked away a cracker addict and asked—er, begged—Wendy for the recipe. (Wendy, in turn, had found the recipe in one of her favorite cookbooks,* The Sprouted Kitchen, *by Sara Forte.) This is a an oil-free variation of what Wendy calls "the best crackers ever."*

½ cup almonds
½ cup raw cashews
2 tablespoons ground flaxseed or flaxseed meal
⅓ cup sesame seeds
2 teaspoons dried thyme
2 teaspoons dried rosemary
½ teaspoon onion powder
½ teaspoon sea salt
1 tablespoon pure maple syrup
2 tablespoons water

In a food processor, combine the almonds, cashews, ground flaxseed, sesame seeds, thyme, rosemary, onion powder, and salt and blend for 3 minutes. Add the maple syrup and water, and continue to process until the ingredients begin to stick together.

Mold into a ball and wrap tightly with plastic wrap. Refrigerate for several hours or overnight.

Preheat the oven to 325°. Line a baking sheet with parchment paper and set aside.

Roll the chilled dough between two pieces of parchment paper until it is ⅛-inch thick. Cut the crackers to desired size with a pizza cutter.

Using a spatula, transfer them to the prepared baking sheet. Bake for 15 minutes. Cool completely. Serve or store for another day.

NUTRITION (1/10 recipe/22g): Calories 100, Calories from Fat 70, Total Fat 8g, Saturated Fat 1g, Trans Fat 0g, Cholesterol 0mg, Sodium 105mg, Total Carbohydrate 6g, Dietary Fiber 2g, Sugars 2g, Protein 3g

TO-DIE-FOR DIPS AND DRESSINGS

Face it: We don't pick from the veggie platter because we love raw cauliflower—we do it because we love rich, creamy dip. Now we can dip (and dress) guilt-free.

Smoked Sardine Dip

SERVES 8

My beloved coauthor, Lisa, gently encouraged (um, forced) me to write a recipe incorporating these tiny savory gems (something about them being "super healthy"). After much kicking and screaming, I created one of my favorite all-time dips. No kidding. Lisa knows best.

¼ cup raw cashews
¼ cup water
2 (3¾-ounce) cans smoked sardines, packed in water, drained
2 tablespoons minced shallot
1 scallion, chopped
2 tablespoons plus 1 teaspoon minced flat-leaf parsley
½ teaspoon salt or more to taste
¼ teaspoon pepper

In a blender or food processor, purée the cashews and water until smooth.

Add the sardines, shallot, scallion, 2 tablespoons of the parsley, salt, and pepper. Process until well blended.

Transfer to a serving bowl and top with the remaining 1 teaspoon of parsley.

Refrigerate until ready to serve.

Quick (healthy) cracker hack: Split whole-wheat pitas to create two circles. Toast and cut into triangles.

NUTRITION (1 serving/45g): Calories 70, Calories from Fat 40, Total Fat 4.5g, Saturated Fat 0.5g, Trans Fat 0g, Cholesterol 35mg, Sodium 210mg, Total Carbohydrate 2g, Dietary Fiber 0g, Sugars less than 1g, Protein 6g

Caesar Salad Dressing and Dip

16 SERVINGS (2 TABLESPOONS EACH)

For many vegan years, I made a fish-free version of this. I balked when Lisa told me I had to create a recipe with anchovies. Then I realized I could enhance my delicious healthy Caesar salad dressing with this savory addition. Voilà. Now it's better than ever. (Thanks, partner.)

1 (16-ounce) can chickpeas
¼ cup fresh lemon juice
6 anchovies fillets packed in water, drained
2 cloves garlic
¾ teaspoon Dijon mustard
¾ teaspoon black pepper
Salt to taste

Purée all the ingredients with an immersion (stick) blender or in a food processor or blender until creamy.

Serve as is for salad dressing or chill for a yummy veggie or healthy chip dip.

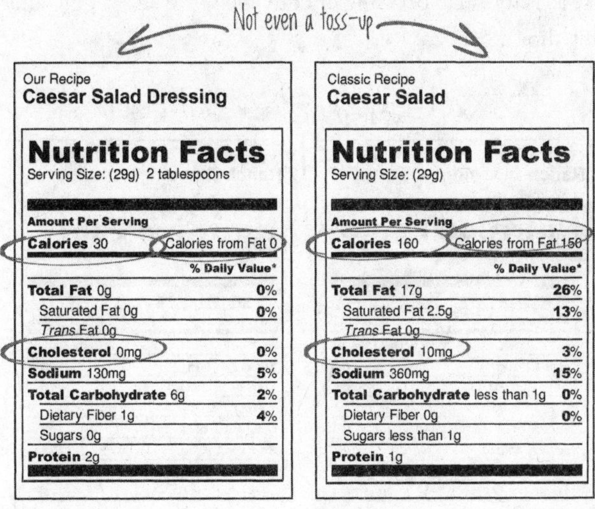

Our Recipe
Caesar Salad Dressing

Nutrition Facts
Serving Size: (29g) 2 tablespoons

Amount Per Serving	
Calories 30	Calories from Fat 0
	% Daily Value*
Total Fat 0g	**0%**
Saturated Fat 0g	**0%**
Trans Fat 0g	
Cholesterol 0mg	**0%**
Sodium 130mg	**5%**
Total Carbohydrate 6g	**2%**
Dietary Fiber 1g	**4%**
Sugars 0g	
Protein 2g	

Classic Recipe
Caesar Salad

Nutrition Facts
Serving Size: (29g)

Amount Per Serving	
Calories 160	Calories from Fat 150
	% Daily Value*
Total Fat 17g	**26%**
Saturated Fat 2.5g	**13%**
Trans Fat 0g	
Cholesterol 10mg	**3%**
Sodium 360mg	**15%**
Total Carbohydrate less than 1g	**0%**
Dietary Fiber 0g	**0%**
Sugars less than 1g	
Protein 1g	

Ranch Dressing and Dip

12 SERVINGS (2 TABLESPOONS EACH)

Even after all these years as veggie lovers, Lisa and I agree that a crudité platter is just not the same without a side of ranch dressing. Here's my delicious healthy version of the fatty classic. Pass the celery sticks, please.

1 (12-ounce) package silken light tofu, drained
2 tablespoons chopped fresh dill
2 tablespoons onion powder
2 tablespoons fresh lemon juice
¾ teaspoon salt
¼ teaspoon ground black pepper

In a blender or food processor, combine all the ingredients and blend until smooth.

Use as is for salad dressing or chill and serve as a veggie and chip dip.

You had us at "no fat"

Our Recipe
Ranch Dressing

Nutrition Facts
Serving Size: (30g) 2 tablespoons

Amount Per Serving	
Calories 15	Calories from Fat 0
	% Daily Value*
Total Fat 0g	**0%**
Saturated Fat 0g	**0%**
Trans Fat 0g	
Cholesterol 0mg	**0%**
Sodium 140mg	**6%**
Total Carbohydrate 1g	**0%**
Dietary Fiber 0g	**0%**
Sugars 0g	
Protein 2g	

Popular Brand
Ranch Dressing

Nutrition Facts
Serving Size: (30g)

Amount Per Serving	
Calories 130	Calories from Fat 120
	% Daily Value*
Total Fat 13g	**20%**
Saturated Fat 2g	**10%**
Trans Fat 0g	
Cholesterol 10mg	**3%**
Sodium 270mg	**11%**
Total Carbohydrate 2g	**1%**
Dietary Fiber 0g	**0%**
Sugars 1g	
Protein 0g	

WAKE-UP CALL—BEST BREAKFASTS

Good morning! Awaken your taste buds with these rise-and-shine recipes—perfect for brunchtime, too.

Buttermilk Biscuits

MAKES 12

Long ago, I gave up any hope of enjoying a healthy version of the flaky Southern classic. How was I supposed to make buttermilk biscuits without buttermilk? Aha! I just added vinegar to the almond milk!

1½ cups plain almond milk
1½ tablespoons white vinegar

¼ cup raw cashews

¼ cup water

2¼ cups white whole-wheat flour or whole-wheat pastry flour

1 tablespoon baking powder

1 tablespoon organic sugar or vegan cane sugar

1½ teaspoons salt

½ teaspoon baking soda

Preheat the oven to 450°.

In a small bowl, combine the almond milk and vinegar and set aside to curdle.

In a blender or food processor, purée the cashews and water until smooth and set aside.

In a bowl, sift together the flour, baking powder, sugar, salt, and baking soda. Stir in the almond milk mixture and the cashew cream until all of the ingredients are combined. Do not overmix.

Let the batter stand for 5 minutes.

In heaping tablespoons, drop 10 to 12 dollops of batter onto a baking sheet.

Bake for 8 to 10 minutes, or until lightly browned. Serve warm.

NUTRITION (1 biscuit /60g): Calories 110, Calories from Fat 15, Total Fat 2g, Saturated Fat 0g, Trans Fat 0g, Cholesterol 0mg, Sodium 510mg, Total Carbohydrate 20g, Dietary Fiber 3g, Sugars 1g, Protein 3g

Crunchy French Toast Casserole

SERVES 4

I was tired of being left out of brunchtime fun, so I came up with this sweet delight that will please everyone.

1 cup almond milk
2 tablespoons pure maple syrup
1½ tablespoons chia seeds
1 teaspoon ground cinnamon
½ teaspoon vanilla extract
¼ teaspoon salt
4 to 6 slices whole-grain or gluten-free bread
¾ cup sliced or chopped almonds

Preheat the oven to 400°.

In a medium bowl, mix the almond milk, maple syrup, chia seeds, cinnamon, vanilla, and salt. Let stand for 5 minutes.

Place half the sliced bread in the bottom of an 8-by-8-inch casserole dish to form a single layer.

Pour half of the almond milk mixture over the bread. Sprinkle with half the almonds. Layer the remaining bread and almond milk mixture and top with the remaining almonds.

Bake, uncovered, for 15 minutes.

Enjoy warm from the oven or make in advance and reheat when ready.

NUTRITION (1 serving/129g): Calories 250, Calories from Fat 110, Total Fat 13g, Saturated Fat 1g, Trans Fat 0g, Cholesterol 0mg, Sodium 340mg, Total Carbohydrate 28g, Dietary Fiber 6g, Sugars 9g, Protein 10g

Granola

SERVES 10 TO 12

Why it is so hard to find granola without added oils? This is a perfectly simple adaptation of Rebecca's from Vegan Sweet Tooth (vegansweeettoooth.com). Change up the nuts, add seeds, and make it your own.

2½ cups rolled oats
2 tablespoons ground cinnamon
¼ cup unsweetened applesauce
¼ cup pure maple syrup
½ cup raisins or dried cranberries
½ cup sliced almonds
¼ teaspoon salt

Preheat the oven to 400°.

Mix all the ingredients together in a large bowl and spread in a thin layer on a baking sheet.

Bake for about 15 minutes. Let cool, then crumble.

Leave the granola out in a bowl on your countertop for in a perfect on-the-go snack.

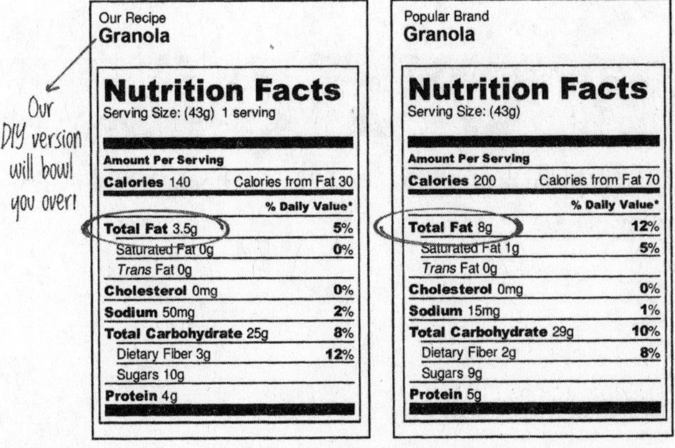
Our
DIY version
will bowl
you over!

Our Recipe
Granola

Nutrition Facts	
Serving Size: (43g) 1 serving	
Amount Per Serving	
Calories 140	Calories from Fat 30
	% Daily Value*
Total Fat 3.5g	**5%**
Saturated Fat 0g	**0%**
Trans Fat 0g	
Cholesterol 0mg	**0%**
Sodium 50mg	**2%**
Total Carbohydrate 25g	**8%**
Dietary Fiber 3g	**12%**
Sugars 10g	
Protein 4g	

Popular Brand
Granola

Nutrition Facts	
Serving Size: (43g)	
Amount Per Serving	
Calories 200	Calories from Fat 70
	% Daily Value*
Total Fat 8g	**12%**
Saturated Fat 1g	**5%**
Trans Fat 0g	
Cholesterol 0mg	**0%**
Sodium 15mg	**1%**
Total Carbohydrate 29g	**10%**
Dietary Fiber 2g	**8%**
Sugars 9g	
Protein 5g	

Banana Overnight Oatmeal

SERVES 3

No more frantic morning breakfasts with a piece of burned toast. Prep this scrumptious breakfast before you hit the sack.

4 cups water
1 cup steel-cut oats (not rolled oats)
2 ripe bananas, cut into small chunks
¼ teaspoon salt
½ teaspoon ground cinnamon (optional)

In a small heavy saucepan, bring the water to a boil. Add the oats, bananas, salt, and cinnamon. Stir and cover. Remove the pot from the heat, leave on counter, and *do not uncover* until morning.

Reheat when ready to eat.

NUTRITION (1 serving/447g): Calories 270, Calories from Fat 30, Total Fat 3.5g, Saturated Fat 0g, Trans Fat 0g, Cholesterol 0mg, Sodium 15mg, Total Carbohydrate 53g, Dietary Fiber 7g, Sugars 11g, Protein 10g

INDULGENT DESSERTS

This is our favorite section in the entire book. Nothing more to say here.

Mocha-Chip Shake

SERVES 2 TO 4

What? A healthy chocolate shake? Pour me a tall one anytime.

1½ cups coffee, chilled
½ cup almond milk
2 tablespoons unsweetened cocoa powder
¼ cup pitted dates
½ cup chocolate chips
6 to 12 ice cubes

Place all the ingredients in a blender and purée until smooth and creamy. (Use more or less ice, depending on the desired texture.)

Pour into tall glasses and serve. (Then, with the added energy, go for a long walk or run.)

Time to shake off the fat and calories!

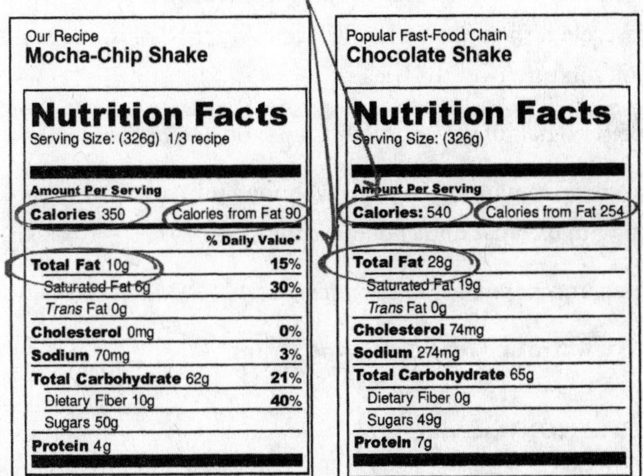

Our Recipe
Mocha-Chip Shake

Nutrition Facts Serving Size: (326g) 1/3 recipe	
Amount Per Serving	
Calories 350	Calories from Fat 90
	% Daily Value*
Total Fat 10g	**15%**
Saturated Fat 6g	**30%**
Trans Fat 0g	
Cholesterol 0mg	**0%**
Sodium 70mg	**3%**
Total Carbohydrate 62g	**21%**
Dietary Fiber 10g	**40%**
Sugars 50g	
Protein 4g	

Popular Fast-Food Chain
Chocolate Shake

Nutrition Facts Serving Size: (326g)	
Amount Per Serving	
Calories: 540	Calories from Fat 254
Total Fat 28g	
Saturated Fat 19g	
Trans Fat 0g	
Cholesterol 74mg	
Sodium 274mg	
Total Carbohydrate 65g	
Dietary Fiber 0g	
Sugars 49g	
Protein 7g	

Chocolate Chip–Banana Bread Pudding

SERVES 4

I barely got to sample this, since my son and husband devoured it as soon as I placed it on the counter. Thanks, guys.

1 cup almond milk
2 tablespoons pure maple syrup
1½ tablespoons chia seeds
½ teaspoon vanilla extract
4 slices whole-grain bread or gluten-free bread
2 ripe bananas, sliced into ¼-inch-thick coins
¾ cup dark chocolate chips

Preheat the oven to 400°.

In a medium bowl, mix the almond milk, maple syrup, chia seeds, and vanilla. Let stand for 5 minutes.

Place half the sliced bread in the bottom of an 8-by-8-inch casserole dish to form a single layer. Pour half of the almond milk mixture over the bread.

Top with half of the chocolate chips and half of the bananas.

Layer the remaining bread and almond milk mixture and top with bananas and chocolate chips.

Bake, uncovered, for 15 minutes.

Serve warm and repeat after me: "Yum!"

NUTRITION (1 serving/192g): Calories 360, Calories from Fat 140, Total Fat 16g, Saturated Fat 8g, Trans Fat 0g, Cholesterol 0mg, Sodium 170mg, Total Carbohydrate 49g, Dietary Fiber 7g, Sugars 26g, Protein 8g

Quick Tiramisu

SERVES 4

A sophisticated interpretation of the beloved classic—without all the fuss . . . or fat. Dress it up by making it in individual ramekins. This one is for my ever-loving chocoholic, Nana.

1 cup almond milk
1 shot espresso (optional)
2 tablespoons pure maple syrup
1½ tablespoons chia seeds
1 tablespoon unsweetened cocoa powder
5 slices whole-grain bread or gluten-free bread, crusts removed
½ cup dark chocolate chips

Preheat the oven to 400°.

In a medium bowl, mix the almond milk, espresso, if using, maple syrup, chia seeds, and cocoa powder. Let stand for 5 minutes.

Place 3 slices of bread in the bottom of a non-stick bread pan to form a single layer that goes up the sides.

Pour half of the almond milk mixture over the bread. Top with half of the chocolate chips.

Layer the remaining bread and remaining almond milk mixture and finish with chocolate chips.

Bake, uncovered, for 15 minutes. Serve warm or chilled with chopped fresh strawberries, if desired.

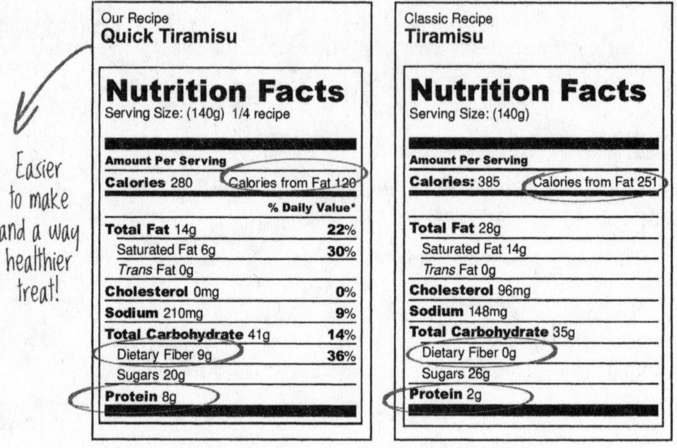
Easier to make and a way healthier treat!

Our Recipe
Quick Tiramisu

Nutrition Facts
Serving Size: (140g) 1/4 recipe

Amount Per Serving	
Calories 280	Calories from Fat 120
	% Daily Value*
Total Fat 14g	**22%**
Saturated Fat 6g	**30%**
Trans Fat 0g	
Cholesterol 0mg	**0%**
Sodium 210mg	**9%**
Total Carbohydrate 41g	**14%**
Dietary Fiber 9g	**36%**
Sugars 20g	
Protein 8g	

Classic Recipe
Tiramisu

Nutrition Facts
Serving Size: (140g)

Amount Per Serving	
Calories: 385	Calories from Fat 251
Total Fat 28g	
Saturated Fat 14g	
Trans Fat 0g	
Cholesterol 96mg	
Sodium 148mg	
Total Carbohydrate 35g	
Dietary Fiber 0g	
Sugars 26g	
Protein 2g	

Peanut Butter Cookies

MAKES 24 COOKIES

My first kitchen assistant, the talented Rebecca, was a baker at heart who somewhat lacked in onion-chopping skills. She more than made up for it in her genius baking though, and went on to launch the spectacular vegan bakery Vegan Sweet Tooth. This recipe is pure genius, with no compromise in flavor or texture.

- 1 cup peanut butter
- 1 cup organic sugar or vegan cane sugar
- ⅓ cup hemp milk
- 1 cup white whole-wheat flour or whole-wheat pastry flour
- ¼ teaspoon baking powder
- ¼ teaspoon salt

Preheat the oven to 350°. If you don't have a nonstick baking sheet, line a baking sheet with parchment paper and set aside.

Cream together the peanut butter, sugar, and hemp milk.

Sift the dry ingredients into the creamed mixture.

Using a tablespoon, drop individual cookies on the prepared baking sheet and flatten with the palm of your hand.

Bake for 15 minutes. Leave on the baking sheet until cooled.

Hide these immediately so your family doesn't scarf the entire batch.

NUTRITION (1 cookie/22g): Calories 110, Calories from Fat 50, Total Fat 6g, Saturated Fat 1g, Trans Fat 0g, Cholesterol 0mg, Sodium 50mg, Total Carbohydrate 14g, Dietary Fiber 1g, Sugars 4g, Protein 9g

Chocolate Brownies with Fudge Icing

SERVES 10 TO 12 (OR 1 IF YOU'RE LISA)

This was my clients' favorite dessert from Rebecca of Vegan Sweet Tooth. Kudos to my friend and loyal recipe tester, Meg, for her genius addition of balsamic vinegar to bring out the chocolate in the icing.

BROWNIE INGREDIENTS:

1⅔ cups applesauce
¾ cup plus 2 tablespoons organic sugar, or vegan sugar
1 teaspoon vanilla extract
1½ cups white whole-wheat flour or whole-wheat pastry flour
½ cup unsweetened cocoa powder
1 tablespoon baking powder
1 teaspoon baking soda
1 teaspoon salt
¼ cup dark chocolate chips

ICING INGREDIENTS:

¾ cup silken tofu
⅓ cup almond butter
2 teaspoons vanilla extract
2 tablespoons unsweetened cocoa powder
¼ cup confectioners' sugar
¼ teaspoon balsamic vinegar

BROWNIE PREP:

Preheat the oven to 350°.

Mix the applesauce, sugar, and vanilla extract in a bowl.

In a separate bowl, mix together the dry ingredients. Add the dry ingredients to the wet ingredients and fold in the chocolate chips.

Pour into a 10-inch square brownie pan and bake for 30 minutes.

ICING PREP:

Put all of the ingredients in a blender and blend until smooth.

When the brownies are cooled, top with frosting and enjoy.

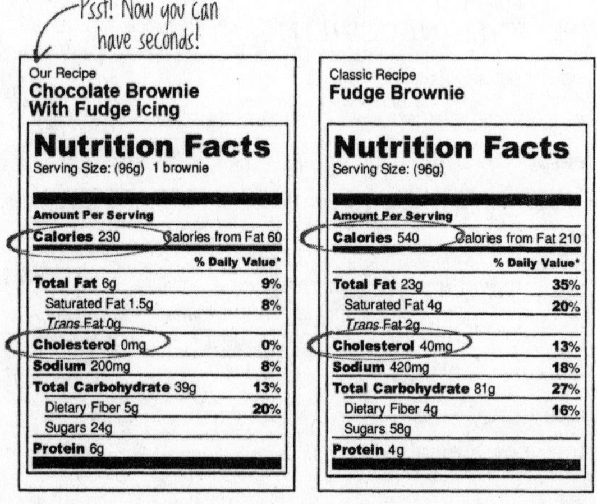
Psst! Now you can have seconds!

Our Recipe
Chocolate Brownie With Fudge Icing

Nutrition Facts
Serving Size: (96g) 1 brownie

Amount Per Serving	
Calories 230	Calories from Fat 60
	% Daily Value*
Total Fat 6g	**9%**
Saturated Fat 1.5g	**8%**
Trans Fat 0g	
Cholesterol 0mg	**0%**
Sodium 200mg	**8%**
Total Carbohydrate 39g	**13%**
Dietary Fiber 5g	**20%**
Sugars 24g	
Protein 6g	

Classic Recipe
Fudge Brownie

Nutrition Facts
Serving Size: (96g)

Amount Per Serving	
Calories 540	Calories from Fat 210
	% Daily Value*
Total Fat 23g	**35%**
Saturated Fat 4g	**20%**
Trans Fat 2g	
Cholesterol 40mg	**13%**
Sodium 420mg	**18%**
Total Carbohydrate 81g	**27%**
Dietary Fiber 4g	**16%**
Sugars 58g	
Protein 4g	

Gluten-Free Double-Chocolate Brownies

SERVES 12

My dear friend and famous cookbook author, Miche Bacher (Cooking with Flowers), *created this magnificent treat exclusively for our book. The first time I tried these, I couldn't stop stuffing brownie after brownie into my mouth as I tried to praise her genius.*

2 tablespoons chia seeds, ground to powder
½ cup water
1⅛ cups (6 ounces) dark chocolate
6 tablespoons silken tofu
⅔ cup coconut sugar or organic cane sugar
2 teaspoons vanilla extract
¼ cup unsweetened cocoa powder
3 tablespoons arrowroot powder
¼ teaspoon salt

Preheat the oven to 350°.

Prepare an 8-by-8-inch baking pan by lining it with a sheet of aluminum foil, leaving a few inches of overhang on the sides to allow for easy removal. Set pan aside.

Mix the ground chia seeds with the water and set aside for 5 minutes.

To melt the chocolate, set a large bowl on top of a 4-quart saucepan half filled with water. Bring the water to a quick simmer over medium heat. Add the chocolate to the bowl and melt, stirring occasionally, 5 to 8 minutes.

Remove from the heat, stir in the tofu, and combine thoroughly.

Using a hand mixer, add the chia mixture, sugar, and vanilla extract to the chocolate mixture and beat until smooth, about 3 minutes.

Reduce the speed to low and add the cocoa powder, arrowroot powder, and salt, mixing until well combined and scraping down the sides of the bowl as necessary. Turn up the speed to high for about 1 minute. The batter should be thick and smooth.

Pour the batter into the prepared pan, spreading it evenly with a spatula.

Bake for 25 to 30 minutes, until the center is set.

Remove from the oven and let cool in pan for about 15 minutes.

Cool completely then cut into squares and devour.

NUTRITION (1 brownie/80g): Calories 200, Calories from Fat 60, Total Fat 7g, Saturated Fat 3.5g, Trans Fat 0g, Cholesterol 0mg, Sodium 50mg, Total Carbohydrate 35g, Dietary Fiber 3g, Sugars 29g, Protein 3g

Power Blondies

SERVES 12

Thanks to my brilliant friend Abby for these scrumptious treats. Once you taste them, you'll want her as a friend, too.

- 3 tablespoons ground flaxseed
- 3 tablespoons warm water
- 2 tablespoons white whole-wheat flour or gluten-free flour
- ¼ teaspoon salt
- ⅛ teaspoon baking powder
- ⅛ teaspoon baking soda

- 1 cup walnuts
- 1 cup almonds
- ¼ cup old-fashioned rolled oats (make sure you buy gluten-free oats if you want these to be gluten-free)
- 1½ cups pitted dates
- 5 tablespoons pure maple syrup
- 1 teaspoon vanilla extract
- ¾ cup dark chocolate chips

Preheat the oven to 325°.

Mix 1 tablespoon of the ground flaxseed with the warm water and set aside.

In a high-powered blender or food processor, add the remaining 2 tablespoons of the flaxseed, the flour, salt, baking powder, and baking soda, and pulse for 5 seconds to mix. Add the nuts and pulse several times, until the nuts are coarsely chopped Add oats and dates and pulse until the mixture is well chopped but still coarse.

In a large bowl, mix the flaxseed-water mixture, maple syrup, and vanilla. Add the blondie mixture from the food processor and combine with your hands, making sure any clumps are separated. Mix in the chocolate chips.

Spread into a 9-by-11-inch nonstick baking dish, pushing the mixture down so that the top is flat.

Bake for 25 to 30 minutes, until set and golden.

Let rest about 10 minutes, then slice into bars. Cool before serving.

NUTRITION (1 blondie/75g): Calories 300, Calories from Fat 130, Total Fat 15g, Saturated Fat 3g, Trans Fat 0g, Cholesterol 0mg, Sodium 65mg, Total Carbohydrate 43g, Dietary Fiber 5g, Sugars 34g, Protein 5g

Caramel Corn

SERVES 6

My super-healthy, strictly vegan husband, Ken, ate the entire test bowl of this one morning. I found an empty, sticky bowl on the counter when I went to try it. He says it's awesome.

⅓ cup organic popcorn kernels
1 large brown paper grocery bag
½ cup pure maple syrup
¼ cup almond butter or peanut butter
¼ teaspoon salt

Place the corn kernels in the bag and fold the bag over twice.

Cook in a microwave oven until the popping slows down, around 3 to 4 minutes; keep watch that bag doesn't catch on fire. Open carefully. Transfer the popcorn to a large bowl.

In a saucepan over medium-high heat, heat the maple syrup until it boils one inch up the sides of the pan. Immediately remove from the heat.

Whisk in the nut butter and salt until smooth. Pour over the popcorn and toss quickly with a spoon (not your hands—ouch).

Cool and serve. Good luck keeping this around for more than thirty seconds.

NUTRITION (1 serving/50g): Calories 190, Calories from Fat 60, Total Fat 7g, Saturated Fat 0.5g, Trans Fat 0g, Cholesterol 0mg, Sodium 100mg, Total Carbohydrate 29g, Dietary Fiber 3g, Sugars 18g, Protein 4g

Maple-Cashew Ice Cream by Hand (No Machine)

SERVES 3

Lisa's omnivorous chef friend, Jason Crispin—owner of the Gourmand Cooking School—makes vegan treats for Lisa's events when she's out promoting The Vegan Cheat Sheet. *The audience always swoons over this Jason creation, which he adapted from my cashew cream recipe. Häagen-Dazs has nothing over Jason's rich, creamy dessert—and second helpings are definitely less guilt inducing. (His version requires an ice-cream maker; ours does not.)*

- 1 cup raw cashews
- ¾ cup plus 2 tablespoons water
- ¼ teaspoon vanilla extract
- ⅓ cup pure maple syrup
- ¾ cup coarse kosher or sea salt for processing

In a blender or food processor, mix all the ingredients until creamy, around 4 to 5 minutes. Chill the ice-cream mixture overnight in the refrigerator in a small covered bowl.

Remove the ice-cream mixture from the refrigerator and beat with a hand mixer for 10 minutes, then cover tightly.

Fill a large bowl halfway with ice. Nest the covered ice-cream bowl inside of the salt-ice bowl so the ice-cream bowl is surrounded by ice.

Place the bowls in the freezer for 45 minutes. Remove the cover of the ice-cream bowl and beat with a hand mixer for 5 minutes. Return the bowls to the freezer and freeze for several hours or longer. I prefer it softer, and I am impatient, so I wait only a few hours before eating.

Quick Option

If you need it now, this version is firm and icy in texture.

Fill a gallon-size zip-top bag halfway with ice.

Add ½ cup salt. Place the ice cream in a zip-top bag inside of the ice bag. Seal the ice bag well. To avoid leaking, double-bag the ice bag.

Shake and rotate the bag continuously for 10 minutes. Carefully remove the inner bag and check the ice cream for firmness.

If firmer ice cream is desired, return it to the ice bag, add more ice, and shake and rotate for another 5 minutes. Scoop out and serve.

NUTRITION (¾ cup/132g): Calories 330, Calories from Fat 170, Total Fat 19g, Saturated Fat 3.5g, Trans Fat 0g, Cholesterol 0mg, Sodium 15mg, Total Carbohydrate 36g, Dietary Fiber 1g, Sugars 26g, Protein 8g

Mocha-Coconut Almond Fudge Ice Cream by Hand (No Machine)

SERVES 4

I impressed myself with this creation. I never knew vegan ice cream could be so delicious and easy to make. When I made this with my dear little neighbors (Anna, John, and Ella), I used the quick two-bag method and divided the ice-cream mixture into three small bags. Then I put each of the bags inside a plastic bag of salt and ice for them to shake. When they were done, each of them could eat their own bag of ice cream.

1 (13.5-ounce) can coconut milk
⅓ cup strong black coffee
¼ cup pure maple syrup
¼ cup unsweetened cocoa powder
¾ teaspoon vanilla extract
½ cup chopped almonds or chopped chocolate chips
¾ cup coarse kosher or sea salt for processing

In a medium bowl, mix all the ingredients except the salt until blended. Chill the ice-cream mixture overnight in the refrigerator in a small covered bowl.

Remove the ice-cream mixture from the refrigerator, beat it with a hand-held mixer for 10 minutes, then cover it tightly. Fill a large bowl halfway with ice. Add the salt. Nest the covered ice-cream bowl inside of the salt-ice bowl so the ice-cream bowl is surrounded by ice.

Place the bowls in the freezer for 45 minutes. Remove the cover of the ice-cream bowl and beat the ice cream with a hand mixer for 5 minutes. Return the bowls to the freezer and freeze for several hours or longer.

I cannot wait that long, and luckily I prefer softer ice cream. Test every hour (yum!) until you're happy with the texture.

Quick Option

If you need it now, this version is firm and icy in texture.

Fill a gallon-size zip-top bag halfway with ice. Add ½ cup of salt. Place the ice cream in a zip-top bag inside of the ice bag. Seal the ice bag well. To avoid leaking, double-bag the ice bag.

Shake and rotate the bag continuously for 10 minutes. Carefully remove the inner bag and check the ice cream for firmness.

If firmer ice cream is desired, return it to the ice bag, add more ice, and shake and rotate for another 5 minutes. Enjoy.

NUTRITION (⅔ cup/167g): Calories 290, Calories from Fat 200, Total Fat 23g, Saturated Fat 15g, Trans Fat 0g, Cholesterol 0mg, Sodium 25mg, Total Carbohydrate 21g, Dietary Fiber 2g, Sugars 15g, Protein 4g

Coconut Whipped Cream/Icing

MAKES 16 SPOONFULS

No one should have to go through life without whipped cream. This vegan version is a simple but outrageous topping from Rebecca of Vegan Sweet Tooth.

1 (14-ounce) can coconut milk, chilled overnight in the refrigerator
½ cup confectioners' sugar
½ teaspoon vanilla extract

Remove the chilled coconut milk from the refrigerator. *Do not shake the can to blend.*

Carefully open the can and remove the thick cream from the top. Discard the remaining watery liquid.

Place the cream in a medium bowl and whip with a hand mixer, 30 to 45 seconds or until creamy.

Add the sugar and vanilla and mix until blended. Store in the refrigerator until ready to use.

NUTRITION (1 serving/29g): Calories 60, Calories from Fat 50, Total Fat 5g, Saturated Fat 4.5g, Trans Fat 0g, Cholesterol 0mg, Sodium 0mg, Total Carbohydrate 4g, Dietary Fiber 0g, Sugars 4g, Protein 1g

CHAPTER 13

RESTAURANT SURVIVAL GUIDE AND SUSHI PRIMER

Once you leave your kitchen and relinquish control of your food prep, you may feel, well, like a fish out of water. Most restaurants accommodate diet requests—from gluten-free to Paleo—so getting the seagan meal you want should be as easy as asking a few questions and making some menu tweaks. Here are our top eating-out tips, plus best menu choices at popular "themed" restaurants.

How to Talk to the Server

(Well, nicely, of course.) Tell him or her that you follow a plant-based-plus-fish, low-oil diet. If you get a blank stare, elaborate by saying:

- You eat all vegetables, preferably steamed and with no or very little oil
- You don't eat dairy—no cream, milk, butter, eggs, cheese, or any dishes containing these ingredients
- You eat some fish (consult our Good Catch, Bad Catch list on page 36 for best options); if the server can't answer your questions about the fish's provenance, catch method, etc., ask to speak with the chef

- If ordering pasta (preferably whole-wheat), confirm it doesn't contain eggs (most dried whole-wheat pasta is egg free; fresh varieties usually contain eggs).

How to Order Your Favorite Cuisine

AMERICAN

- Steamed or simply grilled salmon
- Baked potato or sweet potato
- Brown rice and other grains
- Steamed vegetables
- Veggie burgers (confirm if vegan; some are made with eggs and/or cheese)
- Tossed salad with balsamic vinegar and a spritz of lemon

BREAKFAST

- Oatmeal (made with water, not milk)
- Pancakes, if made without eggs or milk (a rarity, but worth asking)
- Veggie "omelet" without eggs—one of Lisa's standbys; basically sautéed vegetables; request with tofu and salsa, if available, and a side of plain corn tortillas
- Veggie "egg" burrito without eggs (yup, just veggies in a burrito)—request with tofu and salsa, if available
- Fruit
- Whole-wheat toast or bagel—with peanut butter and jam

CHINESE

- Steamed vegetables with steamed shrimp, fish, or tofu
- Oil-free sauces for dipping, such as sweet-chili sauce and low-sodium soy sauce
- Brown rice

DELI/BAGEL SHOP

- Whole-wheat bagel with smoked salmon, tomatoes, and onions (no cream cheese or butter, unless nondairy cream cheese is available)
- Whole-wheat wrap with avocado and fresh veggies
- Large mixed salad with all veggies and avocado, topped with balsamic vinegar

DESSERT

- Dark chocolate
- Dark-chocolate-covered strawberries and fruit
- Fresh fruit
- Sorbet

GREEK

- Simply grilled fish or shrimp
- Hummus
- Greek salad (omit the feta cheese; substitute vinegar for salad dressing)
- Stuffed grape leaves
- Tabbouleh
- Baba ganoush
- Falafel (go easy, since these are typically fried)

INDIAN

- Any fish or vegetarian dishes that don't contain ghee (clarified butter) or other dairy products
- Try to avoid dishes with too much rich coconut milk; if you're craving that intensity, ask if they can go lighter in your dish
- Vegan breads; eat in limited quantities, since they often contain oil

- Mango chutney, tamarind, or spicy dipping sauces
- Brown rice

ITALIAN

- Tossed green salad with balsamic vinegar and a squeeze of lemon
- Grilled or baked fish (confirm no butter or cream sauces)
- Pasta (whole-wheat, if possible) with shrimp and marinara sauce (check if vegan and low-oil) and add any of these: artichokes, chopped tomatoes, fresh broccoli, marinara or pomodoro sauce (check if it contains cheese or meat), mushrooms, onions, peppers, spinach, white beans

JAPANESE/SUSHI

For more sushi tips, see page 151.

- Fish, vegetable, sweet potato, or futomaki roll without egg
- Bowl of vegan buckwheat udon soup
- Steamed tofu and veggies with vegan sauce (soy or dumpling) on the side
- Brown rice

MEXICAN

- Plain corn tortillas (not fried) instead of tortilla chips
- Guacamole (ask if vegan; enjoy in limited quantities)
- Salsa fresca/pico de gallo
- Black, pinto, or refried beans (ask if they are vegan and check for fat; refried beans are often just mashed pinto beans with seasoning)
- Rice (ask if vegan and low-oil/no lard)
- Grilled vegetables (request no/little oil)
- Simply prepared shrimp or fish (no butter and limited oil)

PIZZERIA

- Tossed green salad with balsamic vinegar and a squeeze of lemon
- Pizza (whole-wheat if possible; omit the cheese)
- Tomato sauce
- Vegetable toppings

THAI

- Simply grilled or steamed fish
- Steamed vegetables with steamed tofu
- Oil-free sauces for dipping, such as sweet-chili sauce and low-sodium soy sauce
- Rice noodles with vegetables
- Brown rice

Sushi Primer

At first glance, sushi seems like the perfect seagan meal. With veggie-packed rolls, plenty of dairy-free options, and small portions of fresh fish on the menu, what's not to love?

Well, perhaps a few things (sorry, sushi, we hate to do this to an old friend):

Problem: Sushi is generally made with white rice, which is high in carbs and sometimes mixed with sugar.

Solution: Request brown rice or opt for sashimi (raw fish, no rice) or naruto rolls (wrapped in cucumber instead of rice).

Problem: If you're like Lisa, you bathe your sushi in soy sauce—a total sodium bomb; 1 tablespoon contains 1,000 milligrams of sodium, nearly half the RDA.

Solution: Ask for low-sodium soy sauce and use it sparingly.

AVOID ROLLS AND DISHES THAT CONTAIN:

- Tempura (fried) ingredients, which add fat and calories
- Processed ingredients like "crab" (or "krab") sticks
- Teriyaki sauces—very high in sodium
- "Spicy" mayonnaise and cream cheese

DON'T OVERDO IT:

- A "love boat" filled with even the healthiest sushi can be a dietary disaster if you consume thousands more calories than you'd normally eat
- Stick with two rolls max and make one a veggie roll
- If you're not satiated, supplement your meal with healthy appetizers such as miso soup, a green salad, edamame, and other boiled or steamed veggie items

Now for the Good News!

It's possible to have a perfectly healthy meal at the sushi bar.

FRIENDS WITH BENEFITS:

- Sliced pickled ginger contains plant compounds that stimulate digestion and calm nervous stomachs

- Wasabi (green horseradish) has significant antimicrobial properties
- Sushi is typically wrapped in nori, a type of seaweed, which, like all sea vegetables, is rich in vitamins, minerals, phytonutrients, and fiber

So Good for You, but . . .

Many of the fish used in sushi—such as salmon and mackerel—are packed with healthy omega-3s. But all the cautions about mercury, contamination, and sustainability outlined in our Good Catch, Bad Catch (page 36) apply at the sushi bar, too—so please order mindfully.

Raw Fish Make You Nervous?

Most—if not all—fish served in sushi restaurants has been commercially frozen and defrosted prior to serving, which kills off the parasites typically found in fresh-caught fish. It's unlikely you'll contract any dangerous infections from raw fish, but be sure to pick a clean, reputable venue with a reasonably high turnover.

Some of the fish, like eel and shrimp, are generally served cooked. Pregnant woman and people with immune-system issues might want to play it safe and stick with only cooked items.

CHAPTER 14

DISSECTING FOOD LABELS—THE TIPS, TRICKS, AND DIRTY LITTLE SECRETS

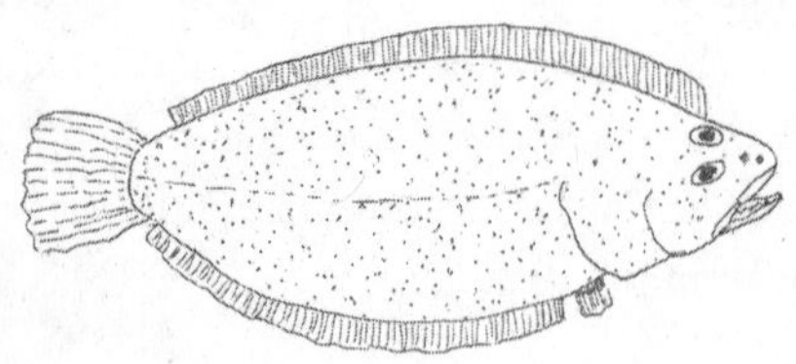

How wonderful it would be to survive solely on fresh-from-the-garden vegetables, nut milks puréed in our blenders, fruit picked from our private orchards, and fish plucked from our backyard streams. But even the healthiest among us have to rely on packaged goods as staples, fill-ins, and full-on meals now and then.

That's why learning to read—and interpret—labels is so important.

There's no other way to get an overall snapshot of what you're putting into your body. Even seemingly healthy fare can be packed with sugar, fat, sodium, and some questionable additives.

But reading labels is no easy feat. For the untrained eye, it can seem like a bunch of gobbledygook, with meaningless numbers and unpronounceable gibberish. So let's try to make sense of it all.

Labeling Gimmicks

First up: those front-of-the-package claims. You know, the brightly colored, bold-type declarations that scream, "I'm

Healthy! Buy Me!" Here's a rundown on what you can believe and what you should take with a giant grain of salt.

Organic!

Foods labeled "organic" may sound impressive, but be careful: "Organic" is not the magic word for "eat as much as you want." These products can still be loaded with fat, calories, and sugar.

ORGANIC CHEAT SHEET

If the product features a USDA label that reads "organic," it means that 95 percent or more of its ingredients were grown or processed without synthetic fertilizers or pesticides. That's good!

If the label reads "made with organic ingredients," it means at least 70 percent of the product's ingredients meet the above standard. That's still pretty good, but not as good as "organic."

Made with Whole Grains!

"Whole grains" are music to our ears. These grains haven't been stripped of their nutrient-packed, fiber-filled germ and bran components. Healthy whole grains include whole wheat, oats, quinoa, buckwheat, brown rice, and many others.

Here's where it gets murky: A "whole grain" label simply means the product was made with at least eight grams of whole-grain ingredients per serving. The rest can be processed, refined flour. Pretty sneaky, eh?

Some dark breads, crackers, and similar "whole-grain" items may *look* like the real McCoy, but they're actually made with refined grains—and then darkened with molasses or other colorant. Bye-bye, health benefits.

Also, the word *enriched* before a grain likely means the

grain has been refined (stripped of germ and bran portions) and then had vitamins and nutrients added back in.

Bottom line: Look for labels that state "100 percent whole grain"—that way, you're truly getting the *whole* grain. At the very least, make sure the first ingredient is a whole grain.

All Natural!

"All natural"—sounds awfully attractive, doesn't it? Most people think this claim means something significant, like the food is free of artificial ingredients, pesticides, or GMOs or that it was processed in an environmentally friendly way.

A brilliant marketing ploy, the "natural" label drives sales (upward of $40 billion worth annually) and brings health-conscious shoppers a sense of comfort and trust.

Curb your enthusiasm: The FDA has no formal definition for this term. As long as the substance contains no added artificial or synthetic ingredients (including all color additives), the feds say, it can qualify as "natural." But there are plenty of "natural" preservatives and chemicals you don't want to ingest. For example, high-fructose corn syrup comes from corn, a product of Mother Nature. But this sugary ingredient could hardly be considered healthy.

Bottom line: Don't trust any label touting "natural." Check the back label's ingredient list for valuable info.

Some watchdog groups are rallying to have the "natural" label banned, since it's ambiguous, confusing, and deceptive, with lots of room for interpretation.

No Sugar Added!

Even if no sugar was added during manufacturing, many foods—including fruits, cereals, and vegetables—naturally contain sugar. And sugar is sugar. So trumpeting "no sugar added" may, well, just be sugar-coating things—these products can still boast plenty of calories, plus blood-sugar-raising carbs. Some "no sugar added" juices, for example, have 26 grams of the stuff or more per serving. Holy sugar coma! (For more sugar scoop, read our Refined White Sugar and Artificial Sweeteners section on page 186.)

Sugar Free!

Tsk, tsk, another potentially misleading term. Presented as healthier, lower-calorie substitutes for your favorite sugary treats, "sugar free" products must have less than 0.5 grams of sugar per serving—but the food can still be packed with fat, carbs, artificial sweeteners, and other junk.

Fat Free!

With all the hoopla surrounding the highly publicized dangers of saturated and trans fats in recent years, the "fat free" label was an instant hit among consumers. But don't be fooled. From a health standpoint, this claim is hollow: Jelly beans are fat free. So are sodas, desserts, cereals, condiments, and "diet" foods. These foods can be loaded with sugar, calories, processed chemicals, and artificial sweeteners.

Zero Trans Fat!

It's no secret that trans fats (or trans-fatty acids) are killer bad for us. Many doctors deem them the worst fats we could eat, because they do double dirty duty by raising our bad (LDL) cholesterol and lowering our good (HDL) cholesterol levels. That leaves us more vulnerable to heart disease and diabetes. The byproduct of partially hydrogenated oils (PHOs), trans fats are commonly found in baked goods, snack foods, stick margarines, coffee creamers, refrigerated dough products (like biscuits), and canned frostings.

But here's the industry's big, fat secret: A food with less than 0.5 grams of trans fat per serving can be labeled 0 grams. If we consume more than one serving, those numbers can quickly add up. Avoid eating *any* artery-clogging trans fat by checking the ingredient list. *If you see shortening, hydrogenated oil, or partially hydrogenated oil listed, the item contains trans fat. Walk away from it. On second thought, run.*

GOOD NEWS: DEATH TO TRANS FATS!

While we were writing this book, the FDA mandated that artificial trans fats (PHOs) be eliminated from food products by 2018. Since trans fats occur naturally in meat and dairy products, they won't be completely eradicated. Still, this move is estimated to prevent 20,000 heart attacks and 7,000 deaths from heart disease each year.

Cholesterol Free!

Cholesterol comes from animals, not plants. Always has, always will. Still, some labels use this throwaway claim to hype up the health benefits of their plant-based products and may hide the fact that they contain other uncool stuff, such as sugar, artificial sweeteners, and fat.

Good Source of Omega-3 Fatty Acids!

Omega-3 fatty acids occur in three forms: eicosapentaenoic acid (EPA), docosahexaenoic acid (DHA), and alpha-linolenic acid (ALA).

ALA, derived from plant-based foods, doesn't have the

same health benefits as EPA and DHA—which are found in many fish. When a product like flaxseed or flaxseed oil is touted to be a "good source of omega-3 fatty acids," it may not be all it's cracked up to be. Your highest, most healthful doses of EPA and DHA omega-3 come from fish. (For more info on omega-3s, check The Health Benefits of Seafood on page 19.)

Ingredient Lists

Manufacturers are required to list their products' ingredients on food labels in order of volume. So the most predominant ingredient appears first, the next most-used second, and so forth. That means it's easy to make snap decisions: If you see high-fructose corn syrup in that number-one (or even number-two) slot, for example, move along.

Just beware—the industry has its little ploys to throw us off kilter. For example, they might split sugar into different types, listing "dextrose," "high-fructose corn syrup," and "cane crystals" as separate items. Lumped together as sugar (which they are), they could very well be the first ingredient. But as distinct ingredients, they appear to carry less importance.

Some General Rules

Avoid products whose ingredient lists include more than one or two forms of sugar. Similarly, steer clear of trans fats, checking for keywords indicating the presence of these chemicals. For example, if it reads "partially hydrogenated," it means "trans fats" or more simply, "Don't buy or eat me."

CHOOSE PRODUCTS THAT CONTAIN:

- the fewest possible ingredients
- minimal quantities of sugar, fat, and sodium
- minimal (or better yet, no) ingredient names you can't pronounce or define

What About the Scary-Sounding Ingredients?

Here's a very short list of ingredients you may want to think twice about. While they all have intimidating names, these are among the many substances the U.S. Food and Drug Administration (FDA) has placed on its GRAS (Generally Recognized As Safe) list. The congressional definition of "safe" is "reasonable certainty that no harm will result from use."

It's not like white-coated FDA technicians with petri dishes are testing these substances. Instead, manufacturers can hire their own "experts" to clear items for GRAS without consulting the FDA. Some harmful substances *are* allowed but only at 1/100th of the amount considered toxic.

We're not sure about you, but we're not keen on phrases like *reasonable certainty* and *generally recognized*. When it comes to our food and our health, we're shooting for "damn well certain." Most of these additives have been associated with illnesses such as cancer, endocrine-system and hormone disruption, heart disease, and more. In small amounts, the risk is likely negligible. But we'll leave that for you to decide.

For a more comprehensive lineup and explanation, consult the Environmental Working Group's website (ewg.org). Whole Foods also posts a fairly current list of ingredients that are banned in products they carry. *(Note: Some of the additives listed below are banned in other countries.)*

Aluminum Additives

Aluminum-based additives such as sodium aluminum phosphate and sodium aluminum sulfate are often used as stabilizers in processed foods.

Artificial Colors

Chemical dyes made from petroleum-derived materials are used to color food and drinks, including candies, pickles, and cake mixes. You'll find them listed by their FD&C (Food,

Drug, & Cosmetics) name, for example, FD&C Blue No. 1 or FD&C Yellow No. 6.

Artificial Sweeteners

These are used to sweeten diet sodas and thousands of other products, from salad dressings to ice creams. (For more info, see our Refined White Sugar and Artificial Sweeteners section, page 186.)

Butylated Hydroxyanisole (BHA) and Butylated Hydroxytoluene (BHT)

Widely used (often in tandem) as preservatives that prevent oils in foods from going rancid, they're commonly found in snack foods, cereals, cookies, breads, gum, vegetable oils, and shortening.

Diacetyl

This is a yellowish liquid or powder primarily used for "butter" flavoring in products such as microwave popcorn, butterscotch, frostings, yogurt, and more. (For more on diacetyl, see our writeup on microwave popcorn and movie-theater popcorn, page 180.)

High-Fructose Corn Syrup

Made from corn, this goopy additive is sweeter and cheaper than sucrose (which is made from sugarcane). It appears in everything from soft drinks to ketchup.

Hydrogenated and Partially Hydrogenated Oils

These oils contain trans fats, which help food retain its freshness—but at a price. Trans fats increase your LDL (bad) cholesterol and decrease your good (HDL) cholesterol. They are commonly found in margarine, vegetable shortening, white bread, nondairy creamers, fast foods, baked goods, and conventional peanut butter.

Hydrolyzed Vegetable Protein (HVP)

Made from cereals, soy, corn, or wheat, HVP—like its relative, MSG (below)—is used as a flavor enhancer in thousands of processed foods, including veggie burgers, soups, sauces, snack foods, dips, and dressings.

MSG (Monosodium Glutamate)

MSG is used as a flavor enhancer in products such as canned and packaged soups, cake mixes, fast foods, chips, snack foods, and salad dressings.

Phosphates

With names like "sodium phosphate," "calcium phosphate," and "phosphoric acid," phosphate food additives are found in frozen dinners, baked goods, sodas, fast food, and restaurant foods.

Potassium Bromate

This chemical bleaches dough and pumps up the volume of bread products to make rolls and breads soft and fluffy.

Propyl Gallate

This preservative—sometimes used in conjunction with BHA and BHT—can be found in microwave popcorn, soup mixes, gum, mayonnaise, and frozen meals.

Propylparabens

Used as an antimicrobial in beauty products, propylparabens can be teamed with other food preservatives to prolong shelf life and prevent mold and staleness in corn tortillas, cakes, pastries, and other baked goods.

Sodium Benzoate

Lab-synthesized sodium benzoate (it occurs naturally in low levels in berries, apples, plums, and cinnamon) is a preservative common in packaged foods such as sodas and other beverages, fruit jams and jellies, relishes, and sauerkraut. (It is also called benzoic acid, benzene, and benzoate.)

Sugars

Sugar has many other names—57 to be exact—which you should keep an eye out for when reading labels. We've listed some of them below. Any given food can contain a variety of these:

Agave nectar
Barley malt syrup
Brown rice syrup
Carob syrup
Corn syrup
Dextrin
Dextrose
Ethyl maltol
Fructose
Fruit juice concentrate
Glucose
High-fructose corn syrup
Honey
Lactose
Malt syrup
Maltodextrin
Maltose
Maple syrup
Molasses
Rice bran syrup
Saccharose
Sorghum and sorghum syrup
Sucrose
Syrup
Treacle
Xylose

Nutrition Facts

The Nutrition Facts label is required on most packaged goods, except for seafood, meat, poultry, fresh produce, and a few other foods. It offers a wealth of valuable information and should be consulted as an important resource for everything you buy. Everything. Once you know what to look for, label reading will be a quick and natural part of shopping.

Math Magic

Manufacturers are permitted to round up or down to the nearest 0.5 gram—so products with less than 0.5 grams of a substance can be rounded down to 0 grams. Therefore, a product with 0.45 grams of trans fats per serving might show "0g" trans fat—even though the entire package may contain several grams.

Imagine you've just plunked down on the couch with the TV remote and an 18-serving bag of chips labeled "0g" trans fats. But in reality, each serving contains .45 grams of trans fat, giving the entire bag 8.1 grams of this crud. If you're like us, you inhale every last chip while watching *Modern Family* reruns—turning your zero-trans-fat snack into an 8-gram artery-clogging nightmare. That's why you have to inspect the ingredient list for hidden intruders, such as partially hydrogenated oil.

Cracking the Label Code

Thanks, FDA, for creating a label so confusing, we need to devote the next few pages to unraveling what it all means. (Really, though, we do appreciate all the great info it gives us. Thanks for that.)

Let's start at the top.

Serving Size

Serving sizes are often deceptive. Although they're based on the amount of food "customarily" eaten in one sitting, a "single serving" can be pretty stingy—like a half-cup of ice cream. Come on, people, who eats a half-cup of ice cream?

If you plan to eat a full cup (or, um, a pint) of Rocky Road, like a normal person, be sure to make the adjustments in calories, fat, and so forth.

DECODING THE LABEL

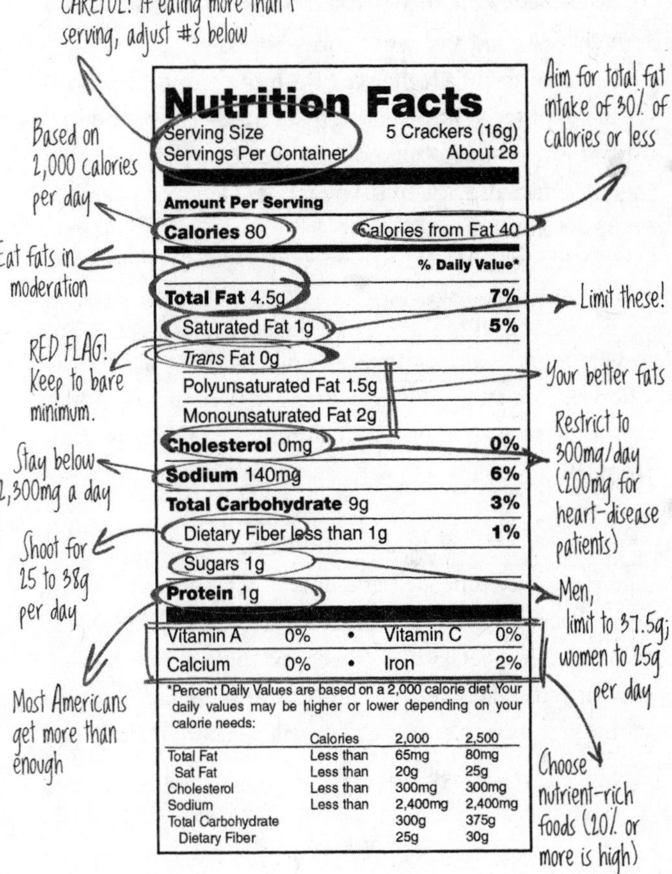

Nutrition Facts

Serving Size 5 Crackers (16g)
Servings Per Container About 28

Amount Per Serving

Calories 80 Calories from Fat 40

	% Daily Value*
Total Fat 4.5g	**7%**
Saturated Fat 1g	**5%**
Trans Fat 0g	
Polyunsaturated Fat 1.5g	
Monounsaturated Fat 2g	
Cholesterol 0mg	**0%**
Sodium 140mg	**6%**
Total Carbohydrate 9g	**3%**
Dietary Fiber less than 1g	**1%**
Sugars 1g	
Protein 1g	

Vitamin A	0%	Vitamin C	0%
Calcium	0%	Iron	2%

*Percent Daily Values are based on a 2,000 calorie diet. Your daily values may be higher or lower depending on your calorie needs:

	Calories	2,000	2,500
Total Fat	Less than	65mg	80mg
Sat Fat	Less than	20g	25g
Cholesterol	Less than	300mg	300mg
Sodium	Less than	2,400mg	2,400mg
Total Carbohydrate		300g	375g
Dietary Fiber		25g	30g

CAREFUL! If eating more than 1 serving, adjust #s below
Based on 2,000 calories per day
Aim for total fat intake of 30% of calories or less
Eat fats in moderation
Limit these!
RED FLAG! Keep to bare minimum.
Your better fats
Restrict to 300mg/day (200mg for heart-disease patients)
Stay below 2,300mg a day
Shoot for 25 to 38g per day
Men, limit to 37.5g; women to 25g per day
Most Americans get more than enough
Choose nutrient-rich foods (20% or more is high)

Calories and Calories from Fat

How many calories are in the serving we're planning to eat—not in the serving size posted on the label?

THINK NUTRIENTS, NOT CALORIES

While Americans are calorie obsessed, it may be healthier to eat a higher-calorie, more nutritious food than opt for a "lite" version that's filled with synthetic and other yucky ingredients. Better yet, go with nutrient-dense, calorie-light foods—then you don't have to bother counting at all.

Calories from fat is a good indicator of a high- versus low-fat food. If the total number of calories is 200 and the calories from fat are 100, you know the product is half fat. Shoot for 30 percent or less of a product's calories to come from fat.

Percent Daily Value

There are recommended amounts of vitamins, fats, carbs, sugars, fibers, protein, and minerals we need daily (RDA, or recommended dietary allowance), and these numbers tell us in what percentage we're getting of those nutrients. A serving with 5 percent or less of the daily value is low, while 20 percent or more is considered high.

Total Fat

Limit the amount of total fat you consume.

Saturated Fat

Most saturated fat comes from animal products (such as meat and dairy products), which also contain cholesterol. Plant-based foods with saturated fat—but no cholesterol—include coconut and coconut oil, palm oil and palm kernel oil, and cocoa butter.

The American Heart Association recommends that healthy people limit saturated fat to 7 percent or less of total calories (on a 2,000-calorie diet, that's about 16 grams)—and even less (6 percent) if you suffer from high cholesterol or heart disease.

Trans Fats

Avoid trans fats whenever possible. Remember, "0g" on the label means there could be up to almost 0.5 grams per serving. Check the ingredient list for any hydrogenated or partially hydrogenated oils (PHOs), which signal the presence of these bad, bad fats. *Note: PHOs will be axed from processed foods by 2018.*

Try to replace saturated and trans fats with unsaturated (monosaturated and polyunsaturated) fats, found in fish, nuts, avocado, and natural peanut butter. All fats are caloric, however, and should be eaten in moderation.

Cholesterol

The American Heart Association recommends that healthy people restrict their average daily cholesterol intake to less than 300 milligrams a day; those with heart disease should stay under 200 milligrams. Only animal products contain cholesterol.

Sodium

It's a salty, salty world. So many of our processed foods are drenched in sodium, which—when eaten in excess—can boost blood pressure and increase the risk of cardiac trouble and stroke.

The USDA recommends no more than 2,400 milligrams (about a teaspoon) of sodium a day (the American Heart Association suggests 1,500 milligrams or less)—way less than the average American's 3,400-milligram intake—so inspect the labels on even seemingly healthy foods carefully for sodium content. One box, one can, one prepared meal can wallop you with half a day's worth or more.

Carbohydrates

Fiber

Fiber is good. Very, very good. The higher this number, the better.

Sugars

Sugar has many aliases—like 57 (view the many names for sugar under What About the Scary-Sounding Ingredients?, page 160). While too much of any sugar is unhealthy, some sugars are better than others. (We elaborate in Refined White Sugar and Artificial Sweeteners, page 186.)

SUGAR HIGH

The American Heart Association recommends that men eat no more than 9 teaspoons (37.5 grams) of sugar a day and women 6 teaspoons (25 grams). We've got some work to do: The market research firm Euromonitor reports that the average American packs in 126 grams of sugar every day.

Protein

Although protein is critical to the healthy function of our cells, muscles, immune system, and more, most Americans get more than enough of this nutrient every day. The National Academy of Sciences recommends that 10 to 35 percent of your daily caloric intake come from protein. Exact amounts depend on many factors, including age, gender, and activity level, so find out where you fall (consult with your doctor or medical professional), and monitor your intake.

Tip: On your vegan (non-fish) days, it's easy to get the protein you need from a well-balanced diet of veggies, grains, beans, nuts, and seeds. The key is variety.

Vitamins and Minerals

The Daily Value (DV) of a vitamin or mineral is the amount the FDA considers sufficient for most healthy adults. Many people believe these recommendations are inadequate—hence the huge market for nutritional supplements. Addressing that debate is beyond the scope of this book, so suffice it to say most experts agree that a food with 10 to 19 percent of a vitamin or mineral is a good source of that nutrient; above 20 percent is high.

CHAPTER 15

TWENTY-THREE VEGAN FOODS YOU SHOULD DITCH

(AND THEIR HEALTHY REPLACEMENTS)

The heart-stopping alerts are everywhere: "Meal Shockers Revealed! Avoid These Foods Like the Plague"; "21 Drinks That Should Never Cross Your Lips"; "Drop That Fork!; These Ingredients Could Kill You."

We agree that some things deserve a spot on the do-not-eat lists, including processed lunchmeats, marshmallow Peeps, and anything called "krab." But given that a huge part of our diet is vegan and all vegan food is healthy, we're exempt from these edicts, right?

If only. The truth is, plenty of animal-product-free foods are health disasters—and it's entirely possible to be a plump, nutrient-deprived vegan (or seagan). Sugar-laden cereals, pastries, and drinks; fat-drenched chips and fries; and sodium-laced soups and packaged meals—they're all vegan, and they're all nutrition nightmares.

So What's a Junk-Foodaholic to Do?

Don't worry, we're not taking the fun out of eating—please, we're foodies, too, and we love donuts as much as the next guy. Instead, we've offered some healthful alternatives to the baddest of the bad convenience foods, along with the semi-confident assurance that you'll love the replacement as much as the original.

And by the way, consuming any of these things every now and then won't kill you. We're not advocating a never-eat-this-again approach. Want a fry? Have a fry. Craving soda? Gulp a glassful. But make these the rare exceptions and not the rules.

Breakfast

You know all the hoopla about breakfast—it's the most important meal of the day, fuels your body, jump-starts your brain, yada, yada, yada. So why do so many of us sabotage it with energy-sapping, mind-dulling rubbish? Is this any way to start the day?

Cereal

What's the Problem?

Even so-called healthy options, such as granolas, mueslis, and "natural" cereals, can be full of fat, salt, carbs, and up to ten different kinds of sugar (look for names like sucrose, cane sugar, agave, fruit-juice concentrate, high-fructose corn syrup, and honey in the ingredient list). What ends up in your bowl is a mound of empty calories.

Healthy Replacement

Choose brands wisely with an eye out for:

- Whole grains—processed grains have been stripped of their fiber and nutrients

- Ample fiber—at least 5 grams per serving
- Minimal sodium—less than 220 milligrams per serving
- Low fat—below 3 grams per serving
- Little sugar—6 grams or less per serving

Find yourself a high-protein brand (at least 6 grams per serving), and you're really in the healthy-breakfast business.

Feel Your Oats

Save yourself all that label reading and go right for the mother lode: oatmeal. It's easy to make and super healthy. Loaded with fiber and protein, oats help stabilize blood sugar, lower cholesterol, and reduce your risk of cardiovascular disease.

Add some almond milk, antioxidant-rich blueberries, strawberries, nuts, seeds, cinnamon, and a splash of maple syrup, and you've got yourself a damn near perfect meal. *Caveat: Don't buy those packets of flavored, sweetened oatmeal, which may contain stuff like sugar, coloring, salt, and "natural and artificial flavors."*

We also love making breakfast porridges with grains like quinoa, amaranth, teff, and even brown rice. Try cooking some Kashi mixed grains in almond milk. Add a splash of maple syrup and a dash of cinnamon.

Donuts

What's the Problem?

Yes, we've heard the news: Donuts are the best thing since sliced bread. Writing this pains us more than you will ever know. But donuts are pretty terrible for you. Most mainstream varieties aren't vegan—but even those free of animal products can be fried in oil, loaded with trans fats, draped in sugary glazes, and jam-packed with sweet fillings. We recommend you dump them entirely from your breakfast repertoire. (There, we said it. Ouch.)

Healthy Replacement

Try sprinkling whole-grain toast with cinnamon—and if you're hankering for something sweeter, add a dash of raw sugar (minimally processed vegan sugar or organic cane sugar) to the mix. Or whip up a batch of our delicious Crunchy French-Toast Casserole (recipe on page 130).

Fruit Juice

What's the Problem?

Disguised as a healthful, vitamin-packed drink, even "100 percent" fruit juice pretty much boils down to sugar water—with some types boasting the same sugar content as soda and other sugary drinks (5 to 8 teaspoons per cup).

When a piece of whole fruit is pressed into juice, all the good, healthy parts are squeezed out, including skin, pulp, flesh, and fiber. What's left is a calorie-dense, sugary-sweet liquid that's quickly absorbed by the body in the form of fructose. Too much of this—or any sugar—can lead to health problems like obesity and diabetes.

Healthy Replacement

Skip the juice and eat the whole fruit instead. Or keep a pitcher of water on hand, along with slices of orange, lemon, lime, and/or grapefruit to squeeze into the water as desired. Garnish with fresh berries and mint. If you insist on having the juice, pour half your normal amount into a glass and fill the rest of the glass with water.

"Nondairy" Creamers and Coffee Whiteners

What's the Problem?

Side of chemicals with your coffee? Many powdered and liquid "nondairy" (some contain the milk product casein) creamers contain bad-for-you stuff such as trans fats, partially hydrogenated oils, food coloring, sugar, sodium, and corn syrup. As java drinkers who just can't tolerate our morning cup without milk, we've found some excellent alternatives to dairy and super-processed options.

Healthy Replacement

Nondairy milks such as almond, soy, or coconut do the trick. Make a latte by heating your milk of choice in a saucepan over a low flame and whisk vigorously until light and fluffy. Pour into a mug and top with coffee.

Lunch and Dinner

It's easy to lean on shortcuts for these meals. Once our days switch into high gear, we're inclined to do what's easiest, fastest—and sometimes unhealthiest. Here are a few things to strike off the menu when you're ready to nosh.

Diet and "Lite" Foods

What's the Problem?

Frozen and prepackaged foods labeled "diet," "low fat," and "lite" appeal to our desire to eat low-impact foods—meaning they have little impact on our waistlines. But when manufacturers take out all the yummy, fattening stuff—such as fats and sugars—to save calories, they have to replace the original textures and flavors with something else—and that something else is usually yucky dreck, including artificial sweeteners, sodium, starches, thickeners, and artificial colors and flavors.

Healthy Replacement

Shy away from overly processed foods and seek out suitable real-food alternatives—even if they contain a little bit of good fat. Better yet, prepare meals from scratch. We've got plenty of super-easy suggestions in our recipe section, beginning on page 64.

French Fries (or Fried Anything)

What's the Problem?

Watch out, kale, you might think you're the hottest thing since iceberg lettuce, but there's another game in town—and it's the most-eaten vegetable in the United States: the potato. Packed with a variety of vitamins, minerals, phytochemicals, and fiber, this low-calorie relative of the tomato and eggplant (all belong to the nightshade family) makes a nutritious side.

But there's a big "but": Stuff it with sour cream and bacon, drown it in cheese, whip it with butter, or deep-fry it in oil, and suddenly the potato is a hot, unhealthy mess, oozing with saturated fat, calories, and sodium.

Now let's focus on that ubiquitous golden-colored, salt-encrusted, awesome-smelling finger food, the French fry. America is madly in love with this potato treat—the average American devours nearly thirty pounds of French fries a year, and probably dunks them in another popular "vegetable," ketchup.

We hate to break up a love affair, but frankly, it's time you do the dirty deed. French fries are one of the unhealthiest foods people eat on a regular basis. What's the big deal? Fries are just that—fried. In oil. That's likely partially hydrogenated. And full of saturated and trans fat—which the American Heart Association says can raise your bad (LDL) cholesterol and increase your risk of heart disease, stroke, and diabetes.

Adding Salt to the Wound . . .

French fries are high in sodium and contain a cancer-causing chemical called acrylamide, which can form in starchy foods like potatoes when cooked at high temperatures. (Note: Potato chips and French fries are notoriously high in acrylamide, but it can also form when baking or roasting potatoes above 250°;

soaking raw potatoes in water for up to 30 minutes prior to cooking may help.)

If you're watching calories, French fries are not your friend: A medium serving typically contains between 300 and 400 calories. Get out of this toxic relationship while you can.

We've come down hard on French fries, but these rules apply to anything that's deep-fried—be it fish, zucchini, onions, sweet potatoes, squash blossoms, Oreos, and whatever else can be dunked in a cauldron of boiling oil.

Healthy Replacement

Cut regular or sweet potatoes into the shape of your choice (disks, slices, wedges), sprinkle with a little salt and your favorite spices (curry, cayenne, black pepper), and bake in a 425° oven, flipping after the first 15 minutes. Continue to check the potatoes every 15 minutes until they are done to your liking. Or cook up our Sweet Potato Chip recipe on page 121.

Frozen Dinners

What's the Problem?

We're all about convenience. And sometimes, frozen dinners are the no-brainer choice when you're pressed for time (like, every day).

But these simple meals may contain substantial amounts of fat, salt, sugar, preservatives, artificial ingredients, and other nasties. And portions can be deceiving. If the box is supposed to feed four people and you wind up eating half of it, you double the fat, salt, sugar, and calories stated on the package.

Healthy Replacement

Choose healthy frozen meals made with whole grains that are low in fat and sugar and high in fiber and nutrients. Even better, dedicate a few hours a week to preparing several days' worth of meals that you can freeze and heat up on a moment's notice.

GRAIN FREEZE

Next time you make a batch of rice, quinoa, or other grain, double the recipe and freeze the leftovers. When you're pressed for time, reheat as part of a quick-and-easy meal. Just add a can of beans and some sautéed onion, peppers, and garlic, and you've got a satisfying lunch or dinner.

Salads and Salad Dressings

What's the Problem?

We're not opposed to salad—we're opposed to slathering a hunk of low-nutrient greens with a boatload of high-fat dressing. So the next time you're tempted to order a wedge of iceberg lettuce coated with blue cheese dressing, down a "healthful" Cobb or chef's salad, or smother your homemade salad with store-bought fat-, chemical-, sugar-, artificial color–, preservative- and MSG-infused dressing, please rethink your choice. By adding the wrong ingredients to an otherwise healthful meal, you could be looking at a high-fat, thousand-calorie disaster.

Healthy Replacement

A super-nutritious salad, built as follows . . .

Forage for the healthiest greens. It's not that iceberg lettuce is bad for you, it's just that it doesn't have the same nutrient value as its darker cousins—romaine, arugula, collard greens, mesclun, spinach, watercress, red- and green-leaf lettuce, and kale. Don't stick with one type: Mix and match a variety.

Shoot for the rainbow. Pile on every color of raw and lightly steamed veggies, including peppers, onions, mushrooms, tomatoes, broccoli, celery, and carrots. For added crunch and sweetness, toss in chopped apples, strawberries, dried (unsweetened) cranberries or cherries, mango, or blueberries.

Power it up with protein. Throw in some cubed organic tofu or tempeh, beans (chickpeas, kidney beans, black beans, pinto beans), wild or canned salmon, light tuna, or sardines.

Accessorize with nuts and seeds. While caloric, these delicious little wonders add a nutritious punch. Try walnuts, pecans, almonds, cashews, macadamia nuts, sunflower seeds, pumpkin seeds, or sesame seeds. Make sure they're raw or dry-roasted, not cooked in oil. (See our Nuts and Seeds chapter on page 194 for more info.)

Dress it up. Many factory-made salad dressings are concocted with icky ingredients such as artificial sweeteners, high-fructose corn syrup, emulsifiers, thickeners, and preservatives. Opt for DIY salad dressings instead. Whip up our easy, oil-free recipes for Caesar Salad Dressing and Dip (recipe on page 126) and Ranch Dressing and Dip (recipe on page 127). Or top with a drizzle of balsamic or red wine vinegar, a spritz of lemon, and a dash of salt.

Snacks and Treats

We want it. We deserve it. We gotta have it. A pick-me-up in the afternoon or some movie-marathon eats on Saturday night are among life's necessities. Don't deprive yourself—just munch wisely.

Chocolate and Candy

We would never, ever, no way, not in a million years *ever* deprive you (or us) of chocolate. That would be wrong. However, there's the good stuff—and there's the not-so-good stuff.

Not-so-good first. That's pretty obvious: Candy bars oozing with caramel, crammed with nougat, dunked in cookie coating, gorged with toffee, and robed in white or milk chocolate serve up heaps of saturated fat, sugar, corn syrup, calories, preservatives, emulsifiers, and assorted artificial substances.

As for candies like licorice, gummy bears, jelly beans, and other rainbow-colored goodies, they may be lower in fat—but their pretty exteriors mask some pretty ugly innards, including sugar, corn syrup, artificial colors, hydrogenated palm kernel oil, and gelatin.

Healthy Replacement

Dark chocolate! Not only is this confection an acceptable treat, but you'll find it on many "superfood" lists. Made with antioxidant-rich cacao, dark chocolate can help lower blood pressure, increase cognitive function, boost your mood, reduce stress, and help control blood sugar. Plus, it contains healthy nutrients like potassium, copper, magnesium, and iron, along with the antioxidant resveratrol—also found in red wine. (Take *that*, milk chocolate!)

Sadly, all these benefits don't give you carte blanche to sit down and eat a case of chocolate: It's still high in fat and calories, so limit your intake (an ounce a day) and stick to varieties that are 70 percent cacao (or cocoa) or more.

Granola and Energy Bars

What's the Problem?

Who doesn't love these portable, energizing snacks you can keep in your purse, throw in your glove compartment, and nosh on the run for a quick boost? Just beware: Not all bars are created equal—you need to vet out the healthful varieties from the highly processed brands that are so loaded with sugar, calories, fat, and artificial flavorings that you might as well just eat a candy bar.

Healthy Replacement

To keep your snack smart, pick vegan bars that meet these criteria:

- **Low in sugar**—look for eight grams of sugar or less
- **High in fiber**—at least five grams
- **Low in fat**—fewer than three grams of saturated fat; *no* trans fat
- **Familiar, natural (not artificial) ingredients**—stick with ingredients you recognize and can pronounce, like fruit, nuts, seeds, and whole grains; the shorter the ingredient list, the better (fewer than ten)
- **Protein**—if you want a jolt of protein, find varieties with six grams or more

Check out our recipe for Granola on page 131.

Microwave and Movie-Theater Popcorn

What's the Problem?

Popcorn is a delicious, high-fiber, whole-grain snack that's low in calories and sodium and free of saturated fat. But step away from your air popper, and the situation gets pretty greasy.

Packaged microwave versions are usually heavily processed, filled with additives and loaded with salt and fat. Their faux-butter flavorings often contain various chemicals, including diacetyl, which is known to cause obstructive bronchitis—aka "Popcorn Workers' Lung"—in workers involved in the manufacturing process.

Adding fuel to the fire, microwave popcorn bags are often lined with the chemical perfluorooctanoic acid, (PFOA), which has been linked to high cholesterol, infertility, ADHD, and an increased risk of certain cancers.

Buying popcorn at the movies is a whole other nutrition drama—it's usually cooked in large quantities of trans-fat oil; doused in artificial flavors, preservatives, and colors (ever notice that yellow hue?); topped with butter-flavored oil; and capped with salt, giving you a giant caloric tub of saturated fat, carbs, and sodium. Wash that all down with a giant soda, and you've got yourself one horror show.

Healthy Replacement

Buy organic popping corn and pop it yourself on a stovetop or in an air popper. To cook it in the microwave, toss kernels into a brown paper bag and set the timer for 3 to 4 minutes, until all of the kernels are popped. (Listen closely: When you no longer hear kernels popping, your snack is ready. Be careful the bag doesn't catch on fire, and open it carefully—the corn will be piping-hot.)

For a real treat, pop out a batch of our Caramel Corn (recipe on page 142).

Potato Chips and Vegetable Chips

What's the Problem?

Chips often include combinations of salt, trans fats, starch, artificial flavors, preservatives, coloring, and other elements that make them undesirable.

And while veggie chips sound like a nobler choice, don't

let them fool you. They're often deep-fried in oils; contain substantial amounts of fat, calories, and salt; and barely live up to their name—with hardly a vegetable in sight. The primary ingredient in most varieties is corn flour or potatoes, with some veggie powder or purée thrown in for good measure.

Healthy Replacements

Store-bought baked chips are lower in fat and calories than their fried counterparts, but for a truly healthy option, make your own baked chips. For inspiration, see our recipes for Sweet Potato Chips (page 121) or One-Minute Tortilla Chips (page 122).

Smoothies

What's the Problem?

Smoothies are a hot "health" trend, and they're everywhere—prepackaged in our supermarket fridges, on the menus of coffee chains and fast-food joints, and, of course, in our own blenders. All that fruit, all those vitamins and antioxidants, all that meal-on-the-go convenience—what could be more perfect?

Here's a bubble-burster we're still trying to recover from: Smoothies are not so cool. When you throw a cup of OJ, some berries, bananas, and soy yogurt into your blender and give it a whirl, you end up with a giant glass of . . . sugar. Buy it from your favorite smoothie vendor, and things get even stickier: High-fat, high-sugar ingredients like sweetened syrups, chocolate syrups, and sherbet can slap you with a thousand-calorie beverage drenched in 100 grams of sugar. Yikes.

Healthy Replacement

If you're jonesing for a smoothie, stick to the occasional DIY version—just watch your fruit (sugar) intake, and throw in some greens for added nutrition and heft. Your best low- and no-sugar ingredients include kale, spinach, avocado, broccoli, cranberries, raspberries, blackberries, and strawberries.

Use water or unsweetened almond milk—not juice—for your liquid, and supplement with nutrient-dense add-ins, such as nut butters, flaxseed meal, chia or hemp seeds, cacao nibs and/or cacao powder, cinnamon, and ginger.

Whipped Topping

What's the Problem?

When Cool Whip—"the world's first nondairy topping"—hit grocery stores in the 1960s, it was vegan. That has since changed: Cool Whip now counts milk products among its many ingredients, but we're including it anyway—because, well, whipped topping is one of those things no human should live without.

This innocent-looking white fluff is guilty of many nutritional crimes, including a host of chemicals, additives, and flavorings that nobody wants, among them: hydrogenated vegetable oil, high-fructose corn syrup, polysorbate-60, and sorbitan monostearate. There is one ingredient known to be healthful, though: water.

Healthy Replacement

Whip up our delicious Coconut Whipped Cream/Icing (recipe on page 146).

Pantry Items

What's in your pantry? It's time to take inventory and do a little cabinet clearing. Some things lurking in innocent-looking cans, bags, boxes, and jars may be, well, not so innocent after all.

Canned Foods

What's the Problem?

As seagans, we keep tons of canned beans, fruits, and vegetables on hand that we can pop open, throw into a pot, and use to create quick, nutritious meals. So when we caught wind of bisphenol A (BPA)—a chemical used in containers that store foods and beverages (like cans and water bottles)—we knew we had to can the cans.

Studies have shown that exposure to BPA can lead to higher risk of developmental, neural, and reproductive problems in infants and children and may contribute to adult cancers, male and female reproductive issues, and much more.

Healthy Replacement

Limit your consumption of canned-food products or look for those labeled "BPA free." Alternatively, cook fresh, buy frozen, or opt for foods packaged in boxes or glass bottles and jars.

Processed Peanut Butter

What's the Problem?

You should never outgrow some favorite childhood staples, especially the healthy ones. Peanut butter spread over whole-grain bread, slathered over fruit, or added to smoothies makes a quick, protein-packed, stick-to-your-ribs snack. But many popular brands are made with nasty stuff like hydrogenated oils, sugar, corn syrup solids, molasses, soy protein, and salt. Peanut butter should contain one ingredient: peanuts.

Healthy Replacement

Buy natural peanut butter or other nut or seed butters (almond, cashew, sunflower). Or make it yourself by tossing

3 cups of peanuts, almonds, or cashews into a high-speed blender or food processor and blending until smooth. Be patient. It will eventually turn to nut butter without any added liquid.

(Author's confession: Amy thought her organic peanut butter was pure health perfection until Lisa asked her to read the label. Oh my.)

White Flour and White-Flour Products

What's the Problem?

White flour has literally been through the mill. Wheat grains get stripped of their bran and germ—along with their fiber, vitamins, minerals, and fatty acids—in order to give the flour a finer texture and longer shelf life. Then the lost natural vitamins are replaced with synthetic versions, giving you "enriched" flour that's barely a shadow of its former healthy self. Finally, the powdery stuff is bleached with more chemicals to give it a snow-white hue.

Processed flour has a very high glycemic rate, which quickly raises blood-sugar and insulin levels and can contribute to diabetes, heart, and other health problems.

Products made from white flour also fall into the avoid-if-at-all-possible category and include white breads, pizza crusts, bagels, pretzels, cakes, crackers, cookies, cereals, and pastas. Don't be misled by labels like "wheat flour" and "multi-grain whatever," which are meaningless terms designed to sound healthy. Instead, look for the verbiage "100 percent whole grain," "whole," or "whole grain," as in whole-wheat flour, whole-grain pasta, and whole-grain cereal.

Healthy Replacements

Whole-grain flours and their food counterparts have more fiber, vitamins, and minerals than the conventional varieties. There's a substantial variety of flours made from grains like wheat, oat, brown rice, spelt, oat, rye, quinoa, and millet; almond flour and meal; chickpea flour; and others. *Note: When substituting other flours for white flour in recipes, you may need to combine several to get a similar texture and taste. Be sure to check for quantities and proportions (the Internet is your best resource).*

Replace white pastas with any number of whole-grain and bean varieties. Eat whole-grain breads and crackers instead of white. Try our Power Crackers recipe on page 123.

White Rice

What's the Problem?

Like white flour, white rice has been denuded of its nutrients, fibers, and antioxidants. It's digested and absorbed quickly, leading to spikes in blood sugar and insulin and contributing to health issues.

Healthy Replacement

Aside from substituting nutrient-rich brown, red, black, or wild rice for white rice, you can also try any number of heart-healthy grains, including quinoa, farro, freekeh, millet, and wheat berries.

Refined White Sugar and Artificial Sweeteners

What's the Problem?

Sorry, sweet tooth—this is the section we dread writing. Sugar tastes delicious. Sugar is comforting. Sugar is addictive. Frosted cupcake? Yes, please! But the added sugars in our diets are—(excuse us while we cry our eyes out)—pretty awful.

Filled with empty calories, and generally devoid of vitamins, minerals, and proteins, excessive amounts of added processed sugar makes us fat, causes tooth decay, and is linked to health problems ranging from diabetes, obesity, and cancer to heart disease, high LDL (bad) cholesterol, and depression. (We're depressed already.)

According to the United States Department of Agriculture (USDA), the average American consumes between 150 and 170 pounds of refined sugar a year. Much of this sweetness is added to foods or beverages during processing—popular sources of added sugar include soft drinks; fruit drinks and punches; candy; baked goods (cookies, cakes, pies, donuts); frozen desserts; and cereals.

Sugar is also disguised under one of 57 names, such as high-fructose corn syrup, dextrose, fructose, glucose, lactose, maltose, sucrose, syrups, and fruit juice concentrates. (Check out our comprehensive list on page 163.) And you'll even find it in such foods as ketchup, barbecue sauces, marinades, salad dressings, canned fruits, yogurts, and many more.

Because we don't believe anyone should be deprived of the occasional treat, we've included some decadent dessert recipes in this book (beginning on page 132), so feel free to indulge now and then. But read labels, break yourself from soda and other sugary addictions, and satisfy your sweet cravings with healthier-than-refined-white-sugar options:

- **Coconut sugar**—Made from the sap of coconut flowers, it's low on the glycemic index and is a rich source of iron, magnesium, zinc, potassium, and B vitamins
- **Pure maple syrup**—It's an excellent source of magnesium and zinc and filled with antioxidants
- **Molasses**—This thick, dark syrup is a byproduct of the refining of raw sugarcane into sugar; it contains potassium, calcium, vitamin B_6, magnesium, and manganese

- **Sucanat**—An acronym for SUgar CAne NATural, this minimally processed, organic cane sugar has less sucrose than refined white cane sugar and contains minerals such as potassium and calcium

Just remember: Sugar is sugar. Eat any form in moderation. The American Heart Association recommends about 6 teaspoons (25 grams) per day for women and 9 teaspoons (37.5 grams) daily for men.

What About Honey?

This centuries'-old sweetener—it's even mentioned in the Bible—is thought to have a treasure trove of nutritional and medicinal benefits, including antibacterial and antifungal properties, along with antioxidants, vitamin B_6, and other nutrients. We prefer to use maple syrup in our recipes, as it is lower in fructose. Honey is *not* vegan. If you do indulge, it's best to choose raw, organic varieties.

What About Agave?

This syrupy sweetener skyrocketed to fame as a healthy, natural, low-glycemic alternative to sugar, but its reputation has since been tarnished. With a higher fructose content than any other common sweetener—including high-fructose corn syrup—agave got knocked off its pedestal. Excessive fructose has been linked to liver disease, obesity, and diabetes. Use *very* sparingly (if at all) or replace with maple syrup. We've removed it from our pantries and shopping lists.

What About Artificial Sweeteners?

Artificial sweeteners have their own health risks and have been associated with increased rates of cancer, neurological problems, migraines, epileptic seizures, brain fog, and aches and pains.

The U.S. Food and Drug Administration deems the top

five sweeteners to have "reasonable certainty of no harm to consumers"—but watchdog groups are barking up another tree, saying the research is flawed and doesn't account for long-term use.

We side with the latter, as we're not inclined to pump these artificial chemicals into our bodies, especially when there's "*reasonable* certainty of no harm." When that changes to "*certain* certainty," we'll take another look.

Here are the five top sweeteners in circulation today. You'll know some by their pink, blue, and yellow packet names.

- Acesulfame potassium (ace-K)—Sunett and Sweet One
- Aspartame—Equal and NutraSweet
- Neotame—based on the aspartame formula
- Saccharin—Sweet'N Low, Sugar Twin
- Sucralose—Splenda

What About Stevia?

Stevia is derived from the herb *Stevia rebaudiana* and has long been popular in South America. With zero calories and 200 times the sweetness of sugar, it has taken American grocery shelves by storm under names like Truvia and PureVia. Some processed liquid and powder brands go through questionable manufacturing processes and contain additives.

While Stevia still makes us a little nervous (we don't use it), your best choice is to go as natural as possible: Grind up leaves from the stevia plant (a totally legal plant you can grow in your garden), buy products made with whole-leaf stevia, or find extract that's 100 percent pure with no added ingredients.

What About Sugar Alcohols?

Sugar alcohols are neither sugars nor alcohols but are so named because their chemical structure resembles that of both sugar and alcohol. (Clever.) These carbs are found naturally in fruits like apples and pears and can also be manufactured.

Sweet to the tongue, low in calories, and boasting a low glycemic index, sugar alcohols are found in many processed foods, including hard candies, ice cream, puddings, baked goods, chocolates, and chewing gum. Some of the most commonly used are: erythritol, glycerol, isomalt, lactitol. maltitol, mannitol, sorbitol, and xylitol.

Like artificial sweeteners, sugar alcohols are included on the FDA's GRAS (Generally Recognized As Safe) list. Because the body can't completely absorb them, many people who use them complain of bloating, gas, diarrhea, and abdominal pain. We don't have those problems, because we don't use them. You decide what's best for you.

Salt

What's the Problem?

The USDA (United States Department of Agriculture) recommends consuming no more than 2,400 milligrams, or one teaspoon, of salt a day. Leading health groups, such as the American Heart Association, argue for 1,500 milligrams or less, especially if you have high blood pressure, diabetes, or chronic kidney disease.

Here's the problem: Americans are crazy about this zippy, flavor-packed mineral—and it's everywhere: in our canned goods, our prepared meals, and our restaurant dishes. A typical can of soup can contain 1,800 milligrams—an entire day's allotment!

Our bodies need sodium to function properly, but consuming too much can lead to such health problems as high blood pressure, heart disease, and stroke.

Healthy Replacement

If you're buying packaged goods, steer clear of high-sodium foods, opting for low- or no-sodium versions when possible. At home, season with sea salt or the pretty pink Himalayan crystal salt, both of which contain minerals and trace elements in their natural form. (Table salt is processed to eradicate minerals and usually contains an anti-clumping additive.)

Even better, spice up your dishes with chopped fresh or dried herbs, such as basil, thyme, dill, tarragon, garlic, and chives.

Beverages

Chugging water all day is a terrific idea. Slurping sugar- and artificial-sweetener-spiked drinks all day? Not so much. If you're addicted to soda, packaged teas, and sports drinks, it may be time to kick the habit.

Soda

What's the Problem?

Little more than liquid candy, sodas are a nutritional zero—and overindulging can adversely affect one's health. Loaded with sugar, mostly in the form of high-fructose corn syrup, these acidic beverages can contribute to obesity, GERD (gastroesophageal reflux disease), diabetes, kidney disease, and heart disease.

Many sodas are made with phosphoric acid, which gives the beverage its tang, inhibits the growth of sugar-loving molds and bacteria—and has been linked to low bone-mineral density in women. An alternative ingredient—citric acid—can damage your smile, as repeated exposure dissolves tooth enamel.

And then there are the artificial colors. While many food dyes haven't been sufficiently tested to determine long-term health hazards, many—including some of the caramel coloring included in brown colas—have been linked to certain types of cancers.

Diet sodas may be free of calories, but they're chock-full of artificial chemicals. And in a cruel twist of irony, artificial sweeteners have been shown to affect your body much like sugar does: They spark insulin production, signaling your body to store fat. The result? Weight gain.

If you must drink regular or diet soda, make it a special-occasion beverage, not a daily ritual. Even one a day can mess with your body.

Healthy Replacements

Make flavored still or sparkling water with a squeeze of vitamin C–packed orange, lemon, lime, or grapefruit, and throw in a few raspberries for fruity essence. On the run? Grab plain or flavored waters with zero sugar or artificial sweeteners. Don't be fooled by "vitamin" waters, which can be loaded with sugar. (One popular brand contains 31 grams of sugar!)

Iced Teas

What's the Problem?

One of America's most popular beverages, tea—especially green and black—is an antioxidant-rich, low-calorie drink, perfect on hot summer days. But prepackaged varieties come with an unsavory crowd of ingredients, among them sugar, high-fructose corn syrup, artificial chemicals, and colorings. Sweetened varieties can cost you more than 200 calories and 60 grams of sugar per bottle—about the same as a similar serving of soda. Low- and no-calorie artificially sweetened versions are laced with artificial chemicals.

Healthy Replacement

Brew your own green, black, or herbal tea, chill it, and serve it with fresh lemon or lime and mint leaves. Add a touch of unrefined sugar or maple syrup if you want added sweetness. When buying prepackaged varieties, choose those with the least number of ingredients, little or no sugar, and no artificial sweeteners or chemicals.

Sports Drinks

What's the Problem?

America's thirst for sports drinks is huge. Some of these vitamin-, protein-, and electrolyte-infused concoctions have their place among athletes—they help replenish lost electrolytes (sodium, potassium, and magnesium) and water after a long run or intense workout.

But guzzling them unnecessarily and frequently can saddle you with unwanted sugar, calories, caffeine, chemicals, and artificial colors. They should not be considered a healthful alternative to soda, sweetened teas, and the like.

Healthy Replacement

If you plan to exercise hard for an hour or more and need an energy boost, choose your sports drink wisely. An 8-ounce serving should contain roughly 14 grams of carbs, 28 milligrams of potassium, and 100 milligrams of sodium. Watch for artificial flavors and colors and high-fructose corn syrup (or make your own). For those armchair or light exercisers who want a pick-me-up, try 100 percent coconut water, which is naturally high in potassium.

CHAPTER 16

NUTS AND SEEDS—TINY NUTRITIONAL POWERHOUSES

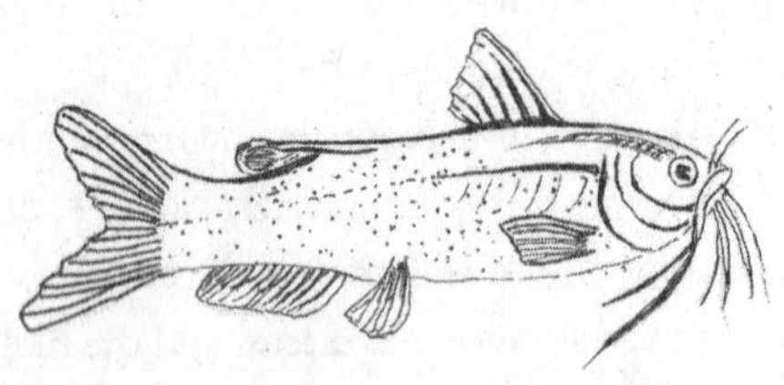

Diet Disasters?

Many weight-conscious folks in the "diet" world have cracked down on nuts and seeds for being high-calorie, high-fat disasters that pack on the pounds. While some of that is true (despite their small size, nuts and seeds are fat and calorie dense), these little nutritional giants should not be shunned.

Eaten in moderation (an ounce a day), they make a healthful addition to any well-rounded diet. A recent *New England Journal of Medicine* study even reports that people who eat a handful of nuts daily live longer than those who don't eat them at all.

So grab a fistful and you'll load up on heart-healthy mono- and polyunsaturated fats, antioxidants, protein, fiber, vitamins, and minerals. Plus, unlike addictive sugary snacks, nuts and seeds can make you feel full faster and reduce hunger pangs. When you're satiated, you're less inclined to raid the cookie jar. That, in turn, can help prevent weight gain. Hello, bikini season!

Stick with raw—and optimally organic—nuts and seeds. They're preferable to dry-roasted varieties, as heating at high temperatures may cause nutrient loss. Snub oily, heavily salted, sugar-coated, honey-roasted, and other processed versions, which often contain saturated fats, corn syrup, artificial flavors, preservatives, and other riffraff.

Nuts

Nutritionally speaking, it's easy to go nutty over which are the "best" and "worst" to consume. Many of the varieties listed here have been hailed as "the It nut" at some point in time.

But it boils down to this: All raw, unprocessed nuts have roughly the same amount of calories and fat per ounce, and the differences in a single serving are pretty miniscule (forty calories or so). So pick and choose your favorites based on taste, nutritional needs, and personal preference. Again, just don't overdo it.

Almonds

High in fiber content and vitamin E—a potent antioxidant—almonds are also a great source of calcium, selenium, protein, and magnesium.

A 1-ounce serving (about 22 almonds) contains 160 calories, 14 grams of fat, 6 grams of protein, and 3 grams of fiber.

GO NUTS!

- Sprinkle whole, sliced, or slivered almonds on your oatmeal, yogurt, or salad
- Use almond flour instead of wheat flour in baked goods
- Spread almond butter on whole-grain toast or apple slices for a satisfying treat

Brazil Nuts

Often left orphaned at the bottom of the mixed-nut can, Brazil nuts deserve some respect. They're a good source of protein, copper, niacin, magnesium, fiber, and vitamin E. Plus, just one nut packs more than 100 percent of the daily value for selenium, a potent antioxidant that may help prevent certain cancers, including bone, prostate, and breast cancers. But go easy on these babies: Eating large quantities could lead to selenosis (selenium poisoning); plus, they're higher in saturated fat than other nuts.

A 1-ounce serving (about 6 kernels) contains nearly 190 calories, 19 grams of fat, 4 grams of protein, and 2 grams of fiber.

GO NUTS!

- Chop them up and add them to cereals, yogurt, and salad
- Eat them with your favorite dark chocolate for a healthy, crunchy boost
- Add a few to a small bag of your favorite nuts and eat on the go

Cashews

These creamy-white wonders (one of our favorite nuts) are especially rich in iron, zinc, and magnesium and are loaded with vitamins B and E, folic acid, and some omega-3 fatty acids. They have a high concentration of heart-healthy oleic acid and contain a fair amount of tryptophan, which can help with insomnia and depression. Cashew cream is a staple in vegan cooking and baking.

A 1-ounce serving (about 18 cashews) contains 157 calories, 12 grams of fat (relatively low compared to other nuts), 5 grams of protein, and 1 gram of fiber.

GO NUTS!

- Whip up our super-easy Cashew Cream (see recipe on page 49) for a luscious addition to soups, pasta sauces, and many other dishes
- Make our Maple-Cashew Ice Cream (recipe on page 143)
- A half-cup of tofu and an ounce of cashews added to a stir-fry can supply about 30 percent of your daily magnesium need
- Add them to oatmeal, yogurt, and salads

Coconuts

The coconut is actually a fruit (well, a type of fruit called a "drupe"). Technicalities aside, we're including it here anyway, because having "nut" in the name is good enough for us—and we're totally crushing on coconuts. Here's why: They're considered antiviral, antifungal, antibacterial, and antiparasitic. They're crammed with fiber, vitamins, minerals, amino acids, and antioxidants and can help lower cholesterol, improve digestion, regulate hormones, and boost metabolism. And they taste decadent and delicious.

A 1-ounce serving (3 tablespoons) contains 100 calories, 9 grams of fat, 1 gram of protein, and 2 grams of fiber.

GO COCONUTS!

- Add unsweetened coconut flakes or shredded coconut to your morning oatmeal, granola, or smoothie
- Use coconut milk in curry and other Asian dishes
- Drink coconut water after exercise to replenish electrolytes

Hazelnuts

Also known as filberts, these delicate-flavored kernels are commonly found in chocolate, baked goods, and confections. They contain high levels of monosaturated fats, are spiked with vitamin E and folate, and boast hefty amounts of manganese and copper. They also contain the highest proanthocyanidin content of any tree nut. This plant-based compound is believed to have anti-inflammatory and other health benefits.

A 1-ounce serving (21 nuts) contains 180 calories, 17 grams of fat, 4 grams of protein, and nearly 3 grams of fiber.

GO NUTS!

- Toss them into oatmeal, yogurt, cereal, and salads
- Add them to grain dishes like rice, quinoa, or risotto for a crunchy treat
- Sauté them with green beans, Brussels sprouts, and other veggies

Macadamia

Round, smooth, and exotic—they hail from Hawaii and other tropical locales—these buttery, sweet-tasting nuts are higher in calories, fat, and saturated fat than other nuts. So if you're addicted (like we are), be extra-careful about overdosing. Macadamias contain the greatest amount of heart-healthy monosaturated fat per serving of any nuts, they're brimming with fiber, vitamin A, iron, protein, thiamine, riboflavin, and niacin and they also contain selenium, calcium, phosphorus, potassium, and magnesium. While people love them, they're toxic to dogs, so avoiding dropping them on the floor when Fido's sniffing around.

A 1-ounce serving (10 to 12 nuts) contains about 200 calories, 21 grams of fat, 2 grams of protein, and 2.5 grams of fiber.

GO NUTS!

- Sprinkle them on salads and toss in recipes
- Add them to healthy granola along with toasted (unsweetened) coconut for an exotic breakfast twist
- Stir them into yogurt

Peanuts

Minor detail: Peanuts aren't nuts. They're actually legumes—like peas, beans, and lentils (they grow underground and not on trees). But let's include these nutlike imposters anyway, because they're inexpensive, easy to eat, loved by all, and astonishingly nutritious. And everyone thinks they're nuts anyway. This humble legume is high in protein, fiber, niacin, folate, pantothenic acid, thiamin, riboflavin, choline, vitamins B_6 and vitamin E, magnesium, phosphorous, potassium, zinc, iron, copper, manganese, and selenium. It also contains resveratrol (found in red wine and dark chocolate as well), an antioxidant believed to have anti-aging benefits.

A 1-ounce serving (28 peanuts) contains about 160 calories, 14 grams of fat, 7 grams of protein, and 2.5 grams of fiber.

GO NUTS!

- Enjoy natural peanut butter on whole-grain bread or spread on apples or bananas
- Toss a tablespoon of peanut butter into your smoothie
- Throw peanuts into yogurt and "ice cream"
- Toss them into Asian stir-fries
- Make a trail mix by combining them with other nuts and dried fruit

Pecans

Among the most antioxidant-rich nuts, pecans are good for much more than just pie. These delicious, potent little packages are loaded with fiber and at least twenty vitamins and minerals, including vitamins A, B, and E; folic acid; calcium; magnesium; copper; phosphorous; potassium; manganese; and zinc.

A 1-ounce serving (18 to 20 halves) contains about 200 calories, 20 grams of fat, 2.5 grams of protein, and nearly 3 grams of fiber.

GO NUTS!

- Add them to your morning oatmeal, porridge, or breakfast cereal
- Spoon them into yogurt with fresh berries
- Toss them into salads
- Add them to baked goods, entrées, and side dishes

Pine Nuts

These rich little guys pack a caloric punch, but they also provide tons of nutritional heft, including vitamins A, B, C, D, E, and K, plus lutein, healthy monosaturated fats, magnesium, copper, iron, and manganese. Oh, and they're packed with protein, too.

A 1-ounce serving (just shy of ¼ cup) contains 190 calories, 19 grams fat, 4 grams of protein, and 1 gram of fiber.

GO NUTS!

- Make a quickie vegan pesto sauce—Toss 1 bunch (1 to 1½ cups) of fresh basil leaves, 2 garlic cloves, 3/4 cup cashew cream, ¼ cup pine nuts, 2 tablespoons nutritional yeast, and ¼ teaspoon salt in a high-powered blender and purée; for a sweet touch, add ¼ cup of sun-dried tomatoes.
- Throw them into salads, pasta dishes (like penne and broccoli), and sautéed veggies
- Add them to rice pilaf, couscous, and other grain dishes

Pistachios

Calorie counters, these nuts are for you. Pistachios contain fewer calories and more vitamin K per serving than their fellow nuts. And there are heaps of other nutrients stuffed inside, including fiber; protein; vitamins A, B_6, and E; as well as thiamine, potassium, and phosphorous. Fattening the deal, they're also rich in plant stanols, which have been shown to reduce LDL (bad) cholesterol.

A 1-ounce serving (about 49 nuts) contains 160 calories, 13 grams of fat, 6 grams of protein, and 3 grams of fiber.

GO NUTS!

- Add them to salads and vegetables
- Toss them into rice and grain dishes
- Combine them with other nuts and dried fruit for an on-the-go hunger buster

Walnuts

Inside a very tough shell is a delicious nut so healthy, it's been dubbed a "superfood"—and for good reason. Walnuts are brimming with alpha-linolenic acid (ALA)—an omega-3 fatty acid—and serve up substantial amounts of vitamin E, copper, manganese, molybdenum, biotin, phosphorous, selenium, protein, and fiber. (Learn more about omega-3s on pages 158 to 159.)

A 1-ounce serving (about 14 halves) contains 185 calories, 18 grams of fat, 4 grams of protein, and 2 grams of fiber.

GO NUTS!

- Make pesto with walnuts instead of pine nuts (see our recipe in Pine Nuts, page 200, and simply replace the pine nuts with walnuts.)
- Eat them with your morning oatmeal or cereal
- Sprinkle them on yogurt, "ice cream," and salads
- Sneak them into pastas, vegetables, and grain dishes

Seeds

Good things come in small packages. And great things come in tiny ones. These itty-bitty parcels of nutrition are jam-packed with fiber, protein, vitamins, minerals, antioxidants, and healthy fats. And they're so easy to toss into other foods for a quick, energizing boost. Here are some of our favorites.

Chia

Yes, these are the same seeds made famous by 1980s Chia Pets, but their history harkens back to the Mayans and Aztecs, who believed these tiny orbs had supernatural powers. Warriors ate them for energy and endurance, and today, they're still revered for their amazing health benefits.

Bursting with fiber, omega-3 fats, protein, vitamins, minerals, and antioxidants, these poppy seed lookalikes help boost energy and metabolism, build muscle, strengthen bones, protect your heart, improve digestion, stall premature skin aging, and more.

A 1-ounce serving (about 2 tablespoons) contains 138 calories, 9 grams of fat, 5 grams of protein, and 10 grams of fiber.

GET SEEDY!

- Sprinkle them on cereal, oatmeal, yogurt, and salad
- These hydrophilic (water-loving) seeds expand when added to liquid—Mix with a glass of water or almond milk for an energizing boost
- Make an egg substitute for recipes—Mix 1 tablespoon of chia seeds with 3 tablespoons of water and let sit for 15 minutes (yields 1 "egg")
- Make a quick, delicious, tapioca-like pudding—In a jar or airtight container, stir together 2½ cups almond milk, 3 tablespoons maple syrup, ½ cup chia seeds, ¼ teaspoon ground nutmeg, and ½ teaspoon ground cinnamon; cover tightly and refrigerate for 4 hours, shaking vigorously after 2 hours; stir well before serving (from *The Vegan Cheat Sheet*)

Flax

This ancient grain was cultivated in Babylon more than 5,000 years ago—so these seeds have staying power, and for good reason. Thirteen centuries later, we know what the

Babylonians didn't: These petite powerhouses are one of the most nutrient-packed foods on the planet, teeming with fiber, omega-3 fatty acids, and lignans—plant compounds thought to protect against certain cancers and other diseases. They're also rich in vitamins B_1 and B_6, manganese, magnesium, phosphorous, selenium, iron, potassium, copper, and zinc.

A 1-ounce serving (around 3 tablespoons) contains 151 calories, 12 grams of fat, 5 grams of protein, and nearly 8 grams of fiber.

GET SEEDY!

- We recommend grinding flaxseed in a blender or coffee grinder to get the full nutritional benefit—because of their very hard shells, seeds may pass through your system undigested if not pulverized first (you can also buy already ground flaxseed or flaxseed meal)
- Add them to smoothies, oatmeal, cereals, and casseroles
- Substitute part of the flour for ground flaxseed in baked goods
- Replace eggs (in recipes) with this flaxseed formula: Per egg, add 1 tablespoon of ground flaxseed to 3 tablespoons of warm water and let sit for 5 minutes

Hemp

Let's clear the air first: Yes, hemp is botanically related to that cannabis stuff people smoke. But, unlike marijuana, hemp has extremely low levels of the high-inducing chemical THC, and therefore has virtually no psychoactive properties. The only thing that will blow your mind is hemp's wealth of nutrients. Stocked with vitamins A, B_1, B_2, B_3, B_6, D, and E—along with calcium, iron, magnesium, manganese, phosphorous, potassium, and zinc—hemp is also rich in protein and gamma linolenic acid (GLA), a natural hormone.

With a healthy balance of omega-3 and omega-6 fatty acids and a dose of the plant-based compounds, phytosterols, hemp seeds contribute to cardiovascular and immune-system health and may help lower cholesterol levels.

Thinking they'd taste like rope, we snubbed hemp seeds for years. When we finally tried them (a vendor was giving out free samples at a vegan food festival), we were bummed we'd waited so long—they're delicious, with a flavor similar to pine nuts.

A 1-ounce serving (almost 3 tablespoons) contains 161 calories, 12 grams of fat, 9 grams of protein, and 2 grams of fiber.

GET SEEDY!

- Toss them into hot or cold cereal, smoothies, salads, and even pastas
- Add them to baked goods
- Sprinkle them on peanut butter–topped whole-grain toast

Pomegranate

Plucked from the pomegranate (Latin for "seeded apple") fruit—one of the oldest known fruits on Earth—these slightly tart, juicy seeds are full of antioxidants, potassium, and vitamin C. They're also high in polyphenols—antioxidants that may help reduce the risk of cancer and heart disease—and blessedly low in calories for those who are counting. The whole seed is edible—not just the fleshy part (as Amy once thought).

A ½-cup serving (about 3 ounces) contains 70 calories, negligible fat, 1 gram of protein, and 3 grams of fiber.

GET SEEDY!

- Throw a handful into your morning cereal or yogurt
- Add them to greens and grain salads and other savory vegetable dishes (they pair beautifully with sweet potatoes and squash)
- Add fresh pomegranate juice to smoothies

- Drop seeds into a glass of sparkling water—or better yet, champagne—for a pretty, healthy garnish

Pumpkin

We remember digging out pumpkin seeds by the shovelful when prepping our Halloween jack-o'-lanterns. Little did we know we were tossing out the healthiest part of the fruit. Also known as pepitas, these little treats are tricked out with heart-healthy magnesium, immunity-boosting zinc, and a host of other beneficial substances, including omega-3 fatty acids, protein, potassium, phosphorous, manganese, and B vitamins.

A 1-ounce serving (about 2 tablespoons) contains around 160 calories, 14 grams of fat, 9 grams of protein, and 2 grams of fiber.

GET SEEDY!

- Next jack-o'-lantern season, don't ditch the pumpkin seeds; roast them! Here's how:
  - After removing as much flesh from the seeds as possible (rinse through a colander to separate the last bits), boil 1 cup of seeds in 4 cups of water and 2 tablespoons of salt for 10 minutes; drain
  - Transfer the seeds to a cookie sheet and add ½ teaspoon salt (optional) or other seasonings, such as paprika, cumin, and/or cayenne pepper
  - Bake at 400° for 20 minutes, allow to cool, and dig in!
- Sprinkle them on your morning hot or cold cereal or granola
- Add them to salads, baked goods, granolas, and trail mixes

Sesame

Those little seeds atop your morning bagel are more than just decoration. Minus the bagel (sorry!), they're bursting with omega-3 fatty acids and other nutritional goodies, including minerals like calcium, iron, magnesium, phosphorous, manganese, copper, and zinc, along with B vitamins, protein, and fiber.

They also contain sesamin and sesamolin—two types of plant lignans that help lower LDL cholesterol, prevent high blood pressure, and increase vitamin E supplies. Finally, they're high in phytosterol, which can help lower LDL cholesterol. Look for raw or roasted varieties in a variety of colors (white, yellow, black, and red) and avoid salted versions.

A 1-ounce serving (around 3 tablespoons) contains about 160 calories, 13 grams of fat, 5 grams or protein, and 5 grams of fiber.

GET SEEDY!

- Sneak them into stir-fries and salads
- Add them to rice and grain dishes for a nutrient-packed crunch
- Top your veggie burger with tahini (sesame spread) or drizzle it on falafel
- Dip raw veggies or whole-grain crackers in tahini

Sunflower

Not just for the birds, sunflower seeds make a nutrient-packed addition to the human diet. Rich in vitamin E and B vitamins, along with magnesium, zinc, selenium, phosphorous, and copper, they're also an excellent source of fiber, amino acids, and essential fatty acids (specifically linoleic acid). These little wonders are loaded with antioxidants that help boost the immune system, lower blood pressure, and decrease LDL (bad) cholesterol.

A 1-ounce serving (just over ¼ cup) contains about 170 calories, 14 grams of fat, 6 grams of protein, and 3 grams of fiber.

GET SEEDY!

- Use them to garnish your oatmeal, cereals, and salads
- Add them to tuna-, salmon-, or chickpea-salad sandwiches for a health boost
- Spread sunflower seed butter on whole-grain toast

Wheat Germ

One of three parts of the wheat seed (the other two are the outer hull and the endosperm), wheat germ is the most healthful of the trio. This bantam seed comes bundled with vitamin E, B vitamins, magnesium, phosphorous, potassium, iron, zinc, healthy fats, and inulin—a type of fiber that helps maintain good digestion. It's also relatively low in calories. Store it in your fridge or freezer, as wheat germ can go rancid once opened.

A 1-ounce serving (about a ¼ cup) contains 102 calories, nearly 3 grams of fat, almost 7 grams of protein, and 4 grams of fiber.

GET SEEDY!

- Sprinkle it into smoothies, breakfast cereals, and salads
- Add a few spoonfuls to recipes for muffins, pancakes, and other baked goods
- Substitute wheat germ for breadcrumbs in recipes

CHAPTER 17

HERBS AND SPICES—THE SPICY SEVENTEEN

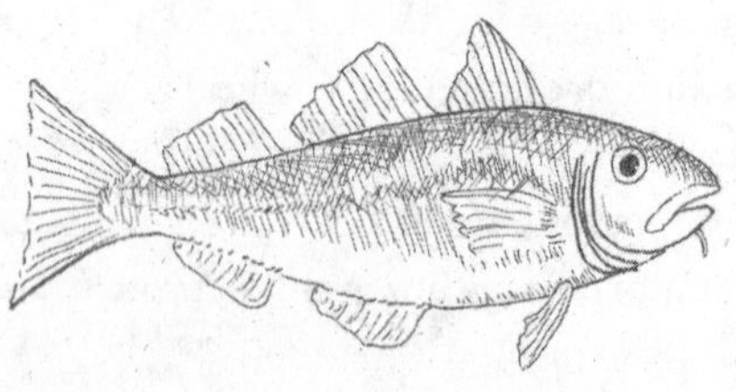

We generally worry about all the things that *shouldn't* be in our food, such as artificial chemicals, colors, and flavors; too much salt and sugar; bad fats; and the like.

But what if we focused on the good stuff that *should* be in our food—and all too often isn't: "additives" that would not only enhance flavors but provide significant health benefits, too? Yes, we're talking about spices and herbs.

Nice (Spice) Rack!

Most of us have spice racks in our kitchens, lined with little jars containing exotic powders and flecks of strange-sounding plants. Admit it—those jars have been there for years. Perhaps your mother gave them to you when you got your first apartment, and you used them once or twice over the years for some special curry-paprika casserole to impress a date. Now they're all but forgotten.

Our advice? Toss them all. It's time to reboot your spice cabinet. Most herbs and spices have a short shelf life (about a year), and that's assuming you've stored them properly—excessive heat and humidity will diminish their potency even faster.

GIVE YOUR SPICES THE SNIFF TEST

If that once-powerful curry powder smells like—nothing—it will probably be tasteless, too. Time to replace it.

Nutrient-Packed Superstars

With an abundance of phytonutrients like carotenoids and flavonoids, herbs and spices have been linked to a number of terrific health perks: Some are thought to lower cholesterol levels, some contain cancer-fighting antioxidants, and others may help manage and prevent chronic conditions like high blood pressure and Alzheimer's. Most are high in B vitamins, contain trace minerals, and have antibacterial and antiviral properties.

The scientific jury is still out on the extent of these health benefits, but as chefs, we know one thing for sure: Adding herbs and spices to your recipes means you can cut back on salt, sugars, and other troublesome ingredients—and your meals will get a hefty dose of flavor.

Note: Be sure to consult your medical professional before using any herb or spice for medicinal or curative purposes. Some may interfere or interact with prescription medications, while others—consumed in extremely excessive amounts—can cause harmful side effects.

Storage and Usage Tips

Keep your herbs and spices fresh by storing them in a cool, dark area—but make sure they're visible, so you remember to use them *every day*. Fresh herbs and spices may need to be refrigerated, of course.

Dried spices and herbs are more concentrated than fresh, so if a recipe calls for fresh and you have only dried, use about a third of the amount called for in the recipe.

Good-quality herbs and spices can be expensive. So let's just focus on a handful that are super flavorful and busting with health benefits.

Our Spicy Seventeen List

Basil

The incredibly aromatic basil leaf is known to have powerful antioxidants that protect against premature aging, common skin issues, and some types of cancers. It even boasts antibiotic/antimicrobial properties, which, in essential-oil form, can be used on wounds to reduce the risk of infection. It's a snap to grow at home—either inside or out.

Spice it up: Use basil to season soups, sauces, and dressings. We especially love chopped fresh basil in our salads and atop our pasta dishes.

Chile Pepper

These hot little numbers get their heat from a chemical compound called capsaicin. Available in dozens of shapes, sizes, and colors, chiles add kick to your dishes, ranging from mildly piquant to blow-steam-from-your-ears hot. Whether you use fresh varieties—such as jalapeño, habanero, and serrano—or packaged versions such as cayenne, red pepper flakes, paprika, and hot sauces—you'll enjoy more than just a dose of pow! Chiles are thought to have loads of health benefits, including improved circulation, reducing the risk of certain cancers, and boosting metabolism. Fresh chile peppers are packed with vitamin C, and red peppers boast tons of beta-carotene.

Feeling the burn? For some brave souls, the hotter the better. Be very careful when handling super-hot varieties like habaneros—even a tiny bit of oil on your fingers can cause serious discomfort later, especially if rubbed in your eyes.

Mouth on fire? If you're packing heat after biting into a fiery pepper, don't guzzle liquids—that just spreads the hot stuff around. Quench the inferno by eating starchy foods, like rice or bread (which sop up the scorching oils), or down a spoonful of sugar.

Spice it up: Toss fresh or dried chiles into hummus, guacamole, salsas, soups, sautéed vegetables, pastas, and nearly any food that's screaming for a pick-me-up.

Cilantro

Rich with phytonutrients and antioxidants, cilantro has the highest vitamin K content of any herb (essential for bone health) and is a good source of vitamins A and C and the minerals calcium, potassium, iron, and manganese.

While it resembles parsley in looks, the taste is completely different—and people seem to love or hate it. We're completely mad about cilantro's bright, fresh flavor. Those who claim it tastes soapy or metallic are thought to have a genetic variation that causes an aversion to the herb. Nonetheless, its worldwide popularity is irrefutable, and cilantro is a staple in many cuisines, including Middle Eastern, Mediterranean, Indian, Mexican, Chinese, African, and Asian.

Spice it up: Sprinkle cilantro on stir-fries; chop and toss it into guacamole, salsas, and salads; add it to curry dishes and sesame-noodle-peanut dishes; throw it into smoothies.

Cinnamon

This fragrant spice is culled from the bark of several varieties of Asian trees long considered to have medicinal properties. Containing high levels of antioxidants, cinnamon can help lower blood sugar, reduce LDL (bad) cholesterol, improve digestive health, and reduce inflammation caused by arthritis and other painful conditions. It's also a good source of fiber.

Spice it up: Substitute it for small amounts of sugar in recipes; add it to baked goods; stir it into oatmeal; sprinkle it on peanut butter toast; use it to spike your coffee, tea, and smoothies.

Cloves

Known as the super spice, cloves are packed with antioxidants; full of manganese; and brimming with antiviral, antibacterial, and antimicrobial properties. They also contain eugenol, a mild anesthetic that can soothe toothaches, burn pain, and sore throats. Plucked from the evergreen clove tree, this spice is also a good source of vitamin K, iron, magnesium, calcium, and fiber.

Spice it up: Add ground cloves and curry power to sautéed vegetables; use it to flavor your oatmeal, yogurt, and baked goods; add it to smoothies, teas, and hot cider.

Cumin

This Egyptian native has been an essential ingredient in Middle Eastern and Indian cuisines for thousands of years. Along with turmeric and coriander, the distinctive, earthy-tasting cumin is one of the main spices in curries. With ample amounts of magnesium and iron, it's believed to have potent anti-inflammatory and antioxidant properties, aid in digestion, and help control blood sugar.

Spice it up: Add it to guacamole, hummus, and other dips; use it to spike your chili, soup, and stew recipes and flavor salad dressings; toss a couple teaspoons into roasted veggie dishes; sprinkle it on popcorn and homemade chips.

Dill Weed

With its wispy, fernlike leaves, this delicate, sweet-tasting plant is related to parsley, cumin, and bay leaf. It has been used since ancient times as an herb and a medicine and is known for its antioxidant, anti-inflammatory, and antiviral properties. Dill is a good source of calcium, manganese, iron, magnesium, and fiber and helps relieve indigestion and insomnia.

Spice it up: Dill complements fish dishes beautifully, especially salmon and trout; use it as a sandwich garnish; mix it with plain nondairy yogurt for a tasty crudité dip.

Garlic

While technically not an herb or spice (it's a member of the lily family, along with onions, shallots, and chives), the "stinking rose" deserves a place of importance in every kitchen. Garlic adds an intense, aromatic accent to your dishes and is healthful to boot—it has been used for millennia by civilizations around the world for its healing and medicinal properties. High in antioxidants, manganese, vitamins B_6 and C, and selenium, garlic is thought to help prevent certain cancers, reduce blood pressure, lower heart-disease risk, improve bone health, and—most famously—ward off vampires.

Spice it up: Add it to salsas, guacamole, dips, and salad dressings; roast a head of garlic and spread it on whole-grain bread; mix it into pasta sauces, mashed potatoes, and stir-fries; use plain garlic powder in place of salt in recipes and on food.

Ginger

The medicinal uses of ginger go back two thousand years or more. Teeming with antioxidants, this flavor-packed root-based herb is antibacterial, antiviral, and anti-parasitic. A digestive aid, ginger helps soothe upset stomachs, relieve heartburn and indigestion, and alleviate nausea. Inflammation-fighting compounds like gingerols help reduce arthritis pain and may help protect against cancer and diabetes. It's available fresh, dried, and powdered, and as a juice and oil.

Spice it up: Add minced fresh ginger to stir-fries, marinades, sauces, and salad dressings—it goes well with soy sauce, citrus fruits, chiles and garlic; sprinkle chopped ginger bits on fruit dishes and desserts or mix it with warm maple syrup to make a terrific glaze for carrots or fish dishes like salmon; eat it pickled, with sushi; toss it fresh or powdered into smoothies; sprinkle powdered ginger into oatmeal; include it in baked goods; make ginger tea (add chopped ginger to boiling water; let steep for 3 minutes; strain and drink).

Marjoram

This member of the mint family is often used interchangeably with its sister herb, oregano, but there are subtle differences. Marjoram is a type of oregano that's sweeter and milder tasting than the more robust, peppery-tasting oregano. A healthful addition to your diet, marjoram contains vitamins A and C, as well as calcium and iron, and has excellent antiseptic, antibacterial, antifungal, and antiviral properties. It's believed to improve digestion, relieve insomnia, boost cardiovascular health, and soothe inflammation.

Spice it up: Use it to season soups, stews, salads, and vegetables; add it to marinades and salad dressings; use it in fish rubs; combine it with dried basil, oregano, thyme, rosemary, and sage for a flavor-packed Italian seasoning.

Nutmeg

Popular in Asian, Middle Eastern, and European cuisines, nutmeg can do your health a world of good. It's chock-full of manganese and contains copper; magnesium; potassium; zinc; iron; antioxidants; vitamins A, B, and C; and disease-preventing phytochemicals. This fragrant spice is thought to promote sleep; help conquer digestive problems; ward off dementia; soothe joint, muscular, and tooth pain; and fight bacteria like listeria, E. coli, and salmonella.

Spice it up: *Nutmeg has a strong flavor, so start with just a dash.* Mix it into soups and stews; toss it on sweet potatoes, squash, carrots, and other vegetables; sprinkle it on raw or cooked apples, pears, peaches, pineapple, and other fruit; stir it into your morning oatmeal and smoothies; add it to recipes for baked goods; pair it with cinnamon in tea, coffee, and hot cider.

Oregano

Anyone who has ever been to a pizza parlor knows oregano—it's that distinctive-smelling green stuff in the shaker next to the crushed red pepper and Parmesan cheese. But this amazing herb can do far more than spice up your slice. Like its relative, marjoram (page 214), oregano has many nutritional and medicinal benefits. Bursting with vitamins A, B_6, C, and K, along with fiber, folate, iron, magnesium, calcium, potassium, and antioxidants, it's believed to support immune-system health, provide powerful antifungal and antibacterial benefits, fight cancer, and relieve respiratory infections.

Spice it up: Use it to season soups, stews, tomato sauces, pasta dishes, and (vegan) pizza; chop fresh oregano into salads; add it to salad dressings, vegetables, and steamed seafood dishes.

Peppermint

Candy canes, peppermint patties, and after-dinner mints: Perhaps peppermint is best known for flavoring refreshing treats like these. But in its natural form, this herb is far more than a palate pleaser—it's a good source of manganese, copper, and vitamin C and is packed with therapeutic benefits that can help stomach upsets, indigestion, irritable bowel syndrome, headaches, muscle pain, asthma, and more.

Spice it up: Add fresh mint leaves to fruit and green salad, gazpacho, and smoothies; make mint tea; add fresh sprigs to iced tea.

Rosemary

With its pinelike fragrance and zingy flavor, rosemary—which grows on small evergreen shrubs—enhances an entire menu of dishes, including entrées, desserts, and drinks. But it also boasts surprising health benefits, ranging from cancer prevention and anti-inflammatory properties to mood elevation and immune system booster. In addition, rosemary can promote digestive health; relieve joint, muscle, and headache pain; and improve memory.

Spice it up: Add rosemary to tofu scrambles, soups, stews, and pasta sauces; use it to season fish dishes and flavor salad dressings; sprinkle it on roasted vegetables and potatoes; use it, along with lemon wedges, to garnish your glass of seltzer; try it in cakes and sweet, quick breads.

Sage

Commonly used in Thanksgiving stuffing, sage belongs to the mint family and has been used for centuries as an herbal remedy. An excellent source of antioxidants; vitamins A, B, C, E, and K; plus fiber, calcium, iron, magnesium, manganese, thiamin, and copper, sage is a natural antiseptic and anti-inflammatory and is believed to help lower cholesterol and blood pressure; calm upset stomachs; soothe sore throats; improve memory and mental focus; prevent diabetes; and decrease inflammation associated with rheumatoid arthritis and asthma.

Spice it up: As Simon and Garfunkel said, sage pairs perfectly with parsley, rosemary, and thyme. Add it to soups, stews, and pasta dishes; toss it on roasted vegetables; freeze it in ice cubes for summer drinks; and use it as garnish with fish dishes.

Thyme

A member of the mint family, thyme contains vitamins A and C, along with iron, manganese, copper, and fiber. It's full of antioxidants that can prevent cellular damage and help ward against cancer, inflammation, and signs of aging. Thyme's antibacterial properties help heal infections, and it has long been used to relieve chest and respiratory ailments.

Spice it up: Mix thyme in salad dressing and dips; use it in sautés and stir-fries; sprinkle it on cooked veggies and fish; add it to pasta dishes, soups, stews, and bean dishes.

Turmeric

This bright-yellow relative of ginger is what makes American mustard yellow. More than just a coloring agent, turmeric is often called a "superspice" and is the main ingredient in curry. Its active component, curcumin, is a potent antioxidant and anti-inflammatory. Studies have shown that turmeric can help prevent or alleviate Alzheimer's disease, arthritic joint pain, certain cancers, and diabetes. It has also been found to curb heartburn, fight inflammation, and tame depression.

Turmeric teas are used to treat colds, and many claim this spice provides pain relief equal to or better than common over-the-counter drugs like acetaminophen and ibuprofen. Applied to the skin, it can help with various inflammatory conditions, insect bites, and other wounds.

Spice it up: Use turmeric in pilaf, rice, and other grain dishes; add it to lentil soups, relishes, and chutneys; use it to make curry dishes and soups; drink turmeric tea.

CHAPTER 18

ORGANIC FOODS—WORTH THE PRICE?

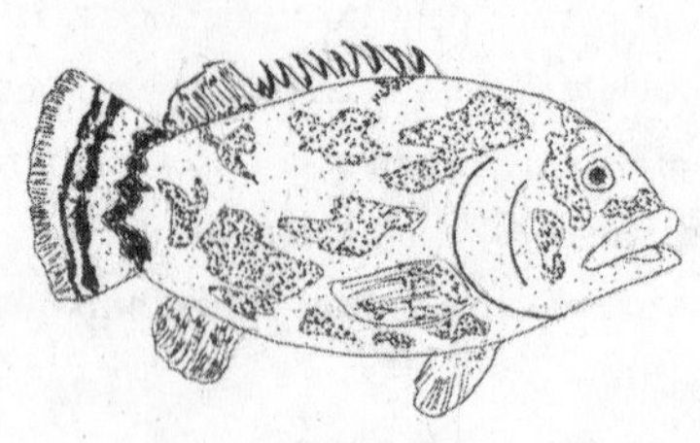

If money is no object, just skip this chapter and buy *everything* organic from now on. Seriously, you can't go wrong buying organic fruits, vegetables, legumes, nuts, seeds, and grains if you can afford it and don't mind forking over the extra bucks.

But if you live in the (real) world of shopping budgets, like we do, things are not so simple. Organic foods can quickly run up your grocery bill, so it's important to discern when it's prudent to buy organic and when conventionally grown food will do.

The trick is to know which foods are likely to have significant amounts of pesticides and chemical residues (spring for organic), and which foods are probably safe (save your pennies).

What Does Organic Mean?

Our quick-and-dirty summary of the USDA's definition:

- Food produced by farmers who use renewable resources and practice water and soil conservation
- Produce grown without the use of most conventional pesticides; synthetic fertilizers or those made with sewage

sludge (ick, really?); bioengineering (genetically modified organisms); and ionizing radiation
- Animals that were not given antibiotics or growth hormones

THE LABELING NITTY-GRITTY

- If a product's USDA label reads "organic," at least 95 percent of the ingredients must have been grown organically.
- If the label reads "made with organic ingredients," 70 percent or more of the ingredients must meet organic standards.

What's Wrong with a Little Pesticide?

It seems pretty obvious that the foods we eat should be free of toxic pesticide residues and other creepy chemicals. So it really bugs us that, according to the Environmental Working Group (EWG), nearly two-thirds of 3,015 produce samples tested by the USDA in 2013 contained chemical residues—from a total of 165 pesticides.

These aren't innocuous chemicals. Insecticides have been connected to a number of health issues, including cancer, birth defects, Parkinson's and Alzheimer's disease, infertility, memory loss, and diabetes.

It's not as if no one cares. The Environmental Protection Agency (EPA) limits the use of pesticides on foods and evaluates chemicals to ensure with "reasonable certainty" that they won't harm infants, children, or adults. Scientists also point out that finding pesticide residue on a fruit or vegetable doesn't automatically mean it's unsafe—residues are said to decrease as crops are harvested, transported, exposed to light, washed, prepared, and cooked.

Why Are Pesticides Even Allowed on Our Foods?

These chemicals are often approved for use on fairly flimsy safety evidence, and then it may take years before enough data piles up to get the chemical banned. Complicating matters, the EPA's limits apply to *individual* chemicals—but food-crop pesticides are often found in combinations. There's little data on the effects of such combinations on our bodies, so limits on individual pesticides may not be as effective as we'd like to think.

Another concern is that pesticides can accumulate in our bodies over decades, with most exposure in children happening during critical formative years. There's no way to tell what the long-term effects might be as these chemicals pile up in our neurons, livers, bones, and other cells.

So while we take comfort in the fact that Uncle Sam's worker bees test pesticides and kinda, sorta regulate their use, we prefer to adopt a "guilty until proven innocent" attitude toward potentially toxic chemicals on or in our foods.

Smart Shopping

Some foods are likelier than others to contain synthetic pesticides, so pinch your pennies where you can: Buy conventionally grown foods if they're deemed free of (or very low in) harmful chemicals.

How to know which are the goodies and which are the baddies? One great resource is the Environmental Working Group's annual "Dirty Dozen" and "Clean Fifteen" lists; you can download wallet-size guides at foodnews.org or grab the app on iTunes.

Following are examples the EWG's 2015 lists. Visit their website (ewg.org) for updates.

EWG's "The Dirty Dozen" 2015

Produce with the highest pesticide-residue content—buy these organic:

1. Apples
2. Celery
3. Cherry tomatoes
4. Cucumbers
5. Grapes
6. Nectarines
7. Peaches
8. Potatoes
9. Snap peas
10. Spinach
11. Strawberries
12. Sweet bell peppers

\+ Hot peppers, kale, and collard greens ("bonus" items found to contain small amounts of particularly dangerous pesticides)

We find this list dismaying, to say the least. Some of our favorite foods are here—and it's especially troubling to see that apples are nearly *always* on the list. An apple a day is supposed to keep the doctor away!

While there may be a price to pay, the solution is simple—buy organic.

What about foods that are safe? The EWG claims there are products we can buy with a clean conscious.

EWG's "The Clean Fifteen" 2015

You can skip the organic versions of these foods:

1. Asparagus
2. Avocados

3. Cabbage
4. Cantaloupe
5. Cauliflower
6. Eggplant
7. Grapefruit
8. Kiwi
9. Mangos
10. Onions
11. Papayas
12. Pineapples
13. Sweet corn
14. Sweet peas (if frozen)
15. Sweet potatoes

Of course, there are other considerations in today's complex, multinational food marketplace. A food deemed low risk in the United States can be high risk when coming from another country, as they may use chemicals there that we don't allow. When in doubt, do your research.

In the end, our advice is simple—go organic to the extent it's economically possible. You'll be doing your family and yourself a big favor.

CHAPTER 19

GMOs—SAFE TO EAT?

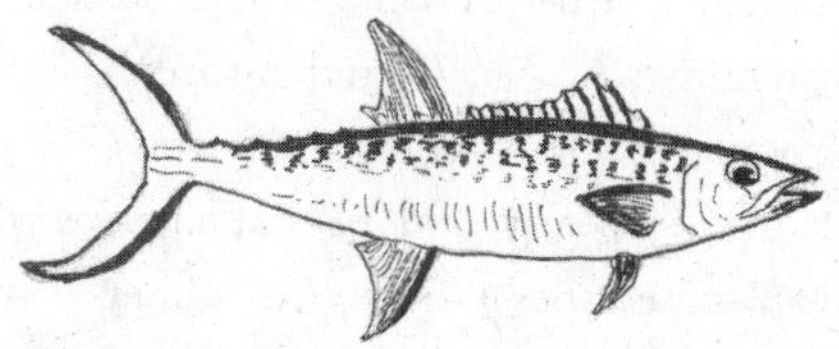

What on Earth Are GMOs?

For starters, GMOs are a lightning rod for controversy (more on that in a sec). But scientifically speaking, GMOs (genetically modified organisms) are plants and animals whose genetic material has been manipulated in the lab to produce a desired trait (such as herbicide resistance).

Most commercially produced GMOs are found in crops like soybeans, corn, and cotton. Scientists insert gene codes from the bacterium Bacillus thuringiensis (Bt) into normal plants, causing the GMO version to produce insect-killing chemicals. In effect, the plant now makes its own insecticide, reducing the need for farmers to spray these crops with other potentially harmful insecticides.

Other plants are genetically modified to withstand colder temperatures, grow more quickly, require less water, or survive application of herbicides like glyphosate (commonly sold as Roundup).

The theory is that genetic-engineering techniques will improve crop yields, decrease dependence on traditional fertilizers and insecticides, and reduce other harms to the environment. Genetic engineering is also being used in the animal world—to speed up the growth rates of food fish like salmon and tilapia, for example.

GMOs—OMG? or OK to Eat?

Many people—and organizations like the Non-GMO Project—argue that there have been no long-term studies of the effects of GMOs on human health. Then there are the ethical issues: Should corporate muckety-mucks and scientists be given carte blanche to, in effect, "play God"? What happens when pollen from GMO plants escapes into the environment? Finally, activists are concerned about the implications of allowing large corporations to patent seeds and other life forms, forcing farmers to buy seeds from them rather than maintaining natural stocks of seeds.

It isn't even clear whether GMOs really provide benefits to farmers or consumers. For example, insects can quickly develop resistance to the insecticides produced by Bt cotton. Bt compounds affect only specific types of insects, leaving other insects unaffected by Bt toxins—so farmers have to apply traditional insecticides to Bt crops anyway.

Concerns about the safety of GMOs have led more than 60 countries, including the European Union, either to ban them outright or to regulate their use tightly. In the United States, however, GMOs are considered substantially similar to normal plants and are, at most, lightly regulated. As a result, GMOs are found in nearly all the food on our supermarket shelves (unless they are organic). It has been estimated that GMOs are in more than 80 percent of the food products sold in North America.

Where Do They Lurk?

According to the Non-GMO Project, the most common GMOs are soybeans, cotton, canola, corn, sugar beets,

Hawaiian papaya, alfalfa, and squash (zucchini or yellow). Since these crops often form the basis of many prepared foods, you may be consuming significant amounts of GMOs even without eating soybeans or drinking soymilk directly.

They're also found in various food ingredients, including amino acids, aspartame, ascorbic acid, sodium ascorbate, vitamin C, citric acid, sodium citrate, "natural" and "artificial" flavorings, high-fructose corn syrup, hydrolyzed vegetable protein, lactic acid, maltodextrins, molasses, monosodium glutamate, sucrose, textured vegetable protein (TVP), xanthan gum, vitamins, and yeast products. Scanning the side of nearly any package will likely reveal one or several of these ingredients.

What's a Health-Conscious Consumer to Do?

First, don't panic. We're not happy about the presence of GMOs in our food, and we're worried about the long-term implications of GMOs on health and the environment. But we're not aware of any hard evidence of harm from GMOs, at least not yet. And while we're suspicious of studies backed by food and seed manufacturers claiming GMOs are safe, we're also cautious about the hysterical claims made by anti-GMO activists.

We would, however, like to know what's in our food! Which brings us to the controversy over labeling laws: Right now, more than 64 countries have policies regarding GMO labeling. But labeling initiatives in the United States remain stalled, thanks to the millions of dollars spent by companies opposing such requirements. Some states like Vermont have passed their own laws, but most of us remain in the dark about GMOs.

For now, the best we can do is rely on independent organizations like the Non-GMO Project to certify foods that don't contain genetically modified ingredients. Look for their label on foods as a guide. The Institute for Responsible Technology (responsibletechnology.org) also publishes a helpful non-GMO shopping guide, and the Environmental Working Group (EWG) is another terrific resource (ewg.org).

Some products *say* they are made without any GMO ingredients, which may or may not be the case. The only way to tell for sure is if the product has been independently tested and verified.

CHAPTER 20

SUPERFOODS—SUPER HYPE? OR SUPERHEROES?

Superfoods are like your favorite comic-book superheroes: They have nutritional powers beyond those of ordinary mortal foods! They're packed with nutrients! They fight off heart disease and cancer! They give you energy and pep! They improve your concentration and memory!

Spoiler alert: Just like Superman, Spider-Man, and Wonder Woman, superfoods don't actually exist—at least, not in the hyped-up way TV health gurus portray them. The term *superfood* is a magnetic marketing gimmick, designed to grab your attention—and ultimately your wallet—as you fall for the miracle product du jour. This term is banned from labels on foods sold in the European Union, unless there's some specific scientific evidence supporting claims of medical benefits.

What Makes a Food "Super"?

Foods might be declared "super" for a variety of reasons. Almost everyone thinks of blueberries as a superfood, for example, because they're relatively high in antioxidants. But lots of foods have similar or higher concentrations of antioxidants—yet, they don't get the prized superfood title.

Other items are "super" based on trends. Superfood arbiters may dismiss amazing foods like kale ("so last year") and tout exotic-sounding fare, such as black garlic, canary seeds, goji berries, maca powder, mangosteen, and za'atar, some of which can be difficult to find or absurdly expensive.

A better way to evaluate foods for "super" status might be to look at nutrient density. How much nutritional value (vitamins, minerals, antioxidants, etc.) does a food have in relation to its caloric content? Nutrient-dense foods give you the most bang for your caloric buck. In this respect they stand in stark contrast to energy-dense foods—items such as sugar, alcohol, or refined grains—that have lots of calories but little or no nutritional value.

Time magazine recently published a list of the 41 most nutrient-dense foods, and guess what? Almost none of the hip superfoods touted in health-food magazines made their cut. Topping the list is watercress, with a 100 percent density rating (all nutrients, no calories), followed by Chinese cabbage, chard, beet greens, and spinach.

You'll note that these are all leafy greens—no surprise! Dark leafy greens have lots of nutrients and almost no calories.

But a list of superfoods that focuses solely on leafy green vegetables isn't much help if you're looking to add "super" foods across your meal plans. That's why we recommend a different approach. To us, superfoods are nutrient-dense foods that are so good, you should try *to include them in as many meals as possible every day.* Ideally, they should represent a variety of food groups and give you a balanced diet.

Here's the most important point about superfoods: *No one food item is "super" all by itself.* We don't claim, for example, that eating whole bunches of watercress, kale, blueberries, goji berries, *or any other single item* on this list will combat heart disease, cancer, aging, or other health problems you may experience.

Rather, it's the *combination* of elements from all these categories that give superfoods their power. So while the scientific jury may still be out on whether the antioxidants in açai berries have any impact on cancer rates or heart disease, there's no doubt that a diet made up largely of these nutrient-dense, mostly plant-based foods will do wonders for your health.

Here then, are our nominations for this year's—and every year's—superfoods. Mix, match, and include a great variety in your daily meal plan.

1. Leafy Greens and Vegetables

As the "nutrient density" ratings discussed above prove, leafy green vegetables are the true superfoods. They're low in calories and fat and high in fiber, vitamin C, carotenoids, folate, manganese, and vitamin K.

You can stir-fry them, include them in soups, steam them, or eat them raw in salads. Or, you can really load up on leafy greens by blending them with fruit and water to make a green smoothie.

See our Seagan Staples Shopping List on page 11 for a rundown of our favorite leafy greens and veggies.

2. Nuts and Seeds

Unlike leafy greens and vegetables, nuts are high in calories, but they're full of healthy unsaturated and monounsaturated fats, vitamins, and essential amino acids.

Check out all their super benefits along with our must-eat list on page 195.

3. Fruits and Berries

Fruits are relatively low in calories and fat but are great sources of dietary fiber, vitamins, and other healthful micronutrient compounds. (Fruits do contain sugar—albeit the natural variety—so you still need to watch your quantities.) In particular, fruits contain various antioxidants, including polyphenolic flavonoids and vitamin C. One type of polyphenolic compound—called anthocyanins—is prevalent in "blue fruits" like dark grapes, mulberries, açai berries, blueberries, and blackberries. Anthocyanins help protect our bodies from oxidant stress, diseases, and cancers and boost our immune systems.

Our top choices for everyday consumption can be found in our Seagan Staples Shopping List on page 11.

4. Herbs and Spices

Herbs and spices provide a rich source of phytonutrients and other beneficial compounds that may do wonders for your health.

We lay out the whole spicy story in our chapter Herbs and Spices—The Spicy Seventeen, on page 208.

5. Grains

First, we're talking only about whole grains here. Refined grains (grains that have been milled to remove the healthy bran and germ portions) aren't likely to be on anyone's list of superfoods. And while "ancient" grains (amaranth, spelt, farro, teff, and quinoa, to name a few) have become popular lately, many whole-grain products have the kind of fiber, healthy fats, vitamins, minerals, and various phytochemicals that qualify them as superfoods.

Consult our Seagan Staples list on page 11 for a list of great grains to include in your diet.

6. Legumes

Almost all legumes have protein, fiber, B vitamins, iron, zinc, magnesium, and potassium, but the dried varieties tend to be richer sources of these nutrients. And as every knowledgeable vegan knows, legumes combined with whole grains provide a complete set of all essential amino acids, meaning you can get all the protein you need simply by eating beans and grain dishes together.

Just about any bean takes the cake. For some recommendations, check our Seagan Staples Shopping List on page 11.

7. *Seafood*

Eaten two to three times a week, the right fish provides a wealth of essential omega-3 fatty acids.

Get the whole scoop in the Health Benefits of Seafood chapter on page 19.

8. *Dark Chocolate*

Thank you, chocolate gods, for giving us a superfood dessert! Dark chocolate (70 percent cocoa or more), along with unsweetened cacao/cocoa powder, contain flavonoids that are known to help lower blood pressure, boost heart health, enhance your mood (duh!), and prevent diabetes.

RESOURCES

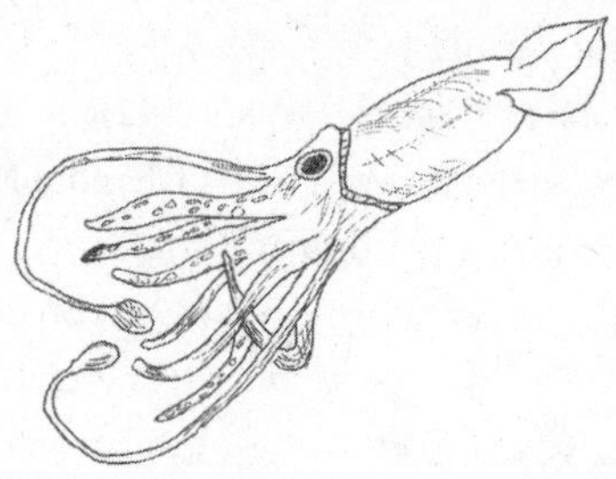

Here are many of the resources we refer to throughout the book, along with some of today's prominent voices in the worlds of wellness, land and sea sustainability, and food safety.

BOOKS

Seafood

Four Fish: The Future of the Last Wild Food, by Paul Greenberg (Penguin Books, 2011)

The Perfect Protein: The Fish Lover's Guide to Saving the Oceans and Feeding the World, by Andy Sharpless and Suzannah Evans (Rodale, 2013)

Sustainable Sushi: A Guide to Saving the Oceans One Bite at a Time, by Casson Trenor (North Atlantic Books, 2009)

Vegan

The China Study, by T. Colin Campbell, PhD, and Thomas M. Campbell II (BenBella Books, 2004)

The Easy Vegan Cookbook, by Kathy Hester (Page Street Publishing, 2015)

Eat Like You Give a Damn, by Michelle Schwegmann and Josh Hooten (Book Publishing Company, 2015)

Food52 Vegan, by Gena Hamshaw (Ten Speed Press, 2015)

Forks over Knives—The Cookbook: Over 300 Recipes for Plant-Based Eating All Through the Year, by Del Sroufe (The Experiment, 2012)

Isa Does It: Amazingly Easy, Wildly Delicious Vegan Recipes for Every Day of the Week, by Isa Chandra Moskowitz (Little, Brown and Company, 2013)

The Oh She Glows Cookbook: Over 100 Vegan Recipes to Glow from the Inside Out, by Angela Liddon (Penguin Books, 2014)

Prevent and Reverse Heart Disease, by Caldwell B. Esselstyn Jr., M.D. (Penguin Books, 2007)

Street Vegan: Recipes and Dispatches from The Cinnamon Snail Food Truck, by Adam Sobel (Clarkson Potter, 2015)

Thug Kitchen: Eat Like You Give a F•ck, The Official Cookbook, by Michelle Davis and Matt Holloway (Rodale, 2014)

The Vegan Cheat Sheet, by Amy Cramer and Lisa McComsey (Penguin Books, 2013)

Healthy Eating and Wellness

The Blue Zones Solution: Eating and Living Like the World's Healthiest People, by Dan Buettner (National Geographic, 2015)

Eat to Live Cookbook: 200 Delicious Nutrient-Rich Recipes for Fast and Sustained Weight Loss, Reversing Disease, and Lifelong Health, by Joel Fuhrman, M.D. (HarperOne, 2013)

Eat Yourself Super One Bite at a Time: A Superfoods Journey for the Happy, Healthy, and Hungry, by Todd J. Pesek, M.D. (Morgan James Publishing, 2012)

8 Weeks to Optimum Health: A Proven Program for Taking Full Advantage of Your Body's Natural Healing Power, by Andrew Weil, M.D. (Ballantine Books, 2007)

The New Whole Foods Encyclopedia: A Comprehensive Resource for Healthy Eating, by Rebecca Wood (Penguin Books, 2010)

Pick Your Poison: How Our Mad Dash to Chemical Utopia is Making Lab Rats of Us All, by Monona Rossol (Wiley, 2011)

The Sprouted Kitchen: A Tastier Take on Whole Foods, by Sara Forte (Ten Speed Press, 2012)

This is Your Do-Over: The 7 Secrets to Losing Weight, Living Longer, and Getting a Second Chance at the Life You Want, by Michael F. Roizen, M.D. (Scribner, 2015)

WEBSITES

GMOS, Organic, Environment, and Food Safety

Center for Food Safety—centerforfoodsafety.org

Environmental Working Group (EWG)—ewg.org

Food & Water Watch—foodandwaterwatch.org

GMO Awareness—gmoawareness.org

The Institute for Responsible Technology (IRT)—responsibletechnology.org

National Resources Defense Council—nrdc.org

Non-GMO Project—nongmoproject.org

Non-GMO Shopping Guide—nongmoshoppingguide.com

Organic Consumers Association—organicconsumers.org

The Organic & Non-GMO Report—non-gmoreport.com

Organic Trade Association—ota.com

Say No to GMOs—saynotogmos.com

U.S. Department of Agriculture (USDA)—usda.gov

U.S. Environmental Protection Agency (EPA)—epa.gov

U.S. Food and Drug Administration (FDA)—fda.gov

Health and Wellness

Andrew Weil, M.D.—drweil.com

Clean Plates—cleanplates.com

DIY Natural—diynatural.com

Dr. Axe: Food is Medicine—draxe.com

Food Babe—foodbabe.com

Nutrition.gov

Prevention—prevention.com

Responsible Eating and Living (REAL)—responsibleeatingandliving.com

SELFNutritionData—nutritiondata.self.com

Well+Good—wellandgood.com

Whole Foods Market: Healthy Eating—wholefoodsmarket.com/healthy-eating

Healthy Eating and Cooking

Fit Foodie Finds—fitfoodiefinds.com

The Kitchn—thekitchn.com

The Roasted Root—theroastedroot.net

Running on Real Food: Life in Healthy Balance—runningonrealfood.com

Sweet Potato Soul (vegan)—sweetpotatosoul.com

Seafood

Aquaculture Stewardship Council—asc-aqua.org

Blue Ocean Guide to Seafood—blueocean.org/seafoods

Colorado Ocean Coalition: Saving Oceans from a Mile High—coloradoocean.org

EDF (Environmental Defense Fund) Seafood Selector—edf.seafood.org

FishWatch—fishwatch.gov

Food & Water Watch—foodandwaterwatch.org

Interstate Shellfish Sanitation Conference (ISSC)—issc.org

Marine Stewardship Council—msc.org

Monterey Bay Aquarium Seafood Watch—seafoodwatch.org

Safina Center Healthy Oceans Seafood Guide—blueocean.org/seafoods

Seafish—seafish.org

Seafood Health Facts—seafoodhealthfacts.org

U.S. Environmental Protection Agency (EPA) Fish Consumption Advisories—water.epa.gov

Vital Choice—vitalchoice.com
Wild American Shrimp—americanshrimp.com

Seagan

Seagan Eating—seaganeating.com

Vegan

One Green Planet—onegreenplanet.org
Thug Kitchen—thugkitchen.com
The Vegan Cheat Sheet—vegancheatsheet.com

Vegan Food Purveyors

Pangea, The Vegan Store—veganstore.com
Vegan Eats—veganeatsusa.com
Vegan Essentials—veganessentials.com
Vegan Sweet Tooth—vegansweettooth.com

BLOGS

Food and Health News

Authority Nutrition—authoritynutrition.com
BuzzFeed *Life*—buzzfeed.com/food
Food Politics—foodpolitics.com
Health Blog (*The Wall Street Journal*)—blogs.wsj.com/health
The Salt: NPR—What's On Your Plate—
npr.org/sections/thesalt
Well (*The New York Times*)—well.blogs.nytimes.com

Healthy Eating and Lifestyle

Diet Blog—diet-blog.com
Eat + Run (*U.S. News & World Report*)—
health.usnews.com/health-news/blogs/eat-run
Examine.com—examine.com/blog
Greatist—greatist.com

Happy Healthy Long Life—happyhealthylonglife.com
Mark Bittman—markbittman.com
Mark's Daily Apple—marksdailyapple.com
MindBodyGreen—mindbodygreen.com
100 Days of Real Food—100daysofrealfood.com
Peace Love Nutrition—peacelovenutrition.wordpress.com
Q by Equinox—q.equinox.com
Say Yes to Salad—Confessions of a Sometimes Vegetarian—thesaladgirl.com
Sonima—sonima.com
This is Why You're Fat—thisiswhyyourefat.com

Vegan

FatFree Vegan Kitchen—blog.fatfreevegan.com
From A to Vegan—fromatovegan.com
Happy Healthy Long Life—happyhealthylonglife.com
Healthy Happy Life—kblog.lunchboxbunch.com
Hell Yeah It's Vegan!—hellyeahitsvegan.com
No Meat Athlete—nomeatathlete.com
Oh She Glows—ohsheglows.com
Post Punk Kitchen—theppk.com
An Unrefined Vegan—anunrefinedvegan.com
Vegalicious—vegalicious.recipes
Vegan Richa—veganricha.com

ACKNOWLEDGMENTS

Somehow, when you and the publisher agree on a book deadline, it feels like you have all the time in the world to get it done (in our case, six months). Then suddenly, you're panicked. What? Six months? What were we thinking? With busy lives, full-time jobs, and families to tend to, writing a book in our "spare time" has been challenging—and would never have been accomplished without the help (and understanding) of so many.

Whether they provided hands-on help, moral support, or just agreed not to break off our friendship because we've been ignoring them for six months, these are just some of the people to whom we're indebted.

First, we'd both like to thank our wonderful agent, Sheree Bykofsky, who encouraged us to go for book number two, believed in the seagan idea, and went to bat for us. And to our amazing editor at Penguin Random House, Jeanette Shaw, thanks for helping us bring our vision to fruition—you always make us look good.

AMY CRAMER

I thank my dear husband, Ken, and my beautiful children, Cai, Liv, and Cam for always loving me, even when I couldn't get dinner on the table because I was ironically too busy cooking for this book.

Thank you to my faithful recipe tester, Meg Rosen, for patiently testing, tasting, and improving my cooking.

Thank you to my armchair editors, Stanley Amelkin (Dad), Ken Cramer (hubby), and Abby Brown (friend). Your excellent catches and edits were invaluable. Thank you to Barbara Amelkin (Mom) for inspiring my love of cooking. And of course, thank you to my dearest friend, confidant, and president of my fan club, Elizabeth Cahn (sister).

Saving the best for last, thank you to my coauthor, Lisa McComsey. Your witty words and beautiful spirit are the most awesome gifts you can share. I am lucky to be the recipient for the past 25 years. I love you, my wonderful friend.

LISA McCOMSEY

While my family believes a life without bacon is not a life well lived, they've been unfailingly supportive of my "crazy" endeavors. Thanks to Mom, the eternal optimist and my tireless promoter, encourager, and eagle-eye editor; and to Dad, our insanely talented illustrator and overall great guy (it's no wonder your initials are GEM). It's a thrill to collaborate with you! My amazing siblings, Scott, Leslie, and Marisa, always have my back, send me meaty ideas, and are tireless brainstormers—quick to respond to panic-filled e-mails with subjects like, "Help! We need a new book title!" Julie Hall, my brilliant sister-in-law, I thank you for all your help, recon, and hours of fun (and wine-ing) in the kitchen.

I am blessed with a circle of smart, loving, witty, and supportive friends who stand by my side, listen to my ramblings, and tolerate the occasional stress-induced grouchiness. What would I do without you? Thanks to you all for keeping me sane. In particular, this project would not have been possible without a few saints:

To my "amanuensis," Rick Askoff, I am indebted. You rescued me from the depths of information overload, got me organized, and kept me motivated. You have been my rock. *Muchas gracias, querido amigo.* And a big shout-out to Rick's "elves," Diane Emerick and Sheila Torpey, for all the laughs and much-needed cocktail breaks.

Weesie Palace, I could never repay all your kindnesses. Thank you for taking such good care of me during this project and throughout all my life's "projects." You are precious to me.

Sherri Muroff Kalt, you are always my lifesaver, but your guidance, ideas, and support during this time were truly a saving grace. Thank you, dear friend.

To my lifelong friend, Sandy Levine, I am grateful for your wisdom, candid feedback, and walking brainstorm sessions by the river. You are always there for me.

Thanks to Lisa Cohan Aronow, the semicolon queen; you keep me on top of my punctuation game (and so much more). You inspire me. And to Loa Heymann, a huge thanks for all your help and clever ideas. Cory Stellmach, you've tolerated my supernumerary health rants during our many runs over the months (and miles), and I am blessed to have you as my friend, sounding board, and vocabulary guru. Ray Moss, you've been my champion and cheerleader for decades, and I value your guidance and encouragement. You've always believed in me—thank you.

Finally, I could write another book on the joys of working, eating, and playing with my coauthor, Amy. You are one special dish, my friend. I love you.

ABOUT THE AUTHORS

AMY CRAMER

Vegan Chef, Coach, Instructor, and Entrepreneur

Following a five-year stint as a marketing executive at *People* magazine, Amy founded a fitness-based direct-marketing company, Highpoint Communications, which she eventually sold. After she and her husband, Ken, converted to veganism in 2007 to combat Ken's chronically high cholesterol, Amy launched the Cleveland-based vegan chef service Dinners Done Now. As owner and head chef, she prepared more than 300 weekly vegan meals for her clients, among them the Esselstyn family (Rip Esselstyn is author of the vegan bestseller *The Engine 2 Diet*; his father, Caldwell B. Esselstyn Jr., MD, penned *Prevent and Reverse Heart Disease).* After moving to Boulder, Colorado, in July 2011, she noticed that supermarkets were greatly lacking in fresh, ready-made vegan foods. To fill the gap, she launched Vegan Eats (veganeatsUSA.com), which manufactures oil-free, gluten-free, and GMO-free vegan dishes—including soups, Alfredo sauces, baked goods, and salad dressings—for supermarket chains (currently in the Midwest and expanding). Along with Lisa McComsey, Amy co-authored *The Vegan Cheat Sheet*, published by Penguin Books in 2013. A graduate of Cornell University, Amy has taught private vegan classes throughout Ohio, in New York City, and in Westchester County, New York, and has been a guest lecturer at Bronx Community College. She also offers one-on-one vegan coaching to those who need more guidance and handholding. Whole Foods Market frequently invites her as a guest instructor. A rising vegan culinary celebrity, Amy is frequently cited in food and health blogs and has been touted in the local press. She lives with her husband and three children—Cai, Liv, and Cam—in Boulder, Colorado.

LISA McCOMSEY

Writer, Marketing Consultant, and Public Speaker

An award-winning copywriter, Lisa has worked on staff and as a freelance copywriter for publications like *Vogue, People, Life, Real Simple, Vanity Fair, Bon Appétit, GQ, House & Garden, Brides,* the *New York Times, Every Day with Rachael Ray,* and *Dr. Oz The Good Life.* She spent three years as copy director of *Allure* magazine and is a two-time recipient of the Time Inc. President's Award for Outstanding Achievement. Lisa cultivated a love for rice and beans while living in Costa Rica and Baja, Mexico, during a three-year volunteer stint as an English teacher—giving her a taste of what was to come when she decided to go vegan in 2009. Following her "conversion," she and longtime friend Amy Cramer co-authored *The Vegan Cheat Sheet*, published by Penguin Books in 2013. An avid bicyclist and runner, Lisa has completed twenty-five marathons, several century rides, and a handful of triathlons. After growing up at the Jersey Shore and vowing "never to go back" once she graduated high school, Lisa attended Bucknell University and then moved to New York City and Latin America—before, yes, returning to her New Jersey roots. She now happily resides near the water, where she continues to write and work as a marketing consultant (lisamccomsey.com).

ED McCOMSEY

Illustrator and Watercolorist

A retired dentist, Ed now works as a professional artist—creating paintings and illustrations instead of crowns and dentures. Under the tutelage of various renowned watercolorists in New Jersey and Key West, he has explored a spectrum of styles and techniques. His work is at times loose and impressionistic, other times calculated and precise, and he enjoys pushing the boundaries and experimenting with color, shape, and methodology. Among his favorite themes—besides fish—are landscapes, seascapes, vegetables (inspired by *The Vegan Cheat Sheet*), and his favorite cocktail, the martini. Ed has exhibited in art shows and galleries in New Jersey, and his works hang in restaurants, hospitals, and many private homes. This is his first book-illustration project. A jazz aficionado who swings to Count Basie, Benny Goodman, and Ella Fitzgerald while painting and drawing, he is affectionately known as the "Jazzy Watercolorist."

INDEX

acrylamide, 175
agave, 188
age of fish, 22
Alaskan salmon
  Maple-Mustard–Glazed Salmon in Foil, 61, 89
  and omega-3 fatty acids, 21
albacore tuna, 21, 34, 42
alcohol, 18
"all natural" claims on packaging, 156
almonds
  health benefits of, 195
  Mocha-Coconut Almond Fudge Ice Cream by Hand, 144–46
aluminum additives, 160
American cuisine in restaurants, 148
American Heart Association
  on cholesterol, 167
  on fish consumption, 2, 21
  on saturated and trans fat, 167, 175
  on sodium intake, 168, 190
  on sugar intake, 168, 188
anchovies
  Caesar Salad Dressing and Dip, 126–27
  as healthy and sustainable option, 33, 36
  and omega-3 fatty acids, 21
  and pantry staples, 34
anthocyanins, 230
applesauce: Chocolate Brownies with Fudge Icing, 137–38
Arctic char
  Arctic Char Puttanesca in Foil, 87
  as healthy and sustainable option, 36
  and omega-3 fatty acids, 21
artificial colors, 160–61
artificial sweeteners, 161, 188–89
Atlantic bluefin tuna, 42, 46
Atlantic flatfish (flounder, sole, halibut), 42

Bácher, Miche, 139
"bacon"
  BLT Sandwich, 56, 63, 110–11
  Pasta Carbonara, 102–4
bagel shops, ordering food in, 149
Baked Ziti with Spinach, 57, 101–2
baking fish, 30
baking ingredients, 11–12
bananas
  Banana Overnight Oatmeal, 56, 57, 132

bananas (*cont.*)
Chocolate Chip–Banana Bread Pudding, 134
barbecuing fish, 29
basil, 210
beans and legumes
pantry staples, 12
Potato-Chip Pie in a Bag, 109–10
superfood status of, 230–31
berries, 229–30
beverages
and bisphenol A (BPA), 184
iced tea, 192
pantry staples, 12
preservatives in, 163
smoothies, 182–83
sodas, 191–92
sports drinks, 193
and sugar, 187
Biscuits, Buttermilk, 128–29
bisphenol A (BPA), 184
bisques: Shrimp Bisque, 97–98
black cod
Black Cod Curry, 57, 75–76
Black Cod Milanese, 68–69
as healthy and sustainable option, 36–37
and omega-3 fatty acids, 21
blender, high-powered, 52
BLT Sandwich, 56, 63, 110–11
blueberries, 227
bluefin tuna, 42, 46
bok choy: Soy-Ginger Halibut with Bok Choy in Foil, 91
Brazilian Fish Stew, 60, 80–81
Brazil nuts, 196
breads
Buttermilk Biscuits, 128–29
Chocolate Chip–Banana Bread Pudding, 134
Crunchy French Toast Casserole, 130
pantry staples, 12
Quick Tiramisu, 60, 135–36
breakfasts, 128–32
Banana Overnight Oatmeal, 132
Buttermilk Biscuits, 128–29
Crunchy French Toast Casserole, 130
Granola, 131
healthy alternatives for, 171–74
in restaurants, 148
Bright-Fallon, Wendy, 123
brownies
Chocolate Brownies with Fudge Icing, 137–38
Gluten-Free Double-Chocolate Brownies, 139–40
Buttermilk Biscuits, 128–29
butylated hydroxyanisole (BHA), 161
butylated hydroxytoluene (BHT), 161
buyers' guide for seafood, 22–28

cabbage: Creamy Coleslaw, 120–21
Caesar Salad Dressing and Dip, 126–27
calories and calories from fat, 166, 167
calzones: Simple Crab-and-Spinach Calzones, 83–84
cancer risk, x, 9, 175
candy, 179
canned goods, 12–13, 34, 183–85
Caramel Corn, 55, 63, 142
carbohydrates, 168
carrots, prepping, 48–49
cashews
cashew cream, 48, 49
health benefits of, 196–97
Maple-Cashew Ice Cream by Hand, 143–44
casseroles
Crunchy French Toast Casserole, 130
Green Bean Casserole, 119–20
Mexican Fish Casserole, 77–78
Tuna Noodle Casserole, 78–79
catch method (farm-raised vs. wild-caught)
buyers' guide for, 22, 23
and pantry staples, 34

catfish
better options for, 43
Catfish with Mango Salsa in Foil, 93
as healthy and sustainable option, 37
imported, 43
White Wine–Tarragon Catfish in Foil, 88
cauliflower
Baked Ziti with Spinach, 101–2
Creamy Cauliflower Mash, 116
Lasagna, 104–5
Spinach and Cheese Empanada, 98–100
cereals, 13, 171–72
Certified Sustainable Seafood label, 23–24
cheese
Crab Mac and Cheese, 65–66
Lasagna, 104–5
pantry staples, 14
Spinach and Cheese Empanada, 98–100
chemical residues on foods, 219, 220, 221
chia, 202
Chilean sea bass, 42
chile pepper, 210–11
Chinese food, ordering, 148
chips
good choices for, 181
One-Minute Tortilla Chips, 122–23
Potato-Chip Pie in a Bag, 109–10
Sweet Potato Chips, 121–22
chocolate
Chocolate Brownies with Fudge Icing, 137–38
Chocolate Chip–Banana Bread Pudding, 55, 134
dark chocolate, 16, 179, 196, 231
Gluten-Free Double-Chocolate Brownies, 139–40
good choices for, 179
Mocha-Chip Shake, 133
Mocha-Coconut Almond Fudge Ice Cream by Hand, 144–46
pantry staples, 16
Quick Tiramisu, 60, 135–36
superfood status of, 231
cholesterol
"cholesterol free" claims on packaging, 158
recommendations for, 167
chowders
Creamy Shrimp and Corn Chowder, 94–95
New England Clam Chowder, 95–96
cilantro, 211
cinnamon, 212
clams, 27, 40
Clean Fifteen list, 220, 221–22
cloves, 212
coconut
Coconut-Crusted Trout, 70–71
health benefits of, 197
coconut milk
Coconut Whipped Cream/Icing, 146
Mocha-Coconut Almond Fudge Ice Cream by Hand, 144–46
coconut sugar, 187
cod (Atlantic), 43
cod (Pacific)
Black Cod Curry, 57, 75–76
Black Cod Milanese, 68–69
as healthy and sustainable option, 36–37
and mercury, 46
and omega-3 fatty acids, 21
and questionable catch methods, 46
Seafood Newburg, 79–80
coffee
Mocha-Chip Shake, 133
Mocha-Coconut Almond Fudge Ice Cream by Hand, 144–46
and "nondairy" creamers, 173–74
Quick Tiramisu, 60, 135–36
Coleslaw, Creamy, 63, 120–21
colon cancer, 9
comfort foods. *See* homestyle classics and comfort foods

condiments, 13–14
cookies and bars
Peanut Butter Cookies, 136–37
Power Blondies, 140–41
cooking fish, 29–31
corn chowder: Creamy Shrimp and Corn Chowder, 94–95
country of origin, 23
crabs
better options for, 43
buyers' guide for, 27–28
Crab-and-Spinach-Stuffed Portabella Mushrooms, 62, 84–85
Crab Mac and Cheese, 56, 65–66
as healthy and sustainable option, 37
king crab, 43
and pantry staples, 34
Seafood Newburg, 79–80
Simple Crab-and-Spinach Calzones, 83–84
crackers: Power Crackers, 123–24
creamers, "nondairy," 173–74
Creamy Cauliflower Mash, 116
Creamy Coleslaw, 63, 120–21
Creamy Shrimp and Corn Chowder, 94–95
Crispin, Jason, 143
Crunchy French Toast Casserole, 56, 130
crustaceans, buyers' guide for, 27–28
cumin, 212–13
curcumin, 217
cured salmon (lox), 30–31
curry
Black Cod Curry, 75–76
Thai Curry Haddock in Foil, 61, 92

dairy substitutes, 14
delis, ordering food in, 149
desserts, 132–46
Caramel Corn, 142
Chocolate Brownies with Fudge Icing, 137–38
Chocolate Chip–Banana Bread Pudding, 134
Coconut Whipped Cream/Icing, 146
Gluten-Free Double-Chocolate Brownies, 139–40
Maple-Cashew Ice Cream by Hand, 143–44
Mocha-Chip Shake, 133
Mocha-Coconut Almond Fudge Ice Cream by Hand, 144–46
Peanut Butter Cookies, 136–37
Power Blondies, 140–41
Quick Tiramisu, 60, 135–36
in restaurants, 149
diacetyl, 161
Dietary Guidelines Advisory Committee, 2015 report, 9
diet or "lite" foods, 174
dill weed, 213
dips and dressings, 125–28
Caesar Salad Dressing and Dip, 126–27
in menus, 54–62
Ranch Dressing and Dip, 127–28
Smoked Sardine Dip, 125–26
Dirty Dozen list, 220–21
diseases and health issues, chronic, 8–9, 19
domestic vs. imported seafood, 22, 34
donuts, 172–73
dressings
Caesar Salad Dressing and Dip, 126–27
in menus, 54–62
Ranch Dressing and Dip, 127–28

Eggplant Parmesan, 58, 105–6
empanadas: Spinach and Cheese Empanada, 98–100
enriched grains, 155
environmental considerations, 9–10
Environmental Defense Fund (EDF) Seafood Selector, 33
Environmental Protection Agency (EPA), 35–36, 219, 220

Environmental Working Group (EWG), 160, 219, 220–22
Esselstyn, Caldwell, Jr., 5
European Union, 224

farmed fish, 44–45
"fat free" claims on packaging, 157
fats on food labels, 166–67
Fettuccine Alfredo with Shrimp, 63, 72–73
fiber, 168
fillets, buyers' guide for, 25
fish, shopping for, 14
Fish Cakes, 59, 76–77
fish markets, 22–23
flax seeds, 202–3
flounder, 42
flour, white, 185–86
foil, preparing fish in, 30, 85–93
- Arctic Char Puttanesca in Foil, 87
- Catfish with Mango Salsa in Foil, 93
- Maple-Mustard–Glazed Salmon in Foil, 61, 89
- in menus, 57, 61
- Salmon with Dill in Foil, 86
- Southwestern Halibut in Foil, 90
- Soy-Ginger Halibut with Bok Choy in Foil, 91
- Thai Curry Haddock in Foil, 61, 92
- White Wine–Tarragon Catfish in Foil, 88

Food & Water Watch Smart Seafood Guide, 33
food labels, 154–69
- amounts listed on, 164
- and buyers' guide for seafood, 23–24
- and claims on packaging, 154–59
- components of, 164–69
- and GMOs, 225
- guidelines for reading, 159–64
- ingredient lists on, 159, 160–63
- Nutrition Facts panel, 163, *165*
- for organics, 219

food processors, 51
French fries, 175–76
French Toast Casserole, 56, 130
frequency of seafood consumption, 2
fried foods
- frying fish, 29–30
- healthy alternatives to, 175–76
- Shrimp Fried Rice, 69–70

frozen foods
- buyers' guide for frozen fish, 26–27
- freezing raw fish, 49
- frozen dinners, 176–77
- staples, 14–15

fruit, 173, 229–30
fruit juice, 173
frying fish, 29–30

garlic, 49, 213
Generally Recognized As Safe (GRAS) standards, 160, 190
genetically modified organisms (GMOs), 223–26
ginger
- guidelines for using, 214
- health benefits of, 213–14
- kitchen hacks for, 50
- Soy-Ginger Halibut with Bok Choy in Foil, 91

Gluten-Free Double-Chocolate Brownies, 139–40
grains
- pantry staples, 15
- superfood status of, 230

granola and energy bars
- good choices for, 180
- Granola recipe, 131

gravy: Mushroom Gravy, 117
Greek food, ordering, 149
Green Bean Casserole, 119–20
greenhouse-gas emissions, 9
grouper, 43

haddock
- as healthy and sustainable option, 37–38
- Thai Curry Haddock in Foil, 61, 92

halibut (Atlantic), 42
halibut (Pacific)
  Halibut à la Vodka, 67
  as healthy and sustainable option, 38
  Southwestern Halibut in Foil, 90
  Soy-Ginger Halibut with Bok Choy in Foil, 91
hazelnuts, 197–98
health benefits of seafood, 19–21
healthy fish choices
  good catches for, 36–42
  and size of fish, 33–34, 35
heart disease, x
hemp seeds, 203–4
herbicides, 223
herbs and spices, 208–17
  basil, 210
  chile pepper, 210–11
  cilantro, 211
  cinnamon, 212
  cloves, 212
  cumin, 212–13
  dill weed, 213
  dried, 210
  garlic, 213
  ginger, 213–14
  health benefits of, 209
  marjoram, 214
  nutmeg, 214–15
  oregano, 215
  pantry staples, 15–16
  peppermint, 215–16
  replacing, 208, 209
  rosemary, 216
  sage, 216
  storage and usage tips, 209–10
  superfood status of, 230
  thyme, 217
  turmeric, 217
herring
  as healthy and sustainable option, 33
  and omega-3 fatty acids, 21
  and pantry staples, 34
high-fructose corn syrup, 161
homestyle classics and comfort foods, 98–112
  Baked Ziti with Spinach, 101–2
  BLT Sandwich, 56, 63, 110–11
  Eggplant Parmesan, 105–6
  Lasagna, 104–5
  Pasta Carbonara, 102–4
  Potato-Chip Pie in a Bag, 109–10
  Spanakopita (Spinach Pie), 112
  Spinach and Cheese Empanada, 98–100
  10-Minute Flatbread Pizza, 106–7
  Vegetable Pot Pie, 107–9
honey, 188
hydrogenated oils, 158, 161
hydrolyzed vegetable protein (HVP), 162

ice cream
  Maple-Cashew Ice Cream by Hand, 143–44
  Mocha-Coconut Almond Fudge Ice Cream by Hand, 144–46
iced tea, 192
icing: Coconut Whipped Cream/Icing, 146
immersion blender, 52
Indian food, ordering, 149–50
ingredient lists on food labels, 159, 160–63
insecticides
  and Dirty Dozen list, 220–21
  and GMOs, 223
  health concerns associated with, 219, 220
  regulation of, 220
Institute for Responsible Technology, 226
Italian food, ordering, 150

Japanese food, ordering, 150
jarred fish, 34

king crab, 43
king mackerel, 21, 34, 38, 43–44
kitchen tools, 51–53

Lasagna, 62, 104–5
leafy greens, 228, 229

lists of recommended seafood, 33
lobsters
  buyers' guide for, 27–28
  questionable sustainability of, 46–47
lox (cured salmon), 30–31

macadamia nuts, 198
Mac and Cheese with Crab, 56, 65–66
mackerel
  better options for, 43–44
  as healthy and sustainable option, 38
  king mackerel, 21, 34, 38, 43–44
  and mercury contamination, 35, 38
  and omega-3 fatty acids, 21
  and pantry staples, 34
  and sushi, 153
mandolines, 52
mango: Catfish with Mango Salsa in Foil, 93
maple syrup
  Maple-Cashew Ice Cream by Hand, 143–44
  Maple-Mustard–Glazed Salmon in Foil, 61, 89
  as sugar substitute, 187
Marine Stewardship Council (MSC), 24
marjoram, 214
mashed-potatoes alternative, 116
meats, x, 9–10
menus, 54–63
mercury
  fish high in, 21, 35, 38, 42, 43, 44, 45, 46
  and pregnant women, 35, 36
  and size of fish, 34, 35
  and sushi, 153
Mexican Fish Casserole, 77–78
Mexican food, ordering, 150
"milks," 14
Mocha-Chip Shake, 133
Mocha-Coconut Almond Fudge Ice Cream by Hand, 63, 144–46
molasses, 187
monkfish, 46
Monterey Bay Aquarium Seafood Watch, 33, 38, 39
MSG (monosodium glutamate), 162
mushrooms
  Crab-and-Spinach-Stuffed Portabella Mushrooms, 62, 84–85
  Mushroom Gravy, 117
mussels
  buyers' guide for, 27
  as healthy and sustainable option, 40
  and omega-3 fatty acids, 21
mustard: Maple-Mustard–Glazed Salmon in Foil, 61, 89

National Academy of Sciences, 169
"natural" claims on packaging, 156
New England Clam Chowder, 95–96
New England Journal of Medicine, 194
"nondairy" creamers, 173–74
Non-GMO Project, 224, 225–26
noodler, 52–53
Nourish (Peterson and Bright-Fallon), 123
nutmeg, 214–15
nuts, 194–201
  almonds, 195
  Brazil nuts, 196
  cashews, 196–97
  coconut, 197
  hazelnuts, 197–98
  macadamia, 198
  pantry staples, 16–17
  peanuts, 199
  pecans, 199–200
  pine nuts, 200

nuts (*cont.*)
  pistachios, 200–201
  superfood status of, 229
  walnuts, 201

oatmeal
  Banana Overnight Oatmeal, 132
  Granola, 131
  as healthy alternative, 172
oils, 10
omega-3 fatty acids
  and claims on packaging, 158–59
  deficiencies in, 19
  fish as best source of, 1, 6, 20–21, 159, 231
  health benefits of, 19–21
  in nuts, 196, 201
  plant-based sources of, 20, 158–59
  in seeds, 202, 203, 205
  in sushi, 153
One-Minute Tortilla Chips, 122–23
onions, 50
orange roughy, 44
oregano, 215
organic foods, 218–22
  and claims on packaging, 155
  and Clean Fifteen list, 220, 221–22
  and Dirty Dozen list, 220–21
  and labeling, 219
  organic seafood, 23
  USDA definition of, 218–19
overweight and obesity, 8
oysters
  buyers' guide for, 27
  as healthy and sustainable option, 40

packaged goods, 12–13
packing fish on ice, 26
partially hydrogenated oils (PHOs), 157–58, 161, 175
pasta
  Baked Ziti with Spinach, 101–2
  Fettuccine Alfredo with Shrimp, 72–73
  kitchen hacks for, 50
  Lasagna, 104–5
  pantry staples, 17
  Pasta Carbonara, 55, 102–4
  in restaurants, 148
Patagonian toothfish, 42
PCBs (polychlorinated biphenyls), 34
peanut butter
  good choices for, 184–85
  Peanut Butter Cookies, 136–37
peanuts, 199
pecans, 199–200
peppermint, 215–16
"Percent Daily Value" on food labels, 166
pesticides
  and Dirty Dozen list, 220–21
  and GMOs, 223
  health concerns associated with, 219, 220
  regulation of, 220
phosphates, 162
pie-style meals and sides
  Potato-Chip Pie in a Bag, 109–10
  Spanakopita (Spinach Pie), 112
  Sweet Potato Pie, 114–15
  Vegetable Pot Pie, 107–9
pine nuts, 200
pistachios, 200–201
pizza
  ordering in pizzerias, 151
  10-Minute Flatbread Pizza, 106–7
plastic packaging, 25
pomegranate seeds, 204–5
popcorn
  Caramel Corn, 142
  good choices for, 180–81
  homemade, 181
  in menus, 57, 58, 59, 62
portabella mushrooms
  Crab-and-Spinach-Stuffed Portabella Mushrooms, 62, 84–85
  Mushroom Gravy, 117
potassium bromate, 162
Potato-Chip Pie in a Bag, 62, 109–10

potatoes
  Scalloped Potatoes, 118–19
  Sweet Potato Chips, 121–22
  Sweet Potato Pie, 114–15
  Twice-Baked Potatoes, 113–14
Pot Pie, Vegetable, 57, 107–9
pots, 51
pouched fish, 34
Power Blondies, 140–41
Power Crackers, 123–24
pregnant women, 35, 36, 153
preparing fish, 29–31
preservatives, 22, 156, 161, 162
Prevent and Reverse Heart Disease (Esselstyn), 5
processed foods, 174
produce, staples, 17–18
propyl gallate, 162
propylparabens, 162
proteins, 168–69
pudding: Chocolate Chip–Banana Bread Pudding, 134
pumpkin seeds, 205
puréeing veggies and tofu, 52

Quick Tiramisu, 60, 135–36

rainbow trout
  as healthy and sustainable option, 38
  and omega-3 fatty acids, 21
Ranch Dressing and Dip, 55, 127–28
raw seafood, 39–40
recipes, hacks for, 48–50
red snapper, 44
refrigerator essentials, 14
resources for recommended seafood, 33
restaurant dining guide, 147–51
  talking to servers, 147–48
  tips for popular cuisines, 148–51
rice
  Shrimp Fried Rice, 69–70
  in sushi, 151–52
  10-Minute Shrimp-and-Spinach Risotto, 82
  white rice, 186
risotto: 10-Minute Shrimp-and-Spinach Risotto, 82
rosemary, 216
Russia, fish from, 43

Safina Center (formerly Blue Ocean Institute) Healthy Oceans Seafood Guide, 33
sage, 216
salads and dressings
  Caesar Salad Dressing and Dip, 126–27
  guidelines for salads, 177–78
  in menus, 54–62
  Ranch Dressing and Dip, 127–28
salmon
  Alaskan salmon, 21, 89
  better options for, 44–45
  Brazilian Fish Stew, 80–81
  farmed, 44–45
  as healthy and sustainable option, 38–39
  lox (cured salmon), 30–31
  Maple-Mustard–Glazed Salmon in Foil, 61, 89
  Mexican Fish Casserole, 77–78
  and omega-3 fatty acids, 21
  and pantry staples, 34
  Salmon with Dill in Foil, 86
  sockeye salmon, 21
  and sushi, 153
salt and sodium, 167–68, 190–91
sandwiches: BLT Sandwich, 56, 63, 110–11
sardines
  as healthy and sustainable option, 33, 39
  and omega-3 fatty acids, 21
  and pantry staples, 34
  Smoked Sardine Dip, 125–26
saturated fats, 9
Scalloped Potatoes, 118–19
scallops
  buyers' guide for, 27
  as healthy and sustainable option, 40–41
sea bass, Chilean, 42

Seafood Newburg, 79–80
seagan food options, 7–8
seeds, 201–7
  about, 194, 201
  chia, 202
  flax, 202–3
  hemp, 203–4
  pantry staples, 18
  pomegranate, 204–5
  pumpkin, 205
  sesame, 205–6
  sunflower, 206
  superfood status of, 229
  wheat germ, 207
serving sizes, 164
sesame seeds, 205–6
shakes: Mocha-Chip Shake, 133
shellfish (bivalve mollusks)
  buyers' guide for, 27–28
  as healthy and sustainable option, 39
  raw, 39–40
shopping list, 11–18
shortening, 158
shrimp
  better options for, 45
  Brazilian Fish Stew, 80–81
  buyers' guide for, 27–28
  Creamy Shrimp and Corn Chowder, 94–95
  Fettuccine Alfredo with Shrimp, 72–73
  as healthy and sustainable option, 41
  labeling for, 41
  Seafood Newburg, 79–80
  Shrimp Bisque, 97–98
  Shrimp Fried Rice, 69–70
  10-Minute Shrimp-and-Spinach Risotto, 82
side dishes, 113–21
  Creamy Cauliflower Mash, 116
  Creamy Coleslaw, 120–21
  Green Bean Casserole, 119–20
  Mushroom Gravy, 117
  Scalloped Potatoes, 118–19
  Sweet Potato Pie, 114–15
  Twice-Baked Potatoes, 113–14
simmering fish in sauce, 31
Simple Crab-and-Spinach Calzones, 83–84
size of fish, 33–34, 35
skipjack tuna, 42
smelling fish, 23
Smoked Sardine Dip, 125–26
smoothies, 182
snacks, 121–24
  One-Minute Tortilla Chips, 122–23
  Power Crackers, 123–24
  Sweet Potato Chips, 121–22
snapper, 44
sockeye salmon, 21
sodas, 191–92
sodium and salt, 167–68, 190–91
sodium benzoate, 163
sodium tripolyphosphate (STPP), 22, 27
sole, 42
soups, 94–98
  Creamy Shrimp and Corn Chowder, 94–95
  New England Clam Chowder, 95–96
  Shrimp Bisque, 97–98
Southwestern Halibut in Foil, 90
Soy-Ginger Halibut with Bok Choy in Foil, 91
Spanakopita (Spinach Pie), 112
spices. *See* herbs and spices
spinach
  Baked Ziti with Spinach, 101–2
  Crab-and-Spinach-Stuffed Portabella Mushrooms, 62, 84–85
  Simple Crab-and-Spinach Calzones, 83–84
  Spanakopita (Spinach Pie), 112
  Spinach and Cheese Empanada, 58, 98–100
  10-Minute Shrimp-and-Spinach Risotto, 82
spoiled fish, 25
sports drinks, 193
The Sprouted Kitchen (Forte), 123
squid (calamari), 41

steaks, buyers' guide for, 25
steel-cut oats: Banana Overnight Oatmeal, 132
Stevia, 189
stew: Brazilian Fish Stew, 80–81
stick blenders, 52
storing fish, 24, 26
STPP (sodium tripolyphosphate), 22, 27
sucanat, 188
sugar
  and claims on packaging, 157
  healthy alternatives to, 186–90
  in ingredient lists, 159
  recommendations for, 168
  various names of, 163, 187
sugar alcohols, 189–90
sunflower seeds, 206
superfoods, 227–31
sushi
  guidelines for ordering, 150, 151
  and mercury contamination, 42
sustainability
  bad catches for, 42–46
  and buyers' guide for seafood, 22
  domestic vs. imported seafood, 34
  good catches for, 36–42
  and size of fish, 33–34
sweet potatoes
  as healthy alternative to fries, 176
  Sweet Potato Chips, 121–22
  Sweet Potato Pie, 114–15
sweets
  healthy alternatives to, 173
  pantry staples, 16
  See also chocolate; desserts
swordfish
  better options for, 45
  toxic contaminants found in, 21, 34, 35

tarragon: White Wine–Tarragon Catfish in Foil, 88
teas, 192
tempeh: Pasta Carbonara, 102–4
10-Minute Flatbread Pizza, 55, 59, 106–7
10-Minute Shrimp-and-Spinach Risotto, 82
Thai food
  in restaurants, 151
  Thai Curry Haddock in Foil, 61, 92
thawing fish, 26–27
thyme, 217
tilapia, 47
Time magazine, 228
Tiramisu, Quick, 60, 135–36
tofu
  Baked Ziti with Spinach, 101–2
  Chocolate Brownies with Fudge Icing, 137–38
  Lasagna, 104–5
  Maple-Mustard–Glazed Salmon in Foil, 61, 89
  Pasta Carbonara, 102–4
  puréeing, 52
  Ranch Dressing and Dip, 127–28
  shopping for, 14
  Simple Crab-and-Spinach Calzones, 83–84
  Spanakopita (Spinach Pie), 112
  Spinach and Cheese Empanada, 98–100
  10-Minute Flatbread Pizza, 106–7
  Thai Curry Haddock in Foil, 61, 92
Tortilla Chips, One-Minute, 122–23
trans fats, 157–58, 161, 164, 167
trawling, 41
trout
  Coconut-Crusted Trout, 70–71
  as healthy and sustainable option, 38
  and omega-3 fatty acids, 21
  and rainbow trout, 21, 38
  Trout Marsala, 74–75
  Trout Piccata, 71–72

tuna
albacore tuna, 21, 34, 42
Atlantic bluefin, 42, 46
and catch methods, 42
as healthy and sustainable option, 42
and mercury contamination, 21, 35, 42
and pantry staples, 34
skipjack tuna, 42
Tuna Noodle Casserole, 59, 78–79
turmeric, 217
Twice-Baked Potatoes, 113–14

United Nations' guidelines for eco-labeling, 24
U.S. Department of Agriculture (USDA)
labeling requirements for seafood, 23
and organic labeling, 155, 218–19
on sodium intake, 168, 190
on sugar intake, 187, 188–89
U.S. Food and Drug Administration (FDA)
on artificial sweeteners, 188–89
and food labels, 156, 164
and Generally Recognized As Safe (GRAS) standards, 160, 190
and trans fats, 158

The Vegan Cheat Sheet (Cramer and McComsey), 1, 4
vegan cheese, 14
vegan foods to replace, 170–93
canned foods, 183–85
cereals, 171–72
chips, 181
chocolate and candy, 179
diet or "lite" foods, 174
donuts, 172–73
fried foods, 175–76
frozen dinners, 176–77
fruit juice, 173
granola and energy bars, 180
iced tea, 192
"nondairy" creamers, 173–74
peanut butter, 184–85
popcorn, 180–81
refined sugar and artificial sweeteners, 186–90
salads and dressing, 177–78
salt, 190–91
smoothies, 182
sodas, 191–92
sports drinks, 193
whipped toppings, 183
white flour, 185–86
white rice, 186
Vegan Sweet Tooth, 131, 136
vegetables
superfoods, 229
Vegetable Pot Pie, 57, 107–9
vegetable spiralizer, 52–53
Vietnam, fish from, 43
vitamins and minerals, 169
vodka: Halibut à la Vodka, 67

walnuts, 201
watercress, 228
water resources and meat production, 9–10
wheat germ, 207
whipped toppings
Coconut Whipped Cream/Icing, 146
good choices for, 183
White Wine–Tarragon Catfish in Foil, 88
whole fish, buyers' guide for, 24
Whole Foods, 160
whole grains
and claims on packaging, 155–56
flours, 186
wild-caught vs. farm raised fish, 22, 23
wine
pantry staples, 18
White Wine–Tarragon Catfish in Foil, 88
World Health Organization, x, 9

yogurt, vegan, 14